Green IT

About the Authors

Toby J. Velte, Ph.D. is an international best-selling author of business technology articles and books. He is co-founder of Velte Publishing, Inc. and the co-author of more than a dozen books published by McGraw-Hill and Cisco Press. Dr. Velte is currently part of Microsoft's North Central practice focused on helping thriving companies with their technology-based initiatives. He works with large organizations to create IT roadmaps that are business focused and practically implemented. He can be reached at tjv@velte.com.

Anthony T. Velte, CISSP, CISA has over 16 years in the information systems industry. He is co-founder of Velte Publishing, Inc. and the co-author of more than a dozen books published by McGraw-Hill and Cisco Press.

Mr. Velte is a Senior Security Engineer for an industry-leading security software company. He frequently speaks at seminars and helps companies large and small protect their information systems infrastructure. He holds a variety of business and technical certifications. He can be reached at atv@velte.com.

Robert Elsenpeter is an award-winning journalist, freelance writer, and author of more than a dozen technology books. He has a bachelor's degree in information technology. He can be reached at rce@velte.com.

Green IT

Reduce Your Information System's Environmental Impact While Adding to the Bottom Line

Toby Velte
Anthony Velte
Robert Elsenpeter

New York   Chicago   San Francisco
Lisbon   London   Madrid   Mexico City
Milan   New Delhi   San Juan
Seoul   Singapore   Sydney   Toronto

The McGraw·Hill Companies

Library of Congress Cataloging-in-Publication Data

Velte, Toby J.
  Green IT : reduce your information system's environmental impact while
adding to the bottom line / Toby Velte, Anthony Velte, Robert
Elsenpeter.
    p. cm.
  ISBN 978-0-07-159923-8 (alk. paper)
  1. Information technology—Management. 2. Information
technology—Cost control. 3. Environmental protection. 4. Computer
systems—Environmental aspects. 5. Green technology. I. Velte, Anthony
T. II. Elsenpeter, Robert C., 1970- III. Title.
  T58.64.V43 2008
  658.4'038—dc22

                                                        2008025478

McGraw-Hill books are available at special quantity discounts to use as premiums and sales promotions, or for use in corporate training programs. To contact a special sales representative, please visit the Contact Us page at www.mhprofessional.com.

**Green IT: Reduce Your Information System's Environmental Impact
While Adding to the Bottom Line**

1234567890 DOC DOC 0198

ISBN   978-0-07-159923-8
MHID   0-07-159923-1

Sponsoring Editor
  Wendy Rinaldi

Editorial Supervisor
  Patty Mon

Project Manager
  Vastavikta Sharma,
  International Typesetting
  and Composition

Acquisitions Coordinator
  Mandy Canales

Copy Editor
  Bart Reed

Proofreader
  Paul Tyler

Indexer
  Jack Lewis

Production Supervisor
  George Anderson

Composition
  International Typesetting
  and Composition

Illustration
  International Typesetting
  and Composition

Art Director, Cover
  Jeff Weeks

Cover Production
  Pattie Lee

Cover Designer
  I2e Design

For Connor and Olivia, striving to improve your future by our actions today. —TJV

For my three amazing sons, Joey, Jack, and Luke. —ATV

For my own royal family, Henry, Elizabeth, and Charles. —RCE

Contents at a Glance

Contents

Foreword

The mere appearance of this book on the market is indication enough of how broad and deep the sustainability movement has evolved. However, don't be mistaken. IT has been part of the movement all along.

The green movement could not have advanced this far and this fast without the nimbleness of communication and information management that the IT community has provided and facilitated. Of course, there are some who will critique IT with as much blame for our energy and material demands and ecologic degradation as any other technology of modern civilization.

We are for them a civilization apparently so hard-wired to maximize productivity and entertainment in every context imaginable, that we have lost our moral compass despite compromise to the Earth's life support systems, much less the claims of the "zombification" of children fueled by an electronic virtual reality.

Regardless, there is also no doubt that we benefit from the evolutionary speed of IT in ways difficult to comprehend. For example, it is IT that has driven how fast we have fortunately come to acknowledge, and increasingly understand, the precarious situation in which we now find ourselves globally immersed—ecologically, socially, and economically.

As Dorothy said in the Wizard of Oz, "Toto, I have a feeling we're not in Kansas any more." The double-edged sword is a cheap, but pertinent metaphor to understanding that we are in relatively uncharted territory in the history of the human species, and IT is a tool with which we can broker a deal for good or for evil on a scale never before imagined. We will either follow the path of least resistance, peak out, and slide down the other side of the Bell curve as the Easter Island, Roman, and British empires before us, or we will look back to see this as an epiphany, with IT as a springboard to an awakening; an enlightenment that will even bring a smile to the face of Mother Nature, and thus to the youth of generations to follow. I obviously hope for the latter….

Little empirical evidence speaks to it directly, but Lester Brown describes it as our "sleep-walking into history." We have come to a point in which our collective conscious and unconscious sense of well-being—our intimate sense of belonging to this place we call Earth—is more in doubt than ever. The exponential trends of disharmony between humans and nature are approaching threshold and tipping points that even the most scientifically uninformed find hard to ignore, such as the melting of the Arctic ice cap, much less the social tipping points for the poverty of the masses seeking access to basic standards of living.

Don't get me wrong. While the issues might seem insurmountable, there is no lack of solutions. There is only a lack of informed awareness, a lack of urgency, and most seriously, a lack of political will and leadership.

We have been in doubt, if not in blind denial, since the beginning of the Industrial Revolution. We as a culture often find great discomfort with any portrayal of the intimate dependency we have upon nature, for our science and technology can overcome any limitation not to our liking…or so we think, despite evidence to the contrary. However, we now obviously have IT systems that will no longer allow us to casually dismiss it as some left-wing politically charged, flower waving, drug-crazed rock and roll, free love conspiracy. Did I forget to blame the hippies and environmentalists?

Seriously, we need to get our heads out of that most uncomfortable of positions and get to work. That is what this book is about.

We now realize that regardless of global issue one wishes to address in personal and professional life, it is only at the community level that the rubber really meets the road for sustainability. It is only at the local community level that fossil fuel dependence, climate change, food shortage, water quality, species extinction, much less the varieties of socio-economic disparity and despair can ever be solved as a result of individual and collective conscience, unless of course, Captain Kirk and Mr. Spock show up pretty soon to carry us off to the hinterlands of the universe. For us, the opportunity is in the crisis. It appears in fact to be one of those moments in history from which could emerge modern day scenarios of Mad Max, or bucolic scenes from the Garden of Eden, or nirvana if you like.

The breadth and depth of the issues are of such complexity and scale that sustainable community development can only be realized through a holistic, systems-thinking approach (such as The Natural Step), with IT at its core as a systemic tool and infrastructure. Whether it is simple provision of email and blogs that vicariously connect each of us to the 6.5 billion other souls and 30 plus million other species in this test-tube, or the gigabytes of raw science data, the Geographic Information System databases of sustainability indicators, the mind-bending public relations media of corporate America having come home to green, or simply a paperless documentation of every moment of our existence; without IT, we are sunk. Yes, the Amish would take issue with such a statement, and rightfully so, but we now need every tool at our disposal for the sake of the common good.

There are over seventy published definitions for sustainability. The most common is from the Brundtland Commission in 1987 where sustainability was defined as "…development that meets the needs of the present, without compromising the ability of future generations to meet their own needs." It certainly sets the ethical foundation, but says little about the principles and best practices. However, make no mistake, the ubiquitous nature of sustainability and its application in personal, professional, and civic life, much less government and industry, is now an assumed responsibility with unprecedented momentum. The data and trend analysis now clearly indicate that sustainability is not a matter of choice. I would suggest the definition is now "leadership in the attempt to avoid un-sustainability."

The ubiquitous nature of sustainability is by itself overwhelming. When tied to the ubiquitous nature of information and the technology that immerses us in a sensual overload of the reality of the human condition almost too rich to comprehend, there is little doubt why many, including the captains, choose to ignore they are clinging to a rudderless ship drifting toward the Bermuda Triangle. *Green IT* is simply the book that sets a powerful new standard for leadership in the field. It will obviously not be the final word, nor should it be. More importantly, however, it forces the conversation to a level that is long overdue.

Like any professional science and technological application that has moved from an annoying adolescence to its Earth-affirming maturity…and thus its humanity…what was once a significant part of the problem is now central to the solution.

Welcome home, *Green IT.*

—Kelly Cain,
Director, St. Croix Institute for Sustainable Community Development
University of Wisconsin, River Falls

Acknowledgments

Like most endeavors in life, a book always starts out as just an idea. It's where everything begins. So we'd like to acknowledge our friend, Darren Boeck, who planted a kernel of an idea that grew into the topic for this book. "I have a good idea, but I don't know how to write a book," Darren said. What else Darren didn't know is that not only did he have a good idea for a book, he had a *great* idea for a book.

These days, it seems like everybody wants to "go green." But it's not just a fad; there are many great reasons why it is in our collective best interests to conserve, to be kinder to Mother Earth, and to make the most of what this amazing universe provides us. It's become quite clear that all we create and all we consume can deeply affect our lives, now and into the future.

This even affects how we use our computers and related technologies. They consume energy and are sometimes made with cutting-edge materials that might not be so healthy for the environment. So learning how we can lessen our organization's impact on the environment, via tweaks to technology, is a very big deal.

We also want to thank the following people:

Larry Aszman, CTO at Compellent Technologies in Eden Prairie, Minnesota. He generously shared information about the green attributes of next-generation storage area networks (SANs) and the initiatives that his company is spearheading, as well as how client companies are using them.

Kelly Cain, professor of plant and earth science, from the University of Wisconsin–River Falls. He turned out to be a wealth of information. Although he was able to talk to us about green efforts in the college's IT system, he really shared a lot of compelling information about the overall system of communities going green and the ability of individuals to live "off the grid."

John Engates, the CTO of Rackspace in Houston, Texas. He shared great information about his company's efforts to offer green technology. The company makes environmental responsibility a high priority. For instance, the company offers a unique option when customers want to buy a server—they can select a "green" option that is more energy efficient. He also talked about how Rackspace integrated "Green Thinking" into the very culture of the company, which has led to several key changes in how it does business.

Lastly, the three of us would like to acknowledge our respective wives for their steadfast support through each and every book project. Thanks, Sandra, Anne Marie, and Janet!

Introduction

Who Should Read This Book

This book was written with a broad audience in mind. If you are part of a business, university, government entity, nonprofit agency, or other organization that uses almost any sort of information system, you'll find the information in this book valuable.

Among other things, this book explains what measures you can take to lessen your IT department's environmental impact. Although you might not think your computers and servers humming away while doing their jobs would really have much of an impact, the reality is that they do. The other reality is that going green responsibly and sensibly is a lot harder than it sounds. It can be a daunting endeavor to sift through all the standards and regulations, technologies, and processes that dot the "green landscape."

If you are a business leader, you can find a lot of good information about the green landscape and learn more about what others are doing—and where they are successful. Drilling further down, you can see how your IT department may be having a negative impact on the environment and how you can make changes that are not only ecologically responsible, but will also save your company money.

If you are an IT manager, you will also get a lot out of this book. For example, this book includes a section that discusses "green" alternatives when it comes time to replace equipment. However, the decision is rarely all in the hands of the IT manager. You might suggest the company purchase servers with efficient power supplies, but as others in the company look at the price tag of those servers (compared to servers with inefficient power supplies), your suggested purchase might get vetoed in favor of the "less expensive" servers. That is why this book is good for the others in the organization who need to understand why these new devices cost more—and why the company will actually save money in the long run.

In short, this book is for the decision makers and anyone else in the organization who is interested in Green IT options—or anyone who needs convincing to pursue green technologies.

What This Book Covers

It's no surprise that the environment is a hot topic these days. Although our overall impact is arguable, it turns out we *are* damaging our planet in many ways. Sure, we've been bombarded with messages about going green. Sure, a lot of times those messages are just like white noise after a while, but it's hard not to acknowledge there is a problem when fossil fuel energy costs are at an all-time high and the emissions from processing and using that energy are choking our atmosphere. And we certainly can't look the other way anymore when mercury, various manmade contaminants, and other toxins as are showing up in our water supplies and our food chain at dangerous levels.

Although we all want to stop destroying our environment, Green IT is as much about doing the right thing as corporate citizens as it is about making the best business decisions from a cost and growth perspective. Adopting Green IT practices will provide you with astonishing financial benefits, and position your company to thrive moving forward.

Although it grabs more than its fair share of headlines and generates considerable consumer angst, it isn't just the price of gas that is causing alarm. As worldwide energy demand increases, coal costs more, too. As you have no doubt noticed, the cost of running your datacenter is more expensive now than it was last year. In addition, operational efficiency, automation, and other business benefits have driven the need for more and more IT infrastructure. That means more power will be consumed with already expensive electricity. What's worse, datacenters around the world are consuming huge amounts of electricity, and demand will only increase. It's starting to look like we could see a future where there just won't be enough power generated to go around, at any price.

But that doesn't mean the game is over just yet. With some forethought followed up by mindful action, you *can* reduce power needs, get energy from alternative sources, and lessen the impact of your company's IT infrastructure. There's a lot you can do to make less of an impact on the planet.

The fact of the matter is, you will likely spend more money on green technology in the short term. Energy-efficient power supplies cost money, even those compact fluorescent light bulbs cost more. But in the long run, you'll save money with a well-thought-out and implemented green plan. Up front it'll cost you some money to install solar panels, for instance. But wouldn't it be a great business advantage to skip paying the electricity bill, and maybe even have enough power to sell back to your utility? What cost money initially, eventually becomes a money saver, and then a money maker. Even if global altruism isn't something you care about, saving money has to be.

You can be as hardcore about this as you want. You can go the Ed Begley route and compost and recycle religiously; get your power from solar cells; use filtered rainwater to flush the toilets; and find each and every way to reduce, reuse, and recycle.

Good for Ed. But in the real world, a business-driven green initiative requires balance, and it will realistically need to be cost-justified. We're not talking only about capital expenditures, though. An assignable dollar value is associated with having a green image—just make sure you are backing it up with more than a pocket full of carbon credits. The more you really do to help save energy and curb pollution, the more your customers will come to appreciate your efforts.

Although we all desire to revamp our IT departments to be as eco-friendly as possible, it is simply not going to happen overnight. However, if you start consolidating your servers onto a few machines, you'll save electricity, and you won't have to buy as many electronic devices. If you start routing incoming faxes to a computer rather than having them spew pages and pages of transferred data, you'll save paper. It's taking a step in the right direction that is important, and every little bit helps. Really.

In this book we'll talk about the different aspects of implementing green changes into your company's IT infrastructure. Let's take a closer look at what we'll be covering.

Part I: Trends and Reasons to Go Green

- **Chapter 1: Overview and Issues** This chapter sets the stage to explain why IT departments are having such a deleterious effect on the environment. We examine computers—from cradle to grave—and show you how they impact the environment, from poor use to their ultimate end. This is a new perspective on IT buying. Before we thought about purchasing computers in terms of the receiving dock to the dumpster. Now we must consider the full life cycle, from production through recycling.

  We'll also talk about your organization and how to determine what sort of impact you're having on the environment. In the end, we'll show how you can save money by going green.

- **Chapter 2: Current Initiatives and Standards** Although it's early in the process of governing bodies creating standards and laws about e-waste, the world knows well enough that electronics make an impact. It wasn't as much of a deal 20 or 30 years ago—before there was a computer on every horizontal surface. But now it is a big deal. To ameliorate those problems, governments and organizations around the world have initiatives in place that will help reduce the impact of electronic waste. This chapter talks about some of the initiatives that aim to lessen IT impact.

Part II: Consumption Issues

- **Chapter 3: Minimizing Power Usage** You probably don't see your datacenter's power bill. If you did, it might shock you (no pun intended) to see how much power you consume. Datacenters and IT departments use a lot of energy. This chapter shows how you can lessen the amount of power you use. If you are looking at a place to pay for your Green IT initiatives, this is likely it.

- **Chapter 4: Cooling** You could probably hang meat in any datacenter you walked into. Because datacenters generate a lot of heat (largely from inefficient power supplies), we tend to crank up the air conditioning to cool things down. Here again is a huge expense. Chapter 4 talks about alternatives for cooling your datacenter, and how you can do so without using more than you need.

Part III: What You Can Do

- **Chapter 5: Changing the Way We Work** Although this book focuses mainly on technology and its environmental impacts, there are some other measures you can take—either on the part of your whole company in general, or your IT department in particular—that can lessen your organization's impact on the planet. This chapter shows you what sorts of things you can do to change your business processes for the better. If you think change is easy when a compelling and obvious path to do the right thing is presented, then you might not remember the challenges the U.S. faced (and lost) when trying to adopt the metric system in the early 1980s.

- **Chapter 6: Going Paperless** We generate a lot of paper, and we don't need to. True, we like holding paper in our hands, but, again, you will save money if you reduce the amount of paper you use—and you'll also save trees. It has been estimated that the cost of handling and processing paper is 31 times that of the paper itself.

We're clear-cutting forests at a breathtaking rate, largely so we can hold that fourth quarter report in our hands. This chapter shows how you can transition your office into a paperless environment.

- **Chapter 7: Recycling**   We're not talking about sorting your different types of glass before pickup. In this chapter, we discuss how you can responsibly get rid of old computers and toner cartridges. It's a huge problem in China and Africa, and by making some extra efforts, you can ensure your computers are disposed of ethically. We feel that legislation will catch up soon to where many of us are ethically, so recycling will not only be the right choice, it'll be the law. You may also consider repurposing old equipment for your organization or donating it to charity. This chapter will show you how to do that.

- **Chapter 8: Hardware Considerations**   You have two options when it comes time to equip for your company's IT needs. You can do it cheaply, initially, or you can do it responsibly (and less expensively in the long run). This chapter will show you how to equip your organization while making as little environmental impact as possible.

Part IV: Case Studies

- **Chapter 9: Technology Businesses**   Think you can't possibly revamp your IT department with eco-friendliness in mind? This chapter discusses two companies—Dell and Hewlett-Packard—that are not only being environmentally responsible, but are also getting their customers involved.

- **Chapter 10: Other Organizations**   Others are making efforts to be environmentally responsible, and we talk about them in Chapter 10. First, the University of Wisconsin–River Falls is going green, and for altruistic reasons. Naturally, the university is saving money from its efforts, but its impetus for going green stemmed from a desire to be responsible. The world's largest retailer—Wal-Mart—is also making huge strides to be green. It is thought that other retailers will follow Wal-Mart's example. This chapter talks about both these organizations and what they're doing to be green.

Part V: The Greening Process

- **Chapter 11: Datacenter Design and Redesign**   The bulk of your power consumption will be in your datacenter. There are steps you can take to ensure you use the best equipment and use the least amount of power. This chapter shows you how to design your datacenter—whether you're totally redesigning it or just replacing old equipment.

- **Chapter 12: Virtualization**   A huge trend in green computing is virtualizing your servers and storage. In other words, it is now possible to put multiple logical servers onto a handful of physical servers. This obviously saves money in hardware acquisition, as well as in the power used to run them. The case is the same for storage. You needn't spend thousands of dollars on data storage—through the use of intelligent SANs, you can save money. This chapter shows you how to do both things.

- **Chapter 13: Greening Your Information Systems**   This chapter brings everything we've talked about together. It shows how the changes discussed in preceding chapters can be applied to your company. We'll talk about not only swapping over your hardware, but also the sorts of initiatives you can make in your organization.

- **Chapter 14: Staying Green** It's great if you make changes, but you don't want to slip into bad habits, and you also want to stay on top of any trends and changes. In the last chapter of this book, we'll show you how you can keep your IT department and your company in the green—both environmentally and monetarily.

Companion Website—www.Greenitinfo.com

We discovered so many things in the process of writing this book that were valuable (like energy calculators), but didn't fit into the book. We wanted to have a way of sharing that information with you, so we created a companion website for our readers—www.greenitinfo.com. It's full of features intended to help you get the most from this book.

For example, you'll see many references to various web links throughout this book. Anytime you see "Link" followed by the chapter number and link number, you will be able to access a clickable version of that link at www.greenitinfo.com/links.

We created the links solution for you because so many of the informational links were far too long and would be quite cumbersome to actually use. We knew that the longer and more cryptic they were, the less likely it would be that anyone would enter them into a browser and see what we were referencing. With a single web page listing all of the links, and having them summarized and clickable, you will be able to access all of the information behind those links and to take more from the book you are holding right now.

The companion website is another reason why you'll find this book so valuable in getting your Green IT initiatives planned and under way. We hope to see you there!

Trends and Reasons to Go Green

CHAPTER

Overview and Issues

The protagonist in the classic children's fable "Chicken Little" would annoy his fellow chickens by constantly insisting that "the sky is falling," when it never was. It was the same sort of deal with the Shepherd Boy in "The Boy Who Cried Wolf." It all ended badly for Chicken Little and the Shepherd Boy, and we run the risk of a similar scenario playing itself out where green computing is concerned.

We've heard so much about global warming; we've heard so much about being eco-friendly; we've seen so many "Think Globally, Act Locally" bumper stickers on VW vans; and Al Gore can't keep himself from talking about the environment. Put simply, we get bombarded by the message so much that it's easy to ignore. But the truth of the matter is that if we don't heed the warnings, the sky will fall and we'll be praying for wolves to eat us.

Being green means different things to different people. Ask ten Chief Information Officers (CIOs) what "being green" means, and you'll get ten different answers. A lot of it depends on what CIOs are particularly interested in. For some, it might mean buying technology that's more energy efficient than what they have. Another might suggest that it's an issue of reducing the amount of electricity a datacenter consumes. For others, it means buying hardware that is made of environmentally friendly components. Yet others might look at the end of hardware life and suggest that Green IT means proper disposal.

Who's right? They all are. Green IT is a combination of all these issues. To be sure, if you make it your mission to tackle just one of these issues, you're doing a good thing for both your organization and the environment. But the more of these issues you go after, the better. Green IT is a complex subject, and it might be tough to decide how to tackle the greening of your organization's IT interests. The global green mantra is "Reduce, Reuse, Recycle." No matter what we do, if we can just keep these ideas at the front of our minds in all our Green IT decisions, we'll be in good shape. But the best advice is to just get started.

Problems

Chances are this isn't the first time you've heard about the need to go green as it relates to your IT infrastructure. But even though the message is out there, not enough organizations are acting on it.

Symantec Corp. released a study that revealed almost 75 percent of datacenter managers do, in fact, have an interest in adopting a strategic green center initiative, but only one in seven has actually done so—Symantec, October 2007.

The reason is obvious—money. Although datacenter managers want to save the environment, they also want to save money. In fact, it's the old business adage that says to be successful, you have to save money and maintain performance. In other words, they're worrying about another type of green.

The truth of the matter is that, yes, adopting a green infrastructure can cost more money up front, but you can save thousands or even millions of dollars (depending on your organization's size) by making some changes.

Although spending that money up front can be a hard pill to swallow, think of it this way—if we don't make meaningful changes, we're contributing to our own downfall. Let's look at the components.

Toxins

According to the U.S. Environmental Protection Agency (EPA), Americans throw out more than 2 million tons of consumer electronics annually, making electronic waste (also known as *e-waste*) one of the fastest growing components of the municipal waste stream. When these electronics break down, they release mercury and other toxins.

E-waste is a concern because of the impact of its toxicity and carcinogenicity when components are not properly disposed of. Toxic substances can include:

- Lead
- Mercury
- Cadmium
- Polychlorinated biphenyls (PCBs)

A typical computer monitor may contain more than 6 percent lead by weight, much of which is in the lead glass of the cathode ray tube (CRT). Components such as capacitors, transformers, and PVC insulated wires that were manufactured before 1977 contain dangerous amounts of PCBs.

We don't mean to frighten you to the point that you never upgrade your computers again. Far from it. You should upgrade, but with environmental responsibility in mind. The good news is that e-waste processing systems have had such a light shone on them recently that they are being forced to—forgive the pun—clean up their acts. More regulation, public attention, and commercial consideration are being paid to the issue.

A major portion of this change is that e-waste is being handled separately from conventional garbage and recycling processes. Far more computers are being reused and refurbished than they were at the turn of the century.

There are lots of benefits to reusing equipment:

- There is less demand for new products and their use of virgin raw materials.
- Less water and electricity is used when reuse lowers the need for the production of new products.
- Less packaging is used.
- Redeployed technology is available to more sectors of society, because computers and other components are often more affordable.
- Less toxins are going into landfills.

Figure 1-1
Computers are loaded with toxins, and if they aren't disposed of properly, those toxins can hurt the environment.

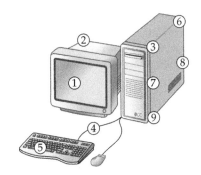

Consider the computer system in Figure 1-1.

This figure shows where various toxins can be found on your desktop computer—or the thousands of desktops in a large organization.

1. Lead in the cathode ray tube and solder

2. Arsenic in older cathode ray tubes

3. Antimony trioxide used as flame retardant

4. Polybrominated flame retardants in plastic casings, cables, and circuit boards

5. Selenium used as a power supply rectifier in circuit boards

6. Cadmium in circuit boards and semiconductors

7. Chromium used as corrosion protection in steel

8. Cobalt in steel for structure and magnetism

9. Mercury in switches and the housing

Power Consumption

On your way to work each day, you drive by a factory and see smokestacks billowing pollution into the atmosphere. You take a measure of comfort when you get to work, knowing that you work in the IT industry and aren't polluting the planet. Unfortunately, although you aren't polluting as demonstrably as that factory, your datacenter is taking its toll.

What You Use

All your desktop PCs, all your servers, all your switches, and so forth use electricity to run. Also, a fair amount of electricity is used to cool your electronics. This electricity not only costs you money to buy from the electrical utility, but the utility has to generate the electricity, quite often by using fossil fuels, which generate more greenhouse gas emissions.

Power usage is an especially relevant issue for operating a green information system—the more power that's used, the more money that's spent and the greater the carbon footprint. The place to start is knowing how much power is being used. However, according to research from Intel, 80 percent of businesses have never conducted an energy audit and only 29 percent of businesses are investing in energy-efficient PCs—Intel, 2006. Those companies are losing money because they don't know just what they're spending and how they can reduce those costs.

It's becoming more expensive to run an IT department, strictly from a power consumption standpoint. International Data Corporation (IDC) notes that ten years ago, around 17 cents out of every dollar spent on a new server went to power and cooling. Today, it's up to 48 cents. Unless things change, that number will get as large as 78 cents or more—IDC, 2007.

Solutions

Conserving power can be realized via technologies such as virtualizing servers. That is, removing the physical server from service and offloading its duties onto another machine. Such a practice saves an organization—per machine—approximately $560 annually in electricity costs.

Another issue isn't so much the planetary impact, but the inability to grow any more. Gartner estimates that by the end of 2008, 50 percent of the datacenters in the world might not have enough power to meet the power and cooling requirements of the high-density computing gear that vendors are offering—Gartner, November 2006.

The point is this: If you have less equipment, you use less electricity and you have less impact on the planet.

There are two ways you can rely less on fossil fuel–based sources of electricity:

- **Virtualization**   Virtualization takes multiple physical servers out of operation and offloads their duties onto a single machine. Specialized software makes it possible to run dozens of servers on one physical machine, thus reducing the amount of power consumed. We'll talk more about this in Chapter 12.

- **Generate your own power**   Many companies are striving to be completely carbon neutral. One way you can cut your electrical bill and make a move toward carbon neutrality is to generate your own power. This is typically done using solar cells or wind turbines. Also, if you generate more power than you need, you can sell it back to your electrical utility. We'll talk about this more in Chapter 3.

Heat

The energy you consume to cool that equipment is also an issue. The more equipment you have (and the less efficient it is), the more heat it generates and the more electricity you use to cool that equipment. We'll talk more about cooling issues in Chapter 4, but the crux of the matter is this: You need less equipment that is more efficient, and you need to employ creative cooling strategies to make the least impact you possibly can.

Consider the Swiss datacenter owned by CIB-Services AG. In 2008, the Uitikon, Switzerland company started using the hot air removed from its datacenter to heat the nearby public swimming pool. What would normally be vented into the atmosphere, and thus wasted, is being utilized for a productive purpose.

Equipment Disposal

The issues go beyond power consumption. Computers and other devices are routinely discarded once they become obsolete. Gartner estimates that 133,000 PCs are discarded by U.S. homes and businesses each day. In 1998 alone, more than 20 million PCs became obsolete in the U.S., but fewer than 11 percent of them were recycled—Gartner, 2003.

Old computers don't need to be looked at like they're infectious materials. Simply by virtue of the fact that they are old and at the end of their life doesn't mean that they are going to hurt you. If they are properly disposed of, they can be a great source for secondary raw materials. On the other hand, if they are disposed of improperly, they can be major sources of toxins and carcinogens.

The problem in many places, including the United States, is that there is no formal, official, legal process in place for the disposal of electronics. There is no umbrella federal law, and individual cities have different requirements for the disposal of electronic waste, but it's a patchwork at best. Other parts of the globe are doing better. Much of Europe and the whole of Japan have policies in place that govern not only what can go inside computer, but also how those devices should be handled when they've reached their end of life.

Electronic waste is a big problem. It represents 2 percent of American landfills, but it accounts for 70 percent of overall toxic waste, as shown next. Much of the e-waste is shipped overseas to China, India, Nigeria, and other places.

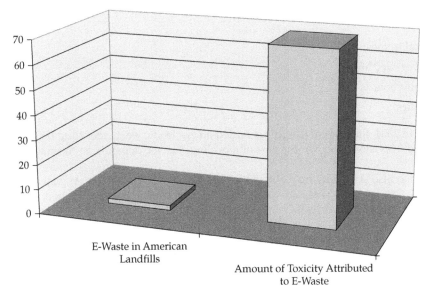

E-Waste Toxicity in Landfills

The Business of Recycling

The International Association of Electronics Recyclers, an industry trade group (www.iaer.org), reports that more than 500 U.S. companies recycle 1.4 million tons of electronics annually, generating US$1.5 billion for recyclers—IAER, June 2008. Recycling e-waste is complicated. First, the metals and plastics must be separated, and then the circuit boards are shredded to separate the aluminum, iron, and copper from the valuable precious metals, such as silver.

NOTE *The plastics might be impossible to reuse if they contain multiple resins.*

Because it's such a labor-intensive and expensive process, many shady "recycling" businesses just sell e-waste to brokers who ship them to developing countries with cheap labor. Dismantling a computer in the U.S. costs about US$35 per hour, while it only costs 25 cents an hour overseas.

Guiyu in the Shantou region of China, as well as Delhi and Bangalore in India, have electronic waste-processing regions. Although these areas can be profitable for the "companies" that import e-waste and extract valuable materials, the environmental and personal costs to the workers are horrendous.

NOTE *We'll talk more about the problems in Guiyu as well as Lagos, Nigeria in Chapter 7.*

Uncontrolled burning, disassembly, and disposal are causing environmental and health problems, including health effects among those who extract precious materials.

The Recycling Process

E-waste processing generally involves first dismantling the equipment into these different components:

- Metal frames
- Power supplies
- Circuit boards
- Plastics

Starting in 2004, the state of California added an electronic waste recycling fee to all new monitors and televisions to cover the cost of recycling. The fee depends on the size of the monitor.

Canada has also started being responsible for electronics recycling. In August 2007, a fee similar to the California fee was added to the cost of purchasing a new television, computer, or computer component in British Columbia. The law also makes it mandatory to recycle those products.

An electronic waste recycling plant found in an industrialized country is able to handle a lot of equipment and effectively sort the components in a safe manner. Material is fed into a hopper, which is then sent up a conveyor and dropped into a mechanical separator. The material is then screened and sorted. This automation limits the amount of human contact with hazardous materials during processing.

Doing It Right

No one has a perfect grip on handling e-waste, but many countries need to be lauded for their efforts. Some do a better job than others, but at the very least something is being done, and it seems like there's enough forward momentum for continual improvement.

The European Union   Europe has taken the lead in the world of e-waste handling. In the 1990s, some European countries banned the disposal of e-waste to landfills. The result of this was a new industry on the continent—e-waste processing.

Responsibly handling e-waste didn't start with computers, but it has grown in scope to include them. The first electronic waste recycling system was mandated by the Swiss in 1991. It started with the collection of old refrigerators. The movement has since snowballed, and since January 2005 it has been possible to return electronic waste to the sales point and other collection points free of charge.

NOTE *In Switzerland, the total amount of recycled electronic waste exceeds 10 kg per capita per year.*

The European Union has mandated a similar system across Europe, known as the Waste Electrical and Electronic Equipment (WEEE) Directive. This directive has been adopted—and subtly modified by member nations—throughout Europe. The directive makes equipment manufacturers financially or physically responsible for obsolete equipment.

This End Producer Responsibility (EPR) policy of the WEEE Directive internalizes the end-of-life costs and provides a competitive incentive for companies to design equipment that is less costly and easier to handle when it has reached end-of-life status.

NOTE   *Under the WEEE Directive, every country has to recycle at least 4 kg of e-waste per capita per year.*

The United States   The United States has led the world in the consumption of many things. However, Americans are sort of stalling when it comes to handling e-waste.

That said, the United States is certainly doing *some* things right. In recent years, some states have banned cathode ray tubes (CRTs) from landfills because of fear that their heavy metals would leach into the groundwater. Circuit boards are also culprits, because the lead in their solder also risks seeping into groundwater. Even worse, if the circuit board is incinerated, air pollution is likely. To counter that, many states have mandated that e-waste be handled separately from regular trash.

Unfortunately, these mandates have had the negative impact of creating "brokers" who collect e-waste and ship it to the aforementioned countries. In Guiyu, for instance, thousands of men, women, and children work in highly polluting environments, extracting the metals, toners, and plastics from computers and other e-waste.

A global agreement known as the Basel Convention prevents the shipment of e-waste to other countries; however, the United States has not signed off on it.

NOTE   *We'll talk more about the Basel Convention in the next chapter.*

The Basel Action Network estimates that 80 percent of the e-waste that is sent out for recycling actually gets loaded onto ships bound for China, India, Kenya, or other countries.

Although the United States doesn't have any federal laws governing e-waste, several states are taking it upon themselves to establish such laws. California was the first state to enact such legislation, followed by Maryland, Maine, Washington, Minnesota, Oregon, and Texas.

Your Company's Carbon Footprint

The term *carbon footprint* is thrown around a lot in green circles. Although we have a general idea of its meaning—one's impact on the planet—there's no standard definition.

In some cases, it might refer just to carbon dioxide output; in other cases it means greenhouse gas emissions. In other organizations, *carbon footprint* might mean that everything is tallied—sourcing materials, manufacturing, distribution, use, disposal, and so forth.

When computing your company's carbon footprint, you need to decide how complete and honest you want to be. Measuring your carbon footprint necessitates gathering a lot of information. Let's consider your carbon footprint as it relates to greenhouse gases. You need to track such areas as

- Facilities
- Operations
- Transportation
- Travel
- Purchases

NOTE   *"Purchases" means everything from raw materials to office supplies.*

You also have to draw some boundaries in your measurements. That is, how far upstream and downstream will your organization measure? For example, when you buy new servers for your datacenter, are you responsible for the greenhouse gases generated to have them delivered, or is that the manufacturer's statistic?

Think about the issue downstream. Is your company or your customers responsible for climatic impacts of the use and disposal of your products? You also need to ensure that all this information is collected consistently so it can be put into reports for different departments, facilities, locations, and so forth.

Although this seems like a lot of work (and it is), it doesn't have to be overwhelming. Fortunately, there is a fairly standard way organizations are measuring their greenhouse gas emissions.

Measuring

Measurement is not a five-minute project. It will take time and expertise. You'll likely want to call in someone who specializes in this work, simply because you'll get better results, it'll free you to do your own work, and you'll be less likely to goof it up.

Four major steps are used to measure your carbon footprint:

- Define what is included in your carbon footprint.
- Set your baseline.
- Track, calculate, and analyze your footprint.
- Report your results to stakeholders.

Let's take a closer look at what's involved in these steps.

Define Your Borders

You first need to define what you are going to be measuring. You can be as liberal with this as you like, but realize that the more you decide to include in your measurement, the more difficult it will be. Realize, also, that while tracking less data is certainly easier, you don't get an accurate accounting.

In your calculations, you might consider both upstream and downstream events. Consider Figure 1-2.

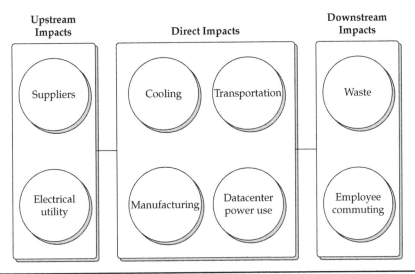

FIGURE 1-2   Defining what you intend to measure also includes establishing boundaries. How far upstream and downstream will you measure?

Will you integrate the impact of your suppliers into your carbon footprint? What about when your product is sold and out the door? Does its use and ultimate end figure into your carbon footprint?

Set a Baseline

Take a look at any available data. You need to establish a baseline year by which your future progress will be measured.

As you look at the existing data, be aware whether anything unusual was going on that year. For instance, were there newly established governmental guidelines that drastically changed your work environment? If so, you might want to look at a different year.

Track and Analyze Your Data

Once you get the data tabulated, it's not only good as a yardstick by which you can measure future performance, but given the right data, you can use it to ferret out problems now. Look at the numbers critically and look for any anomalies.

For instance, if you have three locations that are more or less similar in size, and one has an unusually large reading, you know something's wrong. By the same token, if all three numbers are the same, but the locations are different sizes, you also know there is a problem.

Report

In the end, you want to present your carbon footprint information to important stakeholders in your organization. This can be the CEO, shareholders, and employees. By showing them your study, these people can see the results of which efforts are being made.

Also, as Figure 1-3 shows, if you don't see the improvement you expected, you can study the problem and explain why you didn't reach a given milestone.

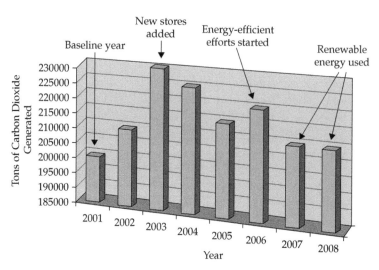

Tracking Carbon Dioxide Annually

Details

It's a daunting task, but it's one you can do. You just need to have a roadmap. First, start with the basics. Take a look at your organization and how people get to and from work each day. Consider the energy used to get your employees to work. There are a number of online calculators you can use to help with the task. They can help you calculate the amount of greenhouse gases generated by your commuting employees. You can also calculate the amount of greenhouse gases you create because of the electricity your datacenter consumes.

NOTE *Lots of calculators are available online, but be aware that many of them are trying to sell you climate offsets, allowing you to purchase renewable-energy credits.*

The next step is to examine your operations. That is, take a look at what you buy, sell, and produce. To figure out your organization's operational impact, you need to get help from an outside consultant or other expert. This is because every organization is absolutely unique. The greenhouse gas emissions from a brewery are going to be drastically different from a company that edits television commercials.

To get the most accurate accounting of your greenhouse gas emissions, you must follow the GHG Protocol Initiative (for more information click Link 1-1 at www.greenitinfo.com/links). It is a globally recognized reporting standard for greenhouse gas emissions.

NOTE *Throughout the book we have included web links to additional information. In many cases, the links we wanted to use in the book were quite long and somewhat cryptic—making them a chore to actually type into your browser. To make it easier to access those URLs and the information they contain, we have created a companion website for the book that has additional information and direct links to those URLs. So any time you see a "Link" reference in the book, you can go to www.greenitinfo.com/links and click the link number specified in the text to access the additional information.*

Based on the protocols, companies must decide how to account for both direct and indirect emissions:

- **Direct emissions**   These are from sources that your company owns or controls, such as factory smokestacks, vents, and company vehicles.
- **Indirect emissions**   These are generated as a result of your company's activities, but occur in sources owned by someone else. For example, if you contract work out or your employees travel, those emissions are generated by a third party, but because of you.

Why Bother?

Why do you care about your carbon footprint? Although measuring your carbon footprint is a good way to measure your overall progress toward becoming green, it isn't just for bragging rights or to keep in the corner of the company newsletter to let everyone know how well you're doing.

A good emissions inventory can help with numerous business goals, including the following:

- Helping your company improve its efficiencies
- Reducing costs
- Getting public recognition for taking action to reduce or eliminate your climate impacts

It can also help your organization if you are part of somebody else's supply chain. Because major organizations are requiring their suppliers to demonstrate their own commitment to minimizing climate impacts, measuring your impacts may help you maintain your link in the supply chain.

Consider, also, the impact on your customers. According to a study by GlobeScan on behalf of AccountAbility and Consumers International, 63 percent of consumers want climate change claims made by businesses to be proven by independent third parties—GlobeScan, 2007.

Plan for the Future

When you measure your carbon footprint, you also need to keep an eye on your crystal ball and think about the future. If your infrastructure is always expanding, even if you virtualize, your virtualized solution will expand as well—just not as greedily as a "conventional" system.

Try to anticipate your future needs when computing your carbon footprint, and take the time now to think about how you can minimize that growth's impact.

Cost Savings

Our primary intent in this book is to show you how adopting Green IT practices can save your business potentially millions of dollars over current practices. Of course, we also want to encourage you to adopt ecologically responsible practices, so that we don't wind up living on a cinder with no atmosphere. Oh yeah, we'd also like to avoid getting cancer from drinking groundwater. But even if you have absolutely no interest in helping the environment, the changes in business processes, practices, and behavior outlined in this book can have an overwhelmingly positive impact on your business.

Can a company be green and churn a healthy profit? Are these two concepts contradictory? Not at all. Even better, not only are they not contradictory, one actually builds on the other. By lessening your organization's impact on the environment, you're going to spend more—at first. After that, you save money—you save *a lot* of money.

The number-one reason businesses either decide to go green or are prevented from going green is cost. Unless equipment is planned to be replaced or there's a datacenter design in the works, most businesses aren't likely to replace their equipment just for the sake of duty to society. But when the cost of power starts taking a bigger and bigger bite out of the IT budget, organizations start really looking at green computing, according to research by Forrester.

Hardware

There are a number of ways that specific hardware and hardware deployments can affect the environment—and your bottom line. The biggest way you can reduce your impact on the environment and the amount of money you're paying for hardware is to simply buy less equipment. We'll talk more about virtualization in Chapter 12, but let's talk a little about the benefits to reducing the amount of hardware you use.

Taking the Steps, Reaping the Rewards

Consider the savings that Nashville's Vanderbilt University and the state of Oregon are going to experience. Both groups have begun datacenter virtualization projects (as of early 2008) and expect to save millions of dollars by the time the projects are finished.

Vanderbilt's Information Technology Services organization is using server virtualization to reduce its energy use. By reducing the number of physical servers they're using, they save money and they do less damage to the environment. They have virtualized 35 percent of the servers they manage, which is the equivalent of saving 20,575 watts per hour. The organization's goal is to get up to 80 percent virtualization on its servers.

The state of Oregon is taking on an even bigger project. It is combining 11 separate state agency datacenters by June 2009. The centers will be combined into a new center in the state capital, Salem, and will combine both servers and storage. The project costs US$43 million up front, but will save US$12 million per year after that, and will reduce power consumption by up to 35 percent.

Use What You Have

Although purchasing new, energy-efficient equipment is a good idea, it's only a good idea if you actually need new equipment. If you have old computers that can be repurposed, you've just administered a one-two punch. You don't have to recycle anything and you don't have to spend money on something new.

For instance, you can take an older computer and turn it into a thin client. With a thin client, the processing and storage duties are conducted at the server. The client just needs enough power to be able to display what is going on at the server.

If you don't like the idea of having old equipment in use—even as a thin client—consider still using the thin-client model, just buy new thin clients. On average, a thin client uses 15 watts of energy instead of the 150 watts that workstations use, as shown next. If you deploy them across your organization, your energy bill will be ten times less than what it is now.

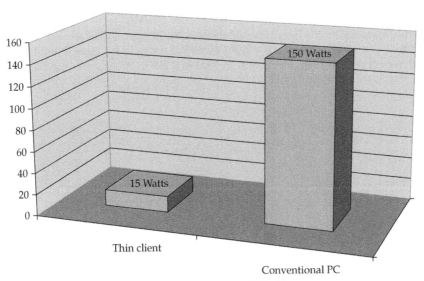

Watts used-PC versus Thin Client

NOTE *We talk more about thin clients in Chapter 8.*

Power

Let's look at the numbers. Buying computers and then disposing of them is a one-time issue—you pick out the computers, you buy them, and you're done. When it's time to get rid of the computers, you find a responsible recycler, you hand them over, and you're done. But the issue of power consumption is ongoing. In fact, you'll be reminded of it every month when the electrical bill shows up.

NOTE *Actually, your facilities manager will be reminded of it. Unless he or she shares the electrical bill with you each month, you may live blissfully unaware of how much electricity you use.*

The issue of power consumption is important on two levels. First, consider your bottom line. The more power you use, the more money you spend. Next, consider the issue on an environmental level. The more power you use, the more fossil fuels the local electrical utility has to burn, thus causing more greenhouse gases to be generated.

Desktops

Power can be managed easily enough throughout your user base, just be sure to enable power management settings.

Consider this: An average desktop PC requires 85 watts just to idle, even with the monitor off. If that computer is only in use or idling for 40 hours a week instead of a full 168, over US$40 in energy costs will be saved annually from that workstation alone. Think about the savings that can be recognized if those savings are multiplied by thousands of computers across your organization.

Datacenters

Networked computers are the backbone of business, but the growth in servers and network infrastructure has caused a sharp spike in the electrical usage in the datacenter. Power consumption per rack has risen from 1 kW in 2000 to 8 kW in 2006 and is expected to top 20 kW in 2010, as shown next.

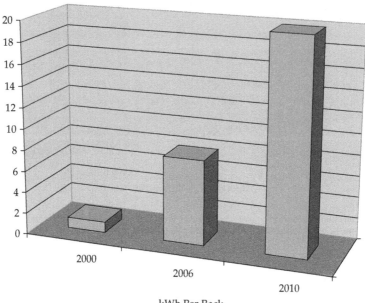

kWh Per Rack

This 20-fold demand in energy consumption isn't just due to more servers. A lot of the increase comes from the additional network infrastructure needed to support additional servers. Of the US$29 billion spent each year on server power and cooling, just 30 percent actually goes to the IT load.

Consider a 24-port Ethernet switch. On the low end, it uses 250 watts of power (most switches use more) and it is in continuous use. Each 1U rack switch uses 2,190 kW each year. If the electricity generated to power this switch comes from a coal-fired plant, 1,780 pounds of coal are needed to produce the 2,190 kW, as illustrated next.

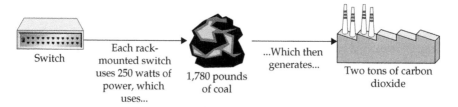

Switch — Each rack-mounted switch uses 250 watts of power, which uses... 1,780 pounds of coal ...Which then generates... Two tons of carbon dioxide

Burning 1,780 pounds of coal releases over two tons of carbon dioxide into the atmosphere, along with other pollutants, such as sulfur dioxide and nitrogen oxide.

NOTE *That doesn't even take into consideration the pollutants generated during mining and transportation.*

But that's just for one rack switch. Multiply those numbers (1,780 pounds of coal and two tons of carbon dioxide) by the millions of switches in the world, and you can see that we have a big problem on our hands.

Consumption

The EPA estimated that datacenters consume 1.5 percent of the nation's electrical power, as shown next—US EPA, 2007. That's barely enough to even show up on a pie chart, but it still equates to about 61 billion kWh per year. That's twice as much power as was consumed five years ago, and that number will double again by 2011 to more than 100 billion kWh.

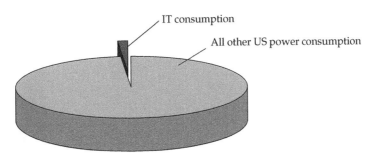

IT consumption

All other US power consumption

Unless CIOs do something to change that trend, 100 billion kWh will require the equivalent of 15 new power plants to be constructed. It would churn out as much as 47 million metric tons of carbon dioxide per year.

NOTE *That's not exactly true. We wouldn't have to build that many power plants—they can't be built that quickly anyway. Instead of building all those power plants, we could just have brownouts and rolling blackouts during peak usage times.*

The EPA has suggested a number of ways in which datacenters can be more energy efficient, ranging from properly organizing physical space to reduce cooling loads to using energy-efficient power supplies.

Higher energy-efficient power supplies can lower your datacenter's electrical bill dramatically. Annual savings of US$2700 to US$6500 per rack are possible simply by moving to energy-efficient power supplies.

The ideal power supplies are at least 80 percent efficient. Supplies reaching that level of efficiency are certified as 80 Plus. To get an idea of what you can save by using an 80 Plus certified power supply, go to www.80plus.org/80sav.htm. There, you'll see a calculator like the one in Figure 1-4.

The calculator allows you to enter the number of 80 Plus certified computers and servers your organization is using, and then it allows you to put in the average price for electricity (expressed in kWh). A link to the calculator can be found at www.greenitinfo.com/links listed as Link 1-2.

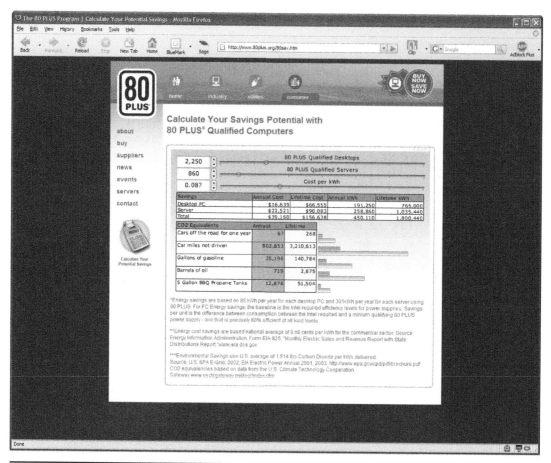

Figure 1-4   A calculator at the 80 Plus website can show you how much money you can save by using energy efficient power supplies in your computers.

Now, this isn't an expressly scientific model of how much you'll save if you adopt overall green strategies, but with a couple clicks of the mouse, you can see approximately how much money you'd save if you use equipment that is 80 Plus certified.

Although it would be great for all organizations to altruistically embrace the notion of going green, that isn't happening. As such, it's up to the government to legislate ethical behavior for companies and individuals. Governments around the world have their own rules and regulations governing the handling of electronic equipment. In the next chapter we'll take a closer look at what rules are on the books around the world.

Current Initiatives
and Standards

It wasn't really treasure that was sunken in that Minnesota lake, but something was down there. In the spring of 2006, discarded computer monitors started bobbing to the surface of Rice Lake and then washing ashore. By the fall, authorities had collected 64 monitors and other e-waste that had been criminally dumped into the lake. The notion of a monitor popping up next to your fishing boat can be comical, until you consider what's involved.

In this case, computer monitors pollute with mercury, cadmium, and lead. Other forms of e-waste—discarded central processing units, batteries, cellular telephones, and so forth—contribute those toxins and many others that can be released into our environment if improperly disposed of. And it's that e-waste that poses a threat to the environment, around the world.

Just like speed limits, how long your grass can grow, and how loud your party can be before the police arrive, different regions have different requirements for the disposal of e-waste. Not every country has established rules, but those who do have different rules. And even within countries, regional differences still occur. For instance, the state of Massachusetts simply prohibits cathode ray tubes (CRTs) from landfills, whereas Minnesota requires product manufacturers to have a complex reclamation program in place.

NOTE *Legislation in general is a moving target. What is true today will be changed tomorrow. As such, be sure to check with your national and local rules and laws to see what applies to you.*

In this chapter we'll look at what different countries and different states require for the disposal of e-waste. Requirements vary drastically, so we'll also look at worldwide initiatives to reduce e-waste. We'll kick off our discussion with an examination of the United Nations and its efforts to ameliorate the e-waste problem.

Global Initiatives

Although the Keokuk County, Iowa waste management plan forbids the dumping of hazardous wastes, the issue isn't just a local-level concern. Let's take a look at some initiatives that can affect the whole planet—from the residents of Keokuk County to those in Bukoba, Tanzania.

United Nations

At the highest level of global governance is the United Nations. Seeing that e-waste is a international concern, it has stepped forward and implemented its Solving the E-waste Problem (StEP) program.

Solving the E-Waste Problem

Don't misunderstand—StEP isn't some sort of military organization where a strike force wearing hemp berets and carrying weapons made from recycled materials rappels into office buildings where CRTs are being disposed of unsafely. Rather, StEP is a program that is open to companies, governmental organizations, academic institutions, nongovernmental organizations (NGOs), and nonprofit organizations around the world. To be involved with StEP, an organization has to commit to active and productive involvement in the StEP program.

StEP's prime objectives are as follows:

- Optimizing the life cycle of electrical and electronic equipment by improving supply chains
- Closing material loops
- Reducing contamination
- Increasing the utilization of resources and the reuse of equipment
- Exercising concern about disparities such as the digital divide between industrializing and industrialized countries
- Increasing public, scientific, and business knowledge
- Developing clear policy recommendations

StEP is based on five principles:

- Work is based on scientific assessments and incorporates a comprehensive view of the social, environmental, and economic aspects of e-waste.
- StEP conducts research on the entire life cycle of electronic and electrical equipment and their corresponding global supply, process, and material flows.
- StEP's research and pilot projects are meant to contribute to the solution of e-waste problems.
- StEP condemns all illegal activities related to e-waste, including illegal shipments and reuse and recycling practices that are harmful to the environment and human health.
- StEP seeks to foster safe, ecological, and energy-efficient reuse and recycling practices around the globe in a socially responsible manner.

Task Forces

StEP gets its work done by members within five task forces. These task forces address e-waste issues at varying levels. These task forces focus on the research, analysis, and facilitation of pilot projects. The work is executed by a secretariat hosted by the United Nations University, and progress is monitored by an international steering committee, composed of key stakeholder groups.

The task forces are concerned with issues ranging from policy and legislation to designing e-waste management models.

NOTE *Additional information about the United Nations' StEP program can be found at www.greenitinfo.com/links under Link 2-1.*

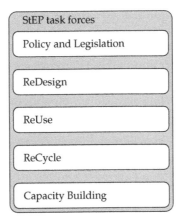

StEP task forces

- Policy and Legislation
- ReDesign
- ReUse
- ReCycle
- Capacity Building

Policy and Legislation   The Policy and Legislation task force reports and analyzes the status of existing techniques and policies for managing e-waste. Based on its research and study, the Policy and Legislation task force makes recommendations for future e-waste management solutions.

Specifically, the task force does these things:

- Analyzes and evaluates national legislation and the international framework for controlling and enforcing trade of e-waste and electronic recycling. Specifically, it examines how the European Waste Electrical and Electronic Equipment (WEEE), Restriction of Hazardous Substances (RoHS), and energy-using products legislation, as well as the Basel Convention and other agreements on the national and international level, achieve their aims with regard to recycling and minimizing environmental impacts and how they contribute to sustainable development.

- Studies green purchasing schemes, especially how they apply to e-waste, in various countries and how that purchasing affects the trade of e-waste and used electronics products.

- Examines how to manage the e-waste problems in industrializing regions such as Africa and Eastern Europe, Latin America, and Southeast Asia.

- Serves as a resource for organizations in that it points out existing business models to support the sustainable use of Information and Communications Technology (ICT) in industrializing countries.

ReDesign   The ReDesign task force supports a sustainable solution to the e-waste problem by focusing on the notion of concept and electrical and electronic equipment (EEE) design. The group's main objective is to optimize the life cycle characteristics of EEE and their adaptation to specific end-of-life conditions.

Current "design for recycling" activities now are focused on industrialized nations. This task force makes special efforts in identifying specific issues in industrializing countries around the world.

The task force defines *redesign* as measures that support the optimal lifetime of a specific product through the optimization of design features. Such efforts hope to improve repair, refurbishment, reuse, and recycling of a product and its components.

Specific tasks include the following:

- Identifying and assessing critical design aspects in the end-of-life treatment of EEE. This could include the material composition and toxicity, its design, or any other components that might impact a product's end of life.
- Comparing current industry approaches to product end-of-life to identify current economical, environmental, and regional design considerations.
- Developing and demonstrating new design solutions of various products.

ReUse   The goal of the ReUse task force is to define globally consistent reuse practices, principles, and standards for EEE products from business-to-business (B2B) and business-to-consumer (B2C) users that are economically, socially, and environmentally appropriate for:

- Changing consumer behavior to get acceptance for reuse and early product takeback. The idea is to avoid long storage by the consumer.
- Extending the usage of EEE products and components.
- Reducing the flow of irresponsible reuse between donor and developing countries.

Specific goals of the task force include:

- Developing a common nomenclature for definitions of reuse, refurbishment, EEE products, and other related topics.
- Determining how equipment enters the "reuse" category.
- Developing globally consistent environmental and business principles and guidelines for equipment recovery.
- Designing a global standard and program for maintaining quality in environmentally sound practices, data privacy, and usage extension.
- Identifying the common barriers to product life extension and recommending practices to overcome these barriers.
- Developing cross-border guidelines and developing guidelines to determine when reuse is economically, environmentally, and socially preferable to recycling.

ReCycle   The goal of the ReCycle task force is to enhance global recycling infrastructures, systems, and technologies while realizing sustainable e-waste-recycling systems.

Specific objectives include:

- Gathering and assessing the most relevant environmental, economic, and social characteristics of e-waste recycling in the industrialized world.
- Evaluating recycling systems, leading to recommendations for long-term development of eco-efficient resource cycles.
- Analyzing transboundary shipments and logistics of e-waste and its underlying driving forces, dynamics, and regulations, as well as the constraints for sustainable resource cycles.
- Describing the best available and emerging technologies for large and small volume WEEE treatment in both industrializing and industrialized countries.

Capacity Building   The Capacity Building task force focuses on building infrastructures for sustainable, efficient, effective, and target group–oriented capacity building, covering relevant aspects of the entire life cycle of EEE in order to sustainably solve the ever-growing e-waste problem.

Specific objectives include:

- Organizing mutual learning environments, including the identification of viable approaches adapted by different target countries and groups, and then testing and implementing these projects.
- Setting standards in the form of comprehensive guidelines for capacity building.

For more information about StEP and how your organization can get involved, visit Link 2-1. There you can find out more and follow a link to its website and learn about specific programs and how to contact StEP and get involved.

Basel Action Network

Though the nonprofit Basel Action Network (BAN) is headquartered in Seattle, Washington, it operates globally. It is a worldwide organization, focused on working with the human rights and environmental impacts of e-waste. It also works to ban waste trade and promote green, toxin-free design of consumer products.

BAN performs these broad functions:

- Acts as a source of information on the waste trade for journalists, academics, and the general public. BAN's informational output includes its website (see Link 2-2), as well as an e-mail newsletter and electronic action alerts.
- Provides international policy advocacy. BAN is invited to participate in UN meetings and policy deliberations. BAN has also worked with the Organization of Economic Cooperation and Development (OECD) and the UN Environment Program (UNEP) Chemicals Program and Governing Council. BAN has also produced Model National Legislation on toxic waste trade for developing countries.
- Conducts field research and investigations in developing countries. It also provides photographic and video documentation of e-waste trade.
- Participates with NGOs around the world in campaigns to counter toxic trade.

BAN is active on a number of campaigns, including the following:

- **E-Waste Stewardship Project** A program to ensure that exports of hazardous electronic waste to developing countries are eliminated and replaced with producer responsibility via green design programs and legislation.
- **Green Shipbreaking** A program that ensures hazardous materials have been removed from U.S. government ships prior to export.
- **Zero Mercury Campaign** A program working toward an internationally binding treaty on mercury pollution to eliminate its extraction, use, trade, and recycling. To promote permanent storage and alternative uses, BAN is working particularly to eliminate surplus mercury trade to developing countries.
- **Basel Ban Ratification** BAN promotes the Basel Ban Amendment Ratifications globally and works to prevent the weakening of this amendment.

Basel Convention

The Basel Convention on the Control of Transboundary Movements of Hazardous Wastes and Their Disposal—less verbosely known as the Basel Convention—is an international treaty designed to reduce the transportation of hazardous waste between nations, especially from developed to less developed countries. Further, the convention deals with minimizing the amount and toxicity of generated wastes. The Convention dates back to 1989 when it was opened for signatures, and went into effect May 5, 1992.

NOTE *Despite having "Basel" in their names, the Basel Action Network and the Basel Convention are totally distinct. BAN is an activist group whereas the Basel Convention is a treaty.*

Origins

The Basel Convention was needed because as environmental laws became stricter in the 1970s, shipping of waste became more popular.

One incident that led to the creation of the Basel Convention was the *Khian Sea* waste disposal incident. A ship carrying incinerator ash from Philadelphia had dumped half its load on a Haitian beach. It was forced away and sailed for several months, changing its name numerous times. Since no port would accept it, the crew finally dumped its toxic load at sea.

Another incident was a 1988 case in which five ships transported 8000 barrels of hazardous waste from Italy to the Nigerian town of Koko. A farmer there had agreed to store the waste on his property for $100 per month.

Although the origins of the Basel Convention had nothing to do with e-waste, in recent years, thanks to the increasing trade in recycling electronic components, e-waste has become a large component in the Basel Convention.

Application

The Basel Convention applies various conditions on the import and export of waste, and it also applies strict requirements for the notice, consent, and tracking of movement of waste across national boundaries.

The Basel Convention also prohibits the import or export of waste between parties of the convention and nonparties. There is an exception to this rule, however. If waste is subject to another treaty and does not take away from the Basel Convention, party and nonparty transportation can occur.

This is especially relevant to the United States, because it is a nonparty to the convention, but has a number of similar agreements that allow for the shipping of hazardous wastes to Basel party countries.

Although the United States is a nonparty, it can still ship e-waste to party members, such as China, because it has other treaties in place. This is illustrated in Figure 2-1.

Further, parties to the Basel Convention must honor import bans from other parties.

Additional Regulation

The Basel Convention also calls for an overall reduction of waste generation. This is meant not to meddle within a sovereign country's boundaries, but rather to discourage the generation of e-waste, which might then be transported to other countries.

The convention also calls for parties to adopt a protocol establishing liability guidelines and procedures for damages that stem from the movement of hazardous waste across borders.

Controversy

The Basel Convention has not been a slam dunk, however. Of the 170 parties to the convention, three have yet to ratify it, including the United States, Haiti, and Afghanistan. Additionally, a number of countries support the Basel Ban.

NOTE *A complete list of the countries to have signed and ratified the Basel Convention can be found on the Basel Secretariat's web page via Link 2-3.*

Although the intent of the Basel Convention seems laudable enough, some people, NGOs, and countries aren't clapping. They don't think the convention goes far enough.

Some countries and NGOs have advocated a complete ban on shipping hazardous waste to developing countries. Additionally, the convention does not prohibit waste exports (except to Antarctica), but rather requires a notification and consent system.

FIGURE 2-1
Although the United States is a nonparty, it can still ship e-waste to party members, such as China, because it has other treaties in place.

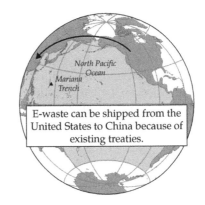

North Pacific Ocean

Mariana Trench

E-waste can be shipped from the United States to China because of existing treaties.

The result of this distaste for the Basel Convention was the drafting—and large approval—of the Basel Ban Amendment. It was the work of developing nations, Greenpeace, and some European countries such as Denmark.

The Basel Ban is not in force yet, but is considered morally binding by signatories. So far 63 countries have signed the ban, but for its adoption three-fourths of the convention's 170 signatories must sign off.

NOTE   *The European Union implemented the Basel Ban in its Waste Shipment Regulation. Therefore, it is legally binding for all EU member states.*

North America

North America is home to two countries that seem to be struggling with implementing e-waste programs. The United States and Canada have both been trying to get national laws on the books, but it hasn't happened yet. Not to be deterred, several states and provinces have taken up the issue at the local level and have developed their own e-waste laws.

This section examines what's going on in the U.S. and Canada. It looks at the issue of e-waste at the national level and also drills down to specific state and province measures.

The United States

Surprisingly, the U.S. doesn't have a national law governing e-waste, but it is making strides. Politicians try to pass legislation, but it seems to run out of gas before passage. Although the country, as a whole, doesn't have any broad e-waste regulation, many states have taken it upon themselves to protect their environments.

EPEAT

Although the federal government hasn't adopted Green IT laws that apply to the entire populace, it is moving forward on rules that apply to itself. And because of the government's sheer buying power (it buys about 2.2 million PCs per year), business is likely to follow suit.

The government is moving forward with a plan requiring federal agencies to buy PCs and monitors that are energy efficient and have reduced levels of toxic chemicals. In December 2007, the U.S. Department of Defense, NASA, and the General Services Administration outlined a rule that requires purchases to be compliant with the Electronic Product Environmental Assessment Tool (EPEAT).

EPEAT was developed by the Green Electronics Council in Portland, Oregon to help institutional purchasers evaluate, compare, and select desktop computers, notebook computers, and monitors based on their environmental attributes.

Electronics can be awarded a gold, silver, or bronze certification, based on how well they meet 51 criteria, including ease of disassembly, chemical content, end-of-life design, and others. Products must meet at least 23 of the criteria for the bronze-level certification.

NOTE *You can download a complete list of the EPEAT criteria via Link 2-4.*

This move is good news for the world of green computing. Because the government is such a big buyer of computers, manufacturers will scramble to make their own EPEAT-certified machines so they can make sales.

At this point, only a handful of vendors have earned gold EPEAT ratings. Dell has six products with gold ratings and 72 at the silver level. Hewlett-Packard has one gold-rated PC and 73 silver. Apple has 17 products meeting silver requirements.

NOTE *Naturally, these numbers are moving targets. Although they were true at the time of writing, it's likely that manufacturers are going to step up their EPEAT-certified machines, so hopefully these numbers will be well out of date by the time you read this.*

For more information on EPEAT, go to its website at www.epeat.net, or via Link 2-5. On the home page is a listing of all the EPEAT-certified electronics, sorted by EPEAT ranking.

National Computer Recycling Act

The United State House of Representatives has twice tried to pass the National Computer Recycling Act. The crux of the act is that consumers would be charged a US $10 recycling fee each time a new computer is sold. It also requires the EPA to take a number of steps to help manage e-waste in the United States.

The act, if introduced again and passed, would do the following:

- Direct the EPA to develop a grant program to encourage municipalities, individuals, and organizations to start e-waste recycling programs.
- Assess a fee of up to $10 on new computers in order to fund the grant program.
- Require a comprehensive e-waste study to be conducted by the EPA, which would make the ongoing recommendations for addressing the problem.
- Require the administrator of the EPA to be in full consultation with manufacturers, retailers, recycling agencies, waste management professionals, and environmental and consumer groups.

The bill was first introduced in 2003 and then again in 2005. Each time the bill was never debated and simply died on the vine. It's not clear if the bill in this form or another will be reintroduced to the House or if similar legislation will be introduced to the Senate.

Individual States

Although the federal government struggles with finding its own voice on the issue of e-waste, individual states are taking the initiative. California, for example, has several measures in place to combat e-waste. But it's not alone. Many others are taking a stab at alleviating e-waste.

Let's take a closer look at one specific state—California—to see how it is regulating the management of e-waste. California is approaching the issue from several angles and seems to be making good progress with its efforts:

- According to state waste and recycling data, California generated approximately 140,000 tons of covered electrical devices (CEDs) in 2005, with more than 60 million pounds of this electronic waste taken back for recycling through the program. In 2006, this number rose to more than 120 million tons recycled, as shown next.

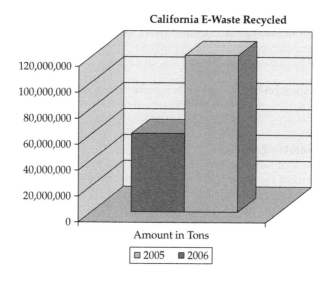

California E-Waste Recycled

- In 2006, the recycling rate for covered electronics was 29 percent, up almost twice as much as 2005.
- The California Integrated Waste Management Board (CIWMB) paid out approximately $61 million in reimbursements to recyclers in 2006.

Electronic Waste Recycling Act   On January 1, 2005, California enacted legislation (formally known as SB 20) to implement an electronic waste recovery and recycling program. The Electronic Waste Recycling Act is modeled after the European Economic Union's Product Stewardship Initiative.

The act's intent is to provide cost-free recycling opportunities to consumers. The goal of it is to prevent the illegal dumping of electronic waste and to discourage e-waste "stockpiling." The larger goal of the act is to decrease the amount of hazardous materials entering the municipal solid waste stream.

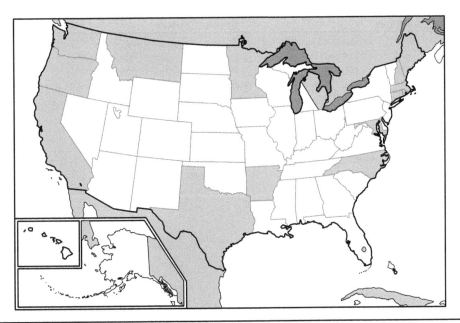

FIGURE 2-2   Several states have already adopted their own e-waste legislation.

Cell Phone Takeback and Recycling   AB 2901 requires some of California's largest cellular telephone retailers to take back used cellular telephones at no cost to the consumer. The phones are then reused, recycled, or properly disposed of.

Rechargeable Battery Takeback and Recycling   Similar to AB 2901, AB 1125 was modeled after the cellular phone takeback bill. This law requires all retailers that sell rechargeable batteries to accept them back at no cost to the consumer. This makes it easy for consumers to drop off end-of-life batteries for recycling or proper disposal.

Other States

There is no single, perfect way to manage e-waste, as you can see from the global initiatives already mentioned. This is also true when comparing the different approaches the individual countries have legislated, as we will explain later in this chapter.

Figure 2-2 illustrates the states that have e-waste laws on the books.

Table 2-1 is a summary of the different laws in the U.S. and how states' borders affect how you're to manage your e-waste.

State	Summary	Covered Devices	Effective Date
Arkansas	HB 2115 imposes a deadline for the disposal of state computer and e-waste in landfills.	Applies only to state agency–generated e-waste. Equipment includes computers, computer monitors, TVs, audio and stereo equipment, monitors, computers, VCRs, keyboards, printers, telephones, and fax machines.	2008
Connecticut	HB7249 establishes a mandatory recycling program for discarded CEDs. CED manufacturers must be part of a program to finance and implement the collection, transportation, and recycling of CEDs. Cities arrange for the collection and transportation to recyclers, and recyclers bill the manufacturers.	TVs, monitors, personal computers, and laptops.	January 1, 2009
Maine	LD 1892 requires municipalities to send waste computer and television monitors to consolidation centers funded by the manufacturers. Manufacturers also pay for shipping and recycling.	TVs, computer monitors, or anything that has a display greater than 4 inches or contains a circuit board.	January 18, 2006
Maryland	In HB 575, a county-by-county collection system is established. Manufacturers are responsible for funding the program or creating their own plans.	Desktop computers, personal computers, laptops, and TVs.	January 1, 2006. Expires 2010.
Massachusetts	CRTs are prohibited from all solid waste disposal facilities.	Cathode ray tubes.	April 1, 2000
Minnesota	HF 854 requires manufacturers to pay a registration fee for setting up their e-waste recycling program, and they must collect 60 percent of the weight of covered electronic devices sold in the state and 80 percent thereafter.	TVs, computer monitors, laptops, computers, printers, scanners, and other computer peripherals.	August 2007
Montana	HB 555 establishes a public education program to provide alternative disposal information for household hazardous waste recycling.	Video, audio, telecommunications equipment, computers, and household appliances.	April 2007

TABLE 2-1   State-Specific Regulations for American E-Waste

State	Summary	Covered Devices	Effective Date
New Hampshire	HB 1455 prohibits disposing of video display devices in solid waste landfills or incinerators.	CRTs.	July 1, 2007
North Carolina	S 1492 requires manufacturers to pay for the transportation and recycling costs for covered devices from collection sites.	Desktops, laptops, monitors, keyboards, and mice.	January 1, 2009
Oregon	HB 2626 requires manufacturers of CEDs to participate in recycling programs and provide collection sites for e-waste. Manufacturers pay for the program, based on how much they sell in Oregon.	TVs, monitors, personal computers, and laptops.	January 1, 2009
Rhode Island	S 2509 bans electronics from landfills. The law will require the Department of Environmental Management and stakeholders to develop the plan for collecting, recycling, or reusing covered products.	Desktops, laptops, monitors (both CRT and flat screen), plasma televisions, and "any similar video display device with a screen greater than four inches diagonally and that contains a circuit board."	July 1, 2008
Texas	HB 2714 requires manufacturers of electronic devices to pay for the collection, transportation, and recycling of covered devices. Manufacturers can also set up their own recycling programs.	Desktops, laptops, and monitors.	September 1, 2008
Washington	SB 6428 will require manufacturers to produce and finance an e-waste recycling program. The measure also encourages manufacturers to design products that are less toxic and recyclable.	TVs, monitors, laptops, and desktop computers.	January 1, 2009

TABLE 2-1 State-Specific Regulations for American E-Waste (*Continued*)

Canada

Canada is managing e-waste in a way similar to the European Union's Waste Electrical and Electronic Equipment (WEEE) Directive. The goal is to reduce the amount of electronic waste going into the general household waste stream.

Environment Canada (the Canadian equivalent of the U.S. EPA) has noted that more than 140,000 tons of used electronics go into Canadian landfills each year.

FIGURE 2-3   Many Canadian provinces have passed e-waste laws.

NOTE   *The WEEE Directive is explained in more depth later in this chapter.*

Many, but not all, of the provinces have adopted e-waste laws. Figure 2-3 illustrates which provinces have current legislation.

Like in the United States, different provinces have different regulations for managing e-waste. Table 2-2 describes how Canadian provinces regulate e-waste.

Province	Description	Covered Devices	Effective Date
Alberta	The Alberta Recycling Management Authority manages a collection and recycling program, collecting fees from retailers, wholesalers, distributors, and manufacturers. The program involves 100 collection points throughout the province.	Laptops, electronic notebooks, printers, computer processors, computer monitors, and TVs.	2004

TABLE 2-2   E-Waste Management by Canadian Province

Province	Description	Covered Devices	Effective Date
British Columbia	Producers are required to develop and fund product stewardship plans or comply with a program for existing products.	Computers, monitors, computer accessories, printers, and televisions. The scope could be expanded later.	January 1, 2008
New Brunswick	The Clean Environment Act establishes a multimaterial stewardship board to manage existing waste programs and create new ones for electronics. There is no formal regulation in place except for the pilot program.		
Nova Scotia	Manufacturers are required to provide collection or enter into a stewardship agreement.	TVs, computers, printers, scanners, telephones, cell phones, and electronic games.	Fall 2007
Ontario	The takeback program will be overseen by Waste Diversion Ontario and managed by Stewardship Ontario.	Household appliances, IT equipment, telecommunication equipment, audio/visual equipment, toys/sports equipment, power tools, as well as navigational, measuring, monitoring, medical, and control instruments.	2008
Quebec	An amendment to the Environment Quality Act to include producer responsibility for WEEE.	WEEE.	2007
Saskatchewan	The Saskatchewan Waste Electronic Equipment Program (SWEEP) is an industry-managed collection system.	CRTs, CPUs, laptops, input devices, printers, and TVs.	February 2006

Table 2-2   E-Waste Management by Canadian Province (*Continued*)

Australia

As of this writing, Australia does not have any formalized, government-mandated rules for the management of e-waste. That doesn't mean that there isn't a program in place to help manage end-of-life electronic equipment. In fact, there is a program that just might serve as a template for the entire nation.

The Byteback program is a fusion of government and industry, aimed toward managing e-waste. The program—serving Australia's southeastern state of Victoria—involves partners Sustainability Victoria (a government environmental group) in conjunction with the Australian Information Industry Association (AIIA) and founding partners Apple, Canon, Dell, Epson, Fujitsu, Fuji-Xerox, HP, IBM, Lenovo, and Lexmark.

With the Byteback program, consumers can bring up to 10 computers to be recycled at no charge to them. Once the devices are accepted by Byteback, printed circuit boards are sent to Canada; nickel and lithium batteries are sent to France; cathode ray tubes are sent to the Netherlands; and LCD screens are sent to the U.S. for processing.

Although this seems to be more transporting of e-waste (and it is), if the Australian government decides to adopt a similar program throughout the entire country, it will have the economy of scale necessary to process materials in-country.

The Byteback program is only a trial. It started in 2005 and will run until the end of 2008. It is expected that what the Victorians learn from the program can be used to prepare the entire country to properly dispose of computer equipment.

NOTE   *In its initial phase, Byteback prevented 300 tons of electronic and electrical waste from entering Australian landfills.*

Europe

The European Union leads the world with its e-waste management WEEE and its RoHs directives. These laws manage not only the resultant recycling and handling of e-waste, but also its creation. In this section, we'll talk about these two directives and how individual European nations are reacting.

WEEE Directive

The Waste Electrical and Electronic Equipment Directive (also known as the WEEE Directive) is the European Union directive on WEEE and became law in February 2003. The directive sets collection, recycling, and recovery goals for used electronic equipment.

NOTE   *The WEEE Directive has become a popular model for managing e-waste. As you already read, several Canadian provinces have modeled their own legislation on Europe's WEEE Directive.*

The directive places the responsibility for the disposal of WEEE on the manufacturers. Manufacturers are required to establish a program for collecting WEEE. The directive states, "Users of electrical and electronic equipment from private households should have the possibility of returning WEEE at least free of charge."

Manufacturers are also required to dispose of, recycle, or refurbish equipment in an ecological manner.

NOTE *The WEEE Directive also has guidelines controlling the transboundary movement of used electrical and electronic appliances.*

When the WEEE Directive became law, it required all of the EU's member states to adopt it into national law by August 13, 2004. The only country to meet this deadline was Cyprus. One year later, all member states except for Malta and the United Kingdom had adopted at least portions of the directive. The United Kingdom finally adopted the regulations, and it went into force on January 2, 2007.

RoHS

Whereas the WEEE Directive is designed to help manage e-waste, the European Union also took steps to reduce how much waste is actually produced. The Restriction of Hazardous Substances Directive (RoHS) was adopted in February 2003 by the European Union.

The directive restricts the use of six hazardous materials in the manufacture of certain types of electronic equipment:

- Lead
- Mercury
- Cadmium
- Hexavalent chromium
- Polybrominated biphenyls (PBBs)
- Polybrominated diphenyl ether (PBDE)

The directive sets a maximum concentration of these materials at 0.1 percent (cadmium is much lower at 0.01 percent) by weight of homogenous material. This means that the weight of these elements—if extracted from the finished product—cannot exceed the aforementioned limits.

National Adoption

Although the WEEE and RoHS Directives come from the EU, countries have to pass their own national laws.

NOTE *To illustrate the importance of managing e-waste, in April 2005, the Royal Society of Arts and Canon presented a 7-meter-tall sculpture called "WEEE Man" on London's South Bank. WEEE Man is made from 3.3 tons of electrical goods—about how much e-waste the average UK citizen creates in a lifetime.*

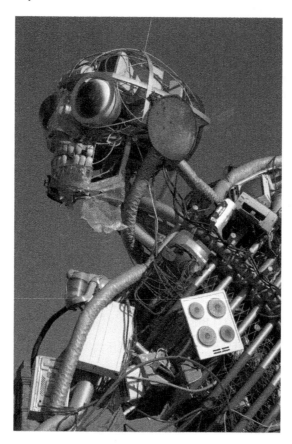

Because each country has adopted varying versions of the WEEE Directive, there are different rules and regulations across Europe. Table 2-3 details specific countries' laws.

Country	Legislation Adoption Date	Details
Austria	April 2005	Austria's WEEE ordinance requires that producers register, mark new equipment for the Austrian market, and finance the collection, recovery, and recycling of WEEE.
Belgium	2004	Belgium is one of three European nations that implemented electronic waste disposal legislation prior to the EU WEEE Directive, but changed its legislation to include the EU's mandates.
Cyprus	July 2004	Companies importing or retailing electronic equipment must register with the Environmental Service.
Estonia	April 2004	Regulations set requirements and procedures for marking electronic equipment, targets for collection, and recovery or disposal of equipment. Estonia has been granted a grace period through December 31, 2008 to meet collection deadlines.
France	November 2006	The French decree implements the concept of producer responsibility for WEEE, and imposes WEEE takeback and recycling obligations. The decree imposes requirements with respect to product design, collection, recovery, financing, marking, and reporting. All producers are responsible for the collection and treatment of household WEEE. The decree also establishes penalties for noncompliance.
Germany	March 2005	Producers or distributors of electronic equipment in Germany must register with a clearing house, a private institution operated and financed by producers. When registering, producers must provide a guarantee for the financing recycling costs and the type and quantity of electronic equipment that will be marketed, collected, recovered, or exported outside the European Union. The law requires manufacturers to use the best available treatment, recovery, and recycling techniques in the disposal of WEEE.
Greece	March 2004	Producers and importers must hold a "certificate of alternative management," which varies depending on the territory in which the products are being marketed. The Greek WEEE regulation varies from the EU directive with a directive that requires that costs for the treatment of WEEE must be clearly visible in all invoices issued throughout the distribution chain.
Hungary	August 10, 2004	Hungarian law requires producers to collect and treat an annually increasing percentage of the EEE they place on the market. Producers must reimburse local authorities if they provide separate collection of WEEE from households.
Ireland	August 2005	Irish law requires producers and distributors of electronic equipment to register with the WEEE Register Society and join a compliance scheme to help meet their collection, recycling, and reporting requirements. Producers are responsible for financing the takeback of WEEE.

TABLE 2-3   Variances in European RoHS and WEEE Laws

PART I

Country	Legislation Adoption Date	Details
Italy	July 2005	Italian law establishes a Supervision and Control of WEEE Management Committee that oversees a central Italian register and clearing house.
		Manufacturers fund the program according to their market share.
		Italian law also requires information to be supplied to consumers, such as the penalties for incorrect disposal.
		Producers must ensure recovery of at least 80 percent of end-of-life goods listed.
		Producers are required to register at their local Chamber of Commerce before placing equipment on the market. They must also provide a guarantee to ensure the financing of the proper disposal of EEE placed on the market after August 13, 2005.
Lithuania	November 2005	Lithuanian WEEE legislation requires producers to register with the Environmental Protection Agency. Lithuania has been granted a grace period through December 30, 2008, to meet collection and recovery targets.
Luxembourg	January 2005	Luxembourg law requires all producers to register and provide a bank guarantee to cover WEEE management costs.
Malta	August 2004	Maltan law requires producers to finance collection, recovery, and recycling of WEEE. It also requires providing information to consumers about treatment sites. Producers should be able to fulfill obligations individually or through a collective.
The Netherlands	July 19, 2004	The Netherlands requires that producers guarantee they will finance the management of WEEE from private households for EEE placed on the market after August 13, 2005. Producers also must pay the costs of WEEE management in proportion to their market share for products placed on the market before August 13, 2005.
Norway	January 24, 2005	Norway had enacted WEEE legislation in 1998, but amended its preexisting law with the EU's RoHS and WEEE.
		The law requires reporting obligations on manufacturers and importers.
		Producers and importers must be members of a takeback company that has been approved by the Norwegian Pollution Control Authority. Businesses can bring WEEE to dealers selling the same types of products, only if they make a new purchase. Businesses can also deliver WEEE to municipalities.
		Consumers can deliver WEEE free of charge to dealers selling the same types of products and can bring WEEE to municipalities, free of charge.

TABLE 2-3   Variances in European RoHS and WEEE Laws (*Continued*)

Country	Legislation Adoption Date	Details
Poland	October 20, 2005	Polish law requires producers to register with the government.
		Fees are calculated according to a producer's annual net turnover. Producers also must keep data and information regarding users and treatment facilities.
		In Poland, point-of-purchase is considered when goods enter the Polish market, offering a narrower definition than under the EU WEEE Directive.
Slovak Republic	April 29, 2005	Slovak law provides for a recycling fund into which producers pay quarterly, based on the difference between the recovery target and their actual recovery rate.
Slovenia	November 2004	Slovenia was granted a grace period until December 31, 2007 to meet EU WEEE Directive collection goals.
Spain	February 25, 2005	Producers may fulfill their WEEE obligations individually or through a collective plan.
		Spain's WEEE law requires producers to design and manufacture equipment that is easier to dismantle, repair, and reuse.
Sweden	2005	Swedish law requires producers to register with the EPA, finance the collection, recovery, and recycling, as well as mark new equipment for the Swedish market.
Switzerland	June 2005	Switzerland had legislation in place in 1998.
		Its version differs from the EU's WEEE Directive in that buyers of EEE pay a recycling fee to finance collection and treatment.
		Retailers, distributors, producers, and importers are required to take back WEEE of the kind of goods they market, manufacture, or import.
United Kingdom	January 2, 2007	The law requires manufacturers to recycle and dispose of used electronic equipment.
		Plans include a national Distributor Takeback Scheme, with treatment facilities to handle recycling and keep producers informed of returned products.

TABLE 2-3   Variances in European RoHS and WEEE Laws

Asia

Asia is a large dumping ground for the world's e-waste, and several countries are trying to minimize the impact on their environments. This section takes a closer look at what's going on in Asia to protect their environment.

Japan

While the bulk of e-waste is shipped to countries in Asia and Africa for recycling, and while the West is getting its e-waste house in order, the Japanese have made great strides in managing their own e-waste problem.

Life Cycle

The Japanese approach to the issue is different from other countries. Whereas Western companies look at the issue as a three-step process—pay a fee, get old materials hauled away, and dispose of them along environmental regulations—the Japanese see the issue in another way.

The Japanese look at the product's end of life as another stage in the product's life cycle. Japan's own WEEE laws took effect in 2001, and the taking back, dismantling, and reuse of materials has become an integral part of the supply chain to create new products. For instance, glass from old televisions is reused in new televisions. Plastic is also reused. This helps Japanese companies meet reuse standards.

NOTE *To help curb e-waste, Sony has even developed a vegetable-based plastic that breaks down faster than other plastics.*

Waste Management

Japan's version of the WEEE Directive came in 1998 with the Japanese Home Electronics Recycling Law. In it, manufacturers were warned to prepare for collection and recycling by 2001. Many manufacturers decided to pool their resources with the Japanese government to open a pilot recycling project while the WEEE legislation was still being tweaked.

The pilot plant was an opportunity to gather important information on cost, personnel, and how to meet reuse targets. This, in turn, helped shape the legislation. By the time the legislation was passed, companies were already prepared.

Japanese electronic waste goes, mainly, to two large, centralized recycling companies, each operated by a consortium of electronics manufacturers. Companies don't involve third parties, but send them to these operations instead. This helps save money, because the middleman has been eliminated from the equation.

China

Although China takes its lumps for being a destination of much of the world's e-waste, the nation is working to get e-waste legislation in place.

The Chinese regulation is normally referred to as China RoHS. Though it is similar to the European Union's RoHS, it does take a different approach. The EU's RoHS lists specific categories of products. Specific products are automatically included in those categories unless specifically excluded. China RoHS, however, contains a list of included products. That list is called the Catalog.

Products

There is, naturally, overlap between the two directives. But many product types that are not within the scope of EU RoHS are within the scope of China RoHS. China RoHS includes the following:

- Automotive electronics
- Radar equipment
- Medical devices

- Semiconductor and other manufacturing equipment, components, and some raw materials
- Some packaging materials

By the same token, some categories of EU RoHS are not within the scope of China RoHS, such as toys and home appliances.

Products shipped to China must be marked as to whether the items are compliant or noncompliant. The Electronic Information Products (EIP) logo or other label is used to mark parts that do not have unacceptable levels of substances listed by China RoHS.

Materials
Products that contain hazardous substances must be marked with the EIP logo and include an Environmental Protection Use Period (EPUP) value listed in years.

Like the EU RoHS Directive, China RoHS bans the following:

- Lead
- Mercury
- Cadmium
- Hexavalent chromium
- Polybrominated biphenyls (PBBs)
- Polybrominated diphenyl ether (PBDE)

Marking
Requirements also differ from the EU RoHS. The initial requirement is for a mark and disclosure of any of the six aforementioned hazardous substances and their locations within the product.

Labels must contain the following information:

- Whether the product contains any of the six hazardous substances. If they are present, the "Environment-Friendly Use Period" (EFUP) must also be determined and indicated.
- Disclosure of which hazardous substances are contained in the product and the component(s) they are present in.
- Packaging material must be disclosed on the outside packaging.
- The date of manufacture.

The regulations have not been implemented yet, being postponed in their formal adoption twice. There is no formal schedule for completion of the Catalog.

Korea
In April 2007, Korea adopted its Act for Recycling of Electrical and Electronic Equipment and Automobiles, also known as Korea RoHS.

The act includes four main requirements:

- Restrictions on hazardous materials
- Design for efficient recycling
- Collection and recycling of WEEE
- Recycling of vehicles at end-of-life

The act went into effect January 1, 2008.

Under the act, producers and importers of EEE or vehicles must make efforts to facilitate the recycling of waste by reducing the use of hazardous substances and making them more easily recyclable.

Producers are required to take back old products when selling a new one, regardless of whether the product was made by them—including packaging—free of charge. Any products to be recycled must be dealt with in an approved manner, by the reseller, by an individual producer or importer, or by a Mutual Aid Association.

It's helpful to realize what laws might apply to you and your company, but in the next section we'll roll up our sleeves and see how you can start making some environmentally and pocketbook-friendly changes to your organization's use of power.

PART

II

Consumption Issues

Minimizing Power Usage

Ask any parent of teenagers and they will tell you that their kids think electricity flows from the wall for free. But it's not free, and mom and dad know it. Cellular telephones, computers, iPods, and whatever else the kids plug in add up in electricity costs. It's costly enough at home, but the issue is even more pronounced in an organization.

Sure, a couple computers here and there take their toll, but what if you've got hundreds of computers, or even thousands? And don't forget the servers and networking gear used to support those workstations (and the necessity to cool those servers, see Chapter 4). To make matters worse, industrywide, costs are going up.

According to the U.S. Environmental Protection Agency's (EPA's) 2006 datacenter energy efficiency report, in 2006, the total amount of power used by datacenters represented approximately 1.5 percent of total U.S. electricity consumption. The cost totaled US$4.5 billion, about as much as was spent by 5.8 million average households for the year—US EPA, July 2007.

NOTE *According to a 2007 study by Gartner Group, information and communications technology accounts for 2 percent of global carbon dioxide emissions, which is roughly the equivalent of what the airline industry produces.*

The fact of the matter is that your computers use juice, and that juice costs you money. To save a lot of money—and to help the environment in the process—you need to reduce how much electricity you use. And to reduce how much electricity you use, you need to know how much you're using and where it can be trimmed.

This chapter looks at the issue of power consumption and offers some recommendations to reduce it across your IT department's infrastructure, from servers to workstations.

Power Problems

Power is a huge issue for businesses. Forget for a moment that this book is largely about minimizing your IT department's impact on the environment, and look at it from a cost point of view. For no other reason than saving a lot of money, energy efficiency is important.

But even beyond saving the planet and saving money, you need to save power, because at some point, you may not have enough power to run your equipment.

Energy-Saving Action	Savings (kW)	Savings (%)
Lower-power processors	111	10
High-efficiency power supplies	141	12
Power management features	125	11
Blade servers	8	1
Server virtualizations	156	14
Cooling best practices	24	2
Variable-speed fan drives	79	7
Supplemental cooling	200	18

TABLE 3-1   The Various Ways You Can Cut Power and Costs

Power isn't cheap. As if rising prices aren't enough, datacenters use a lot of juice. U.S. datacenter power consumption totaled 45 billion kilowatt (kW) hours in 2005. That's more than Mississippi and 19 other states. The entire world used 123 billion kW hours in 2005.

U.S. businesses spent between 4 and 10 percent of their IT budgets on energy. Gartner predicts that this will rise fourfold in the next 5 years.

It gets even more alarming. Power supply vendor Liebert Corp. announced that 33 percent of respondents to a datacenter survey expected to be out of power and cooling capacity by the end of 2007. That number jumped to 96 percent by 2011—Lisbert, 2006.

According to a study by Gartner, 50 percent of datacenters said they will have insufficient power and cooling capacity by 2008—Gartner, November 2006.

So what's the upshot of all this? It's a business imperative to reduce power use wherever you can. It's not just for the planet. It's not just to save some money. It's for the sake of your business.

There are sundry changes you can make in your organization to save power. Some changes are big (such as installing new servers) whereas others are small (such as changing the desktop color of your monitors).

Table 3-1 shows how making corrections throughout your organization can help you save money.

Another way to look at the figures in Table 3-1 is like this: A US$10 billion company spends about 4 percent of its revenue on IT costs. So if we take a couple figures from Table 3-1 (variable-speed fan drives, for instance, at 7 percent), then the company stands to save US$2.8 million a year. That's because 10 billion × 0.07 × 0.04 = 2.8 million.

For your own organization, you can compute savings by plugging in how much your IT department spends and then doing a rough estimate with the numbers in Table 3-1.

Monitoring Power Usage

Obviously, the server room isn't the only place where power gets used. Your whole organization uses power, all the time. The place to start is with an overall assessment of the power you use. As you are an IT professional, you're likely only interested in the computers and network infrastructure, but you can take this task to whatever level of granularity you choose.

For instance, although reducing server power draws and minimizing PC power usage seem obvious, you might decide to implement a plan where lighting automatically turns off. You could get as small as directing laptop and cellular phone users to disconnect their chargers from the wall when they're not using them. Although there's no device plugged into the charger, the charger still sips at the electrical current.

Let's talk about how your organization can study its power usage.

You should consider the costs involved with doing the testing yourself and what it would cost to contract out the project. There's no shame in hiring a professional to do the heavy lifting. They are trained and experienced in this type of work and can give you the results you want more quickly than you are likely able to do on your own—although you can certainly do it on your own.

Servers

To monitor power consumption yourself, you need to use power-monitoring software. Without knowledge of where you're starting, it's impossible to tell how much of a problem you have and to what degree your fixes are helping.

Several vendors offer tools that help monitor datacenter power. For instance, IBM's PowerExecutive provides the tools needed to monitor and manage power consumption accurately. It can measure real-time power consumption and heat emission by individual server, server group, or location. It allows for the optimization of energy use and the lowering of power consumption when low utilization can provide cost savings. These power monitoring and management capabilities are an important tool in achieving energy efficiency in the datacenter.

IBM's PowerExecutive tool is shown in Figure 3-1.

With the results you get from your study, you should be able to do the following:

- Understand the datacenter's thermal traits.
- Locate overlapping areas of cooling capacity. This helps because it shows where you can place high-density or mission-critical equipment because of its ideal cooling location.
- Consider "what-ifs" with the placement of the datacenter

NOTE *Don't just stop with the servers. Don't forget to upgrade transformers, uninterruptible power supplies, and fans, among other devices.*

Low-Cost Options

There are also some very low-cost solutions for checking power on your workstations and standalone devices.

Kill A Watt

The Kill A Watt device is a US$25 product that you plug into the wall and then plug your computer or monitor into the device. The result is that it will show you how much power your device is using.

True, it's not really practical in an environment with hundreds of workstations to run around and plug in this device. However, assuming all the devices' settings are the same (or similar), you can measure a couple workstations and make some easy (and inexpensive) assumptions about power usage.

More information about the Kill A Watt can be found at Link 3-1.

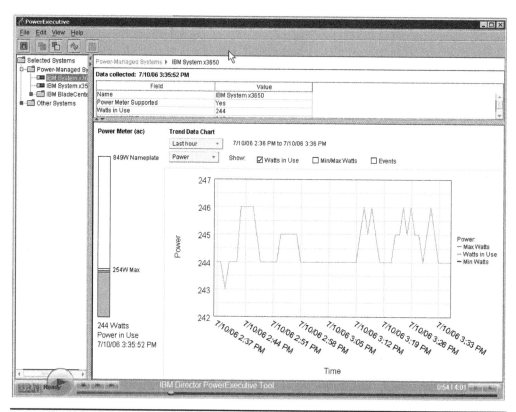

Figure 3-1   IBM offers its PowerExecutive tool to help you monitor power use in your datacenter.

Calculator

Tech Republic offers a free worksheet to help you determine various costs for monitor power. It allows you to do the following:

- Determine how much you spend on electricity to power your existing monitors.
- Compare new LCD and CRT monitors to determine which option is less expensive.
- Compare different models of the same type of monitor to determine which one carries the lowest total cost, when power is considered.
- Compare the same monitor under two different operating scenarios. For example, see how much cost savings you could achieve by implementing a monitor's sleep mode instead of leaving it running at full power when not in use.

The worksheet can be found at Link 3-2. The download does require a free membership on their website.

Reducing Power Use

Once you have an idea of how much power you're using, it's time to take steps. There are a number of ways you can cut your electric bill. In this section, we'll take a closer look at some ideas that can help cut power use.

Data De-Duplication

The mantra of computer use has been (and likely will continue to be) "Back up your data." And that's good advice. It's like "Wear your seatbelt" and "Never play pool against a guy named after a city." It just makes sense.

But are we overdoing it? Although it's never a good idea to hit the freeway without a seatbelt or to play nine-ball with a guy named Cleveland, we tend to back up stuff over and over. Once is often enough. More than that is just wasteful and costly.

So-called "data de-duplication" is a tool for reducing storage and bandwidth consumed from disk-based backup. By eliminating the need to constantly back up the same file over and over again, backup storage consumption is reduced 10 to 50 times. Because less data is sent across your network, overall bandwidth consumption is reduced by almost 500 times.

The obvious benefit is freeing up storage space, but there are energy implications that affect your corporate ledger. Reducing the number of data copies reduces storage capacity needs and storage power consumption. Further, once data storage has been reduced, snapshots and other copies from high-performance disks can be shifted to lower-performance, energy-efficient disks.

The benefit trickles down when you consider your organization's remote sites. Because less data is being replicated, money is saved because network traffic and storage capacity are not being overused.

Virtualization

The biggest power draw to your IT infrastructure is from your servers. In and of themselves, they can gobble up 50 percent of the power coming into your datacenter. The best way to reduce this power usage is to reduce the number of servers you use.

"Madness!" you proclaim. "We have that many servers because we need that many servers."

Although you may have, in the past, needed that many servers to fulfill mission-critical tasks, by consolidating several machines into one and through virtualization, you can wheel out some of those watt-munching behemoths. This is illustrated in Figure 3-2.

NOTE *We'll talk about server virtualization and how to get your hands dirty doing it in Chapter 13, when we discuss configuring the server and using applications such as Virtual PC and Microsoft Virtual Server.*

Data storage is another massive consumer of power. Direct-attached storage can account for as much as 27 percent of your electricity bill. Direct-attached storage units fragment where data is stored in the organization. Also, each device must consume its own power.

Clustering also involves identical hardware and operating systems to ensure a smooth rollover in the event of tragedy. The costs add up, especially when one considers the cost of the hardware and the power draw—especially from a largely unused device.

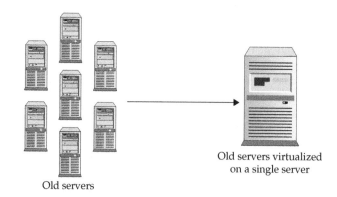

Figure 3-2
Consolidating
servers onto a
fewer number of
units conserves
energy.

Old servers virtualized
on a single server

Old servers

If you virtualize your servers, however, advanced clustering technologies allow them to act as traffic cops and move applications between servers and storage devices with precision. Regardless of what fails, you can still keep working as normal. Further, this causes a reduction in the need for hardware, space, and energy usage.

Storage

If your organization uses a lot of direct-attached storage, you will see a huge power savings if you switch over to a storage area network (SAN). By removing file servers, you see an instant reduction in power usage.

A SAN also allows you to grow in a logical, efficient manner. With direct-attached storage, you have to add file servers to your network. If you've got a SAN, you just have to add disks, which is considerably less expensive.

Case Studies

Vanderbilt University's IT services organization has turned to virtualization with great success.

Realizing that physical servers cost money for power and cooling, as well as their environmental effects, the university decided to host fewer servers and virtualize. IT services officials utilized server virtualization for 35 percent of the servers they manage. They estimate they have been saving 20,575 watts per hour. Officials hope to eventually virtualize 80 percent of their servers. The state of Oregon is taking on a much larger consolidation project. It is combining 11 state agency datacenters by June 2009. The plan is for the centers to be combined at a new datacenter in Salem and involves virtualizing both storage and servers.

The project is estimated to cost $43 million and it is expected to save $10 to $12 million per year, once finished, and reduce power consumption by up to 35 percent.

Management

In most organizations, computers are used for just 4 hours a day. The additional 20 hours, those idle machines are still using energy.

Some estimates say that 65 percent of the energy used by computers and monitors is wasted because workers don't turn off computers when they leave for the day. Additionally, half of computer monitors do not have a power management scheme applied, so more money is wasted when they fail to automatically switch off.

A number of utilities are available that enable system administrators to easily manage power settings. These utilities usually enable sleep features built into prevalent operating systems and allow a computer to go into low-power-consuming sleep mode.

NOTE *Even if you don't want to spend money on an application or don't trust the freeware out there, Policy Manager on Windows lets you establish power settings for your users.*

It's estimated that these toolkits can save between $10 and $50 per computer per year.

Bigger Drives

Another technological boon that can help you conserve power is to ditch all your older, smaller hard drives and install a new, bigger one.

Serial ATA (SATA) drives use about 50 percent less power per terabyte (TB) than Fibre Channel drives. They are also higher in storage density, which also helps reduce power consumption.

For instance, if you replace 11 legacy drives with a modern, high-capacity drive, you get a 16 percent increase on capacity and use 81 percent less power. Further, you save 93 percent more floor space than with the other system.

Involving Your Utility Company

You should also try to involve your utility company in your efforts to reduce power costs. They can offer power-savings tips as well as other services that can save you money.

Monitoring

One way you can monitor how much power you use is simply by contacting your utility company. They can provide you with historical information about how much power was consumed (there is likely a difference since October when you added 25 percent more servers), and they can help you figure out what you're currently using.

Sellback Opportunities

Maybe your organization is especially forward thinking and has turned to Mother Nature for its power needs. If that's the case—or the idea simply piques your interest—you might be fascinated to know that those electrical lines running into your organization send power both ways. That is, if you generate more power than you're using, you can sell it back to the power company, as shown in Figure 3-3.

The practice is called *net metering,* and most states have laws that direct utility companies to buy back power at the same rate you buy it from them.

NOTE *States that don't have legislation in place typically pay the wholesale cost of power—about 1 to 3 cents per kilowatt hour.*

If your organization is considering relying on the sun for its power, and possibly to sell back power to the utility company, you'll need a few things:

- **Photovoltaic panels**   These panels absorb solar radiation. They are made of silicon and coated with tempered glass. Panels are typically mounted on the roof or on a free-standing pole.

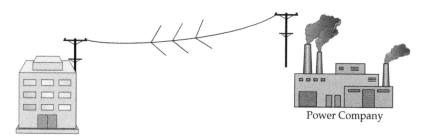

Power Company

Figure 3-3 Net metering allows you to sell power back to the electric company.

> **NOTE** *A company called Sunslates sells roofing tiles with photovoltaic cells built in. They're about double the price of typical solar cells. You can find out more via Link 3-3.*

- **An inverter** This device regulates the power and changes it to alternating current (AC). Inverters for a 6.5-kilowatt system run $3,000 to $4,000.
- **A meter** You need a meter that can run backward and can show how much you're sending back to the utility company.

True, not every utility will pay for incoming electricity. That will depend, however, on your state's energy policies and rules and whether your local utility is willing to work with net metering clients.

> **NOTE** *Some people and organizations use wind power as a form of renewable energy. Wind power requires a more expensive investment (it can cost $70,000 in equipment just to power a home), and wind is more prevalent at higher elevations, which can mean upwards of 120-foot mounting poles.*

There's good news if you are considering renewable energy. The government is encouraging using renewable energy and might offer your organization tax breaks. You can also get rebates for any Energy Star devices you buy—such as monitors.

Low-Power Computers

Computer manufacturers are starting to offer low-power models that consume less power than other computers. Of course, the workstations you need may or may not fall in line with the specs for these machines, but as more and more companies want to save money on power costs, look for more machines to be introduced.

In this section, we take a look at some of the offerings for Windows machines as well as some Linux options.

PCs

Windows-based PCs are the backbone of industry. Sure, there are some Macs and Linux boxes out there, but most companies run on Windows. There aren't too many low-power models out there, but 2008 saw a number of new models introduced.

Intel

At the 2008 Consumer Electronics Show (CES) in Las Vegas, Intel unveiled 16 new products based on the company's first 45 nanometer (nm) processor.

The new processor boosts a PC's speed, reduces power requirements, saves on battery life, helps the environment, and comes in a smaller package for more fashionable and compact computer designs. With the introduction of the new processors, Intel will be offering a total of 32 desktop, laptop, and server processors.

HP

HP has introduced its own low-power PCs, including the rp5700.

The PC touts a specialized design with additional cooling features. This allows it to be in higher temperature environments than most other PCs. Its energy efficiency comes from S3 power management, specialized Intel processors, and 80 Plus power supplies.

NOTE *We'll talk about 80 Plus power supplies later in this chapter.*

The rp5700 also uses postconsumer recycled plastics and packaging as well as exceeds requirements for hazardous material reduction.

Linux

Low-power Linux machines have largely been—like the OS itself—homebrew devices. An enthusiastic tinkerer will decide he wants a low-power file server, so he'll slap one together, put his favorite flavor of Linux on it, and post the video of him doing it on his website. But there are companies that offer their own low-power Linux options. Many of these are not only inexpensive to run, but downright cheap to buy.

NorhTec

The Bangkok-based NorhTec offers a tiny PC (for less than US$100) capable of running Puppy and other lightweight Linux distributions.

NorhTec's MicroClient Jr. is 4.5 inches square and draws 8 watts of power. It uses a 166MHz Pentium–compatible processor.

The MicroClient Jr. is the smallest of the company's line of extremely small, energy-efficient PCs.

In fact, the company's founder says he built the company with the goal of producing sub-$100 PCs. The company has already sold PCs to clients such as McDonalds of Canada.

The MicroClient Jr. boots from CompactFlash rather than a hard drive. Other features include:

- Fanless design
- 128MB SDRAM
- Input/output ports

- IDE
- 10/100 Mbps Ethernet
- 3 USB V1.1 ports
- Optional RS232
- CompactFlash slot for expansion
- 2.5-inch hard drive mounting

NorhTec offers several other models of small, energy-efficient PCs, including the following:

- MicroClient JrSX, with a 486-compatible processor and running DOS ($85)
- MicroClient Sr., with the same form factor as the MicroClient Jr., but with a 500MHz CPU and a WiFi option ($195).

Excito

Swedish company Excito offers a low-power, quiet Linux file and print server based on Debian Linux.

"Bubba" is based on a 200MHz ARM processor, and comes equipped with an 80GB to 500GB drive plus a customizable OS featuring a torrent/http/ftp download manager.

The Bubba server was designed to be left on all the time, without using much power or generating a lot of noise. It draws a maximum of 10 watts.

Bubba's hardware specs include:

- 200MHz ARM processor
- 64MB RAM
- 3.5-inch, 7200rpm 80GB, 320GB, or 500GB IDE hard drive
- 1 x 10/100 Ethernet
- USB 2.0 type A to printer or memory stick connection
- USB 2.0 type B to PC connection
- 7.2 × 4.5 × 1.7 inches
- 3.7 pounds

Bubba's features—including basic file management, Samba file/print sharing, mail transport agent, IMAP server, and webmail—are controlled via a web interface. An interface is also provided for firmware upgrades.

Components

The big power draw is your server room, that's no secret. However, a number of other places within your IT infrastructure can save you some watts. You won't see the huge numbers adding up like they do in the server room, but every bit helps. Plus, if you are replicating a setting change across hundreds or even thousands of workstations, those savings will add up.

Servers

You can reduce the amount of energy your servers use by deploying blade servers and by virtualizing your servers.

Blades are entire computers contained on a card that can be inserted into a larger device. As such, rather than one server taking an entire rack, 20 blades can be installed into one unit.

Usage

Blade servers consume about 10 percent less power than equivalent rack mount servers because multiple servers share common power supplies, cooling fans, and other components.

Blades are popular because they not only reduce the amount of space needed, as Figure 3-4 shows, but also because they use less power.

NOTE *Currently, five manufacturers account for more than 75 percent of all the blade servers on the market. These manufacturers are HP, IBM, Sun, Fujitsu/Siemens, and Dell.*

Many organizations have a large number of servers, each running one application. This separates and isolates the units, and if there is a failure only that application is affected. Although there is some logic behind this setup, the reality is that each server only has a 5 to 10 percent CPU utilization rate. This boils down to a lot of hardware taking up a lot of space, and not doing as much as it should.

NOTE *In 2007, Symantec conducted a study that asked organizations if they were considering server consolidation or virtualization. Of respondents, 51 percent said they were considering consolidation, and 47 percent said they were considering virtualization.*

Case Study

Ask.com has taken a unique tack in its efforts to maximize what its servers do and what it gets from them in return. The company asked its server vendor, Dell, to build servers that are customized for its very specific functions. That is, each server is built with specific memory, processors, disk space, and power supplies, all tuned to the application the server supports.

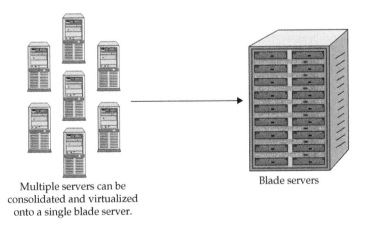

Multiple servers can be
consolidated and virtualized
onto a single blade server.

Blade servers

FIGURE 3-4   The work of many servers can be offloaded onto one server containing many blades.

Each box comes with only the components needed for each application. As such, the overall cost is less than buying a server out of the Dell catalog. On top of that savings, Ask.com has cut server power usage by 30 percent.

NOTE *Ask.com isn't the only company getting its servers custom made. Dell launched a program in 2007 in which it will customize servers for its largest customers—those who buy at least 1000 servers each quarter.*

Computer Settings

Although establishing policies to govern your computers' monitor power settings is a great place to start (and we'll talk about that more in a moment), there are some other places where you can make more precise changes for real savings.

Polling

Periodic polling—that is, the computer automatically checking to see if a given action has been taken—draws power from idling computers, because it automatically wakes the computer up to check for a given event.

Every time an application polls for something, the CPU wakes from an idle state and consumes power.

You might not be able to eliminate all your polling tasks, but you can manage them. Let's say you have 10 polling actions that occur within 1 second. Schedule them so that they run immediately after another, rather than at various times during that period. Figure 3-5 demonstrates this.

NOTE *If a computer is in an idle state, allow it to remain idle as much as possible. The more the computer wakes up (for polling or from someone moving the mouse), the more energy it will consume.*

By grouping them together as the figure shows, the computer only has to come out of an idle state once, rather than multiple times.

Turn Off Unused Devices

This seems like a no-brainer. If a computer or other device is not going to be used in the foreseeable future, turn it off. Failing that, at least set up the computer so that it hibernates after a certain period of nonuse.

FIGURE 3-5
Group your timers together so that they reduce the amount of time the computer has to be polled.

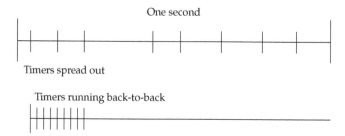

One second

Timers spread out

Timers running back-to-back

Use Large Buffers

If your organization is one where media is played from a CD, DVD, or hard drive, make sure that applications' buffers are set large enough to store as much of the media in memory as possible. Doing this reduces the hard drive, DVD, or CD drive from spinning as much and thus saves power.

Storage

Storage is another big area in the realm of power consumption. Although you want to have a measure of redundancy protecting your data, it's simply wasteful and inefficient to have hundreds of drives spinning away when a couple dozen will do the trick.

Chances are your organization's storage started in one, logical way, but has since become something else. Just by adding to what you have, the reasonable system you had in place a few years ago has become Frankenstorage. Now's a good time to reevaluate your storage and see where you can make logical changes.

Green Drives

Green hard drives are drives that reduce the amount of power they use through a variety of mechanisms, including unloading the heads during idle time to reduce aerodynamic drag. Further, the drives calculate the optimum seek speed to use just the amount of power necessary.

Western Digital is a major producer of green hard drives and estimates that its green drives can shave off US$10 per drive, per year in electricity costs. For example, its 1TB WD Caviar GreenPower hard drive uses about 5 watts less power than drives of the same size, which typically consume 13.5 watts.

NOTE *Western Digital is used here as an example. It is certainly not the only company to produce green drives. Hitachi and Samsung also offer such drives, and the market is only going to open up with more vendors, greater capacities, and speedier seek times. You can compute the math out even further on this. A datacenter with 10,000 drives can save US$100,000 in annual costs. Plus, carbon dioxide emissions are cut by 600 metric tons. That's the equivalent of taking 400 cars off the road for one year.*

NOTE *Solid state drives (SSDs) have no moving parts and use much less energy. Although that fact alone is notable, it is also worth noting that they are very expensive and don't yet hold a great capacity. For the price of one SSD you could buy more than 50 traditional hard drives. We mention it here for the sake of completeness, but it is a very costly option and not as efficient.*

MAID

A massive array of idle disks (MAID) is a system that employs hundreds or thousands of hard drives for near-line data storage.

NOTE *The term* near-line *is used to define the area between online and offline storage.*

MAID is designed for write once, read occasionally (WORO) applications. In this model, drives are spun up only on demand to access data stored on them. Because only a small amount of the data is being accessed, these disks can be powered as needed, thus reducing

Drives powered down, waiting to be accessed   Actively spinning drives

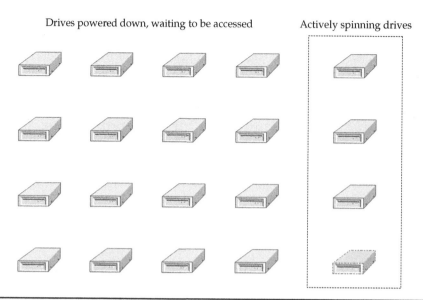

FIGURE 3-6 In a MAID deployment, only a quarter of the disks are spinning at any one time.

the power used to run them as well as reducing the generation of heat, which in turn reduces cooling costs.

MAID differs from RAID in that it has increased storage density and is much less expensive, thus saving power and the need for cooling.

MAID comes with some compromises, however, such as increased latency, lower throughput, and much lower redundancy. Although a MAID solution can be slow—data access can take a few milliseconds up to 10 seconds—it is much faster than tape, which can take 60 seconds or longer to access data.

Also, because large hard drives are designed for constant spinning, continual shutdown and reactivation threatens their reliability. Drives that are designed for repeated spin-up/ spin-down cycles are much more expensive.

The MAID architecture really developed because of the introduction of SATA drives that are designed to be powered up and down. In a large deployment, MAID allows a dense packaging of drives, and typically only 25 percent of the disks are spinning at any given time, as illustrated in Figure 3-6. This helps with the problem of throughput.

The appeal of MAID is also apparent when you consider their use in large environments. SATA drives are rated at 400,000 hours of life. If a datacenter has 1000 drives powered on all the time, a drive would fail every 18 days. Clearly this is no good, so employing a MAID system quadruples the drive's life to 1.6 million hours.

Power-managed RAID

The idea behind RAID has always been to safeguard your data. But employing multiple, always-on drives jacks up your power consumption. To deal with this issue, a new form of RAID has been introduced.

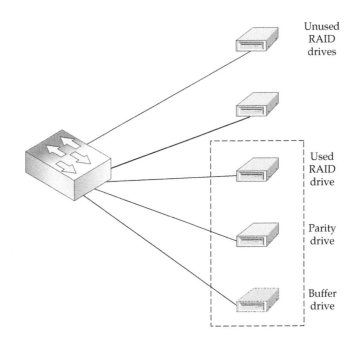

Figure 3-7
Power-managed
RAID only uses the
drive where data is
being stored and
the parity drive.

Unused
RAID
drives

Used
RAID
drive

Parity
drive

Buffer
drive

Power-managed RAID provides parity protection, but with only some of the RAID disks actually turned on. When data is written, only the parity and associated data drives are powered up. When data is read, only the disk being read needs to be powered up. This is illustrated in Figure 3-7.

Nondisruptive and sequential read/writes are accomplished by staging the data to an always-spinning drive, while the next drive is being powered up. The result is that your organization can have hundreds of terabytes in storage in a single footprint.

Monitors

It's no secret that computer monitors are power hogs. Even new monitors can consume 100 W of power while they are on. In sleep mode, they typically use 5 W or less.

Adjusting your monitors to automatically enter sleep mode after a period of nonuse is a quick-and-easy way to reduce costs.

LCD displays aren't necessarily less power hungry that CRTs. It depends on the model and how much power it draws. It's best to evaluate monitor power draws as part of your feature comparison before you buy one.

NOTE *A free tool to tell you how much power your computer monitors are using can be found via Link 3-4.*

Settings

The first place to start is by setting up your monitors to turn off after a certain period of nonuse. However, you can make some subtle changes to your computers' settings that can reduce costs while they are turned on. Specifically, managing the colors on your monitors—especially backgrounds—can save money.

Color	Watts Used
White	74 W
Fuchsia	69 W
Yellow	69 W
Aqua	68 W
Silver	67 W
Blue	65 W
Red	65 W
Lime	63 W
Gray	62 W
Olive	61 W
Purple	61 W
Teal	61 W
Green	60 W
Maroon	60 W
Navy	60 W
Black	59 W

TABLE 3-2   Different Colors Use Different Amounts of Power

White and bright colors can use up to 20 percent more power than black or dark colors. Table 3-2 show how much power colors expend.

Is the difference between a white background (74 W) and a black background (59 W) major? Well, 15 W equates to about $17 a year. Multiply that by the number of computers in your organization and you'll see a difference.

The Power Switch

The best energy saver is, of course, to turn off your monitor. Some users might not know it, but there is a power switch, usually located on the front or the side of the monitor. Turn it off when the computer's not going to be in use for a while, and you get the ultimate savings—zero watts of energy used.

True, you can use the Energy Star settings in Windows to turn the monitor off after a while, but those settings take some time to kick in.

Let's say you're going to lunch. Over your 30-minute break, there will be no savings for the first 5 minutes; 20 percent savings for the next 5 minutes; 90 percent savings for the next 10 minutes; and 95 percent savings for the last 10 minutes. Energy Star saves 65 percent of the monitor's power during the half hour. Powering off saves 100 percent.

NOTE *Screensavers seem like they should save power, but they don't—they just save the screen from burn-in. After all, something is still being displayed on your screen. That said, not all screensavers are created equal. If you must rely on a screensaver rather than powering down the monitor, use a stock Windows screensaver, such as Marquee or Stars. These use less power than custom-made screensavers. Also, have you ever noticed how your CPU (and the fans) goes into hyperdrive when trying to render a complicated, animated screensaver?*

Power Supplies

If you have a say in the components that go into your computers or other devices, use those that conform to the 80 Plus standard. This requires power supplies in computers and servers to be 80 percent or greater energy efficient at 20 percent, 50 percent, and 100 percent of the rated load.

The EPA finalized updated performance requirements for computers and servers that include the more efficient 80 Plus standards. These requirements took effect July 2007.

Wireless Devices

Radios consume power for both transmitting and receiving. Most laptop adapters use their radios, even if they're not connected to an access point (AP). Let's talk about how you can minimize excessive power output from these devices.

WiFi

APs announce their presence at regular intervals by sending a *beacon packet*. The default interval for most APs is set to 100 milliseconds. The impact of the beacon interval is most noticeable when it's trying to find a network to associate with. This is shown in Figure 3-8.

Association requires a WiFi radio to tune to each channel and listen for the AP to broadcast a beacon. The longer between the intervals, the longer the radio must wait on each channel.

In addition to the radio overhead, the downside of a lot of broadcast beacon packets is that with some wireless adapters, the computer must come out of power-saving idle states to process the packets. For laptops that are close to the AP, you may be able to save a little bit of power by going into the administrative page of the AP and increasing the beacon interval.

FIGURE 3-8
APs regularly transmit beacon packets so that wireless clients can find them.

The access point is constantly transmitting beacon packets so the laptops know it is available.

Access point

Laptops

This is a matter of fine-tuning on your part. You may not need a 100ms beacon broadcast. If you can pare that number down, you'll save radio power.

Bluetooth

Most computers now come with a preinstalled Bluetooth radio. Like a WiFi radio, Bluetooth eats up power. A lot of it, actually. But unlike WiFi, Bluetooth is oftentimes enabled even when it is not being used. If your laptops aren't using their Bluetooth for anything, shut off the radios and you'll save energy.

Software

Although it's possible to manage many power settings using Group Policy in Windows or a similar tool in Linux and Mac environments, some companies are making the process even easier and marketing power-saving software.

Seattle-based Verdiem said that by the end of 2007, 500,000 computers were using its Surveyor software.

Surveyor is a networked-computer utility that can cut energy use by 30 percent per machine by switching into low-power mode when a computer is not being used. Verdiem estimates a cost savings of between US$20 and US$60 per machine, per year.

For more information about Verdiem and Surveyor, visit www.verdiem.com, or Link 3-5.

As repeatedly stated in this chapter, power consumption is a major issue. It affects the environment; it affects your bottom line. By using the mechanisms in this chapter, you should be able to see some appreciable cuts in your power usage.

But even as optimal as your system is, it's still going to use power, and that power will generate heat. In Chapter 4, we talk about what you can do to optimize cooling in your server room.

Cooling

In the last chapter, we talked about some strategies to reduce how much power your datacenter consumes. With any amount of power comes heat, and if there's too much heat in the datacenter, you can expect trouble.

There's a fine line to be walked when it comes to cooling your datacenter. You want to keep things cool, but you don't want to walk in and see polar bears curled up on the floor shivering. While many of us have experienced the joys of managing an undercooled data center, overcooling your datacenter is a very common problem too. Datacenter managers don't want their equipment to overheat, but they're throwing money out the window when they use too much cooling power.

This chapter examines cooling issues in the datacenter as well as where you can save money, and it provides some tips for adding cooling capacity without spending more money than you need to.

NOTE *You don't have to get your hands dirty with all the steps and processes we talk about in this chapter. You can certainly hire a datacenter consultant to help you optimize your datacenter. A datacenter consultant should be able to help you consolidate and virtualize your datacenter as well as optimize your cooling.*

Cooling Costs

Some estimates state that cooling can account for upward of 63 percent of your IT department's power usage. That's obviously a big amount and not something that should be overlooked. If you need more cooling power, rather than simply turning up the air conditioning, it's useful to figure out how much you're actually spending and how much you actually need to spend.

How Much Does Power Cost?

Let's take a moment to understand how much power costs and how those costs are computed. Electricity is paid for per kilowatt-hour (kWh). This is a measure of the hourly consumption of electrical power. For the sake of easy math, let's use a basic electrical device—the household incandescent light bulb—to determine how much electricity costs.

A 100-watt (W) bulb uses 100 watt-hours of electricity in 60 minutes. As such, ten 100 W light bulbs will use a total of 1 kWh of electricity per hour. But electrical power costs are different around the country.

For instance, the U.S. Department of Energy reports that in New York in 2007, 1 kWh costs 15.48 cents for commercial use. In Minnesota, the same amount of commercial power costs 7.47 cents. To power those ten light bulbs in New York, 10 hours a day, 5 days a week, 52 weeks a year ($10 \times 5 \times 52$) would cost US$402.48. In Minnesota, those same ten light bulbs would cost US$194.22—U.S. Department of Energy, 2007. We're not trying to build a case to convince you to relocate your business to Minnesota (but if you do, let the Governor know we swayed you), but rather to illustrate a point—electricity costs different amounts in different places.

Table 4-1 compares the average price per kWh for each region of the U.S. and shows how much it has increased in one year.

NOTE *You can see the average for each U.S. state at the Department of Energy website via Link 4-1.*

Because most companies aren't just running on ten light bulbs, let's put the numbers in realistic terms. International Data Corp. estimated that companies worldwide spent about $29 billion to cool datacenters in 2007, up 400 percent from 2000—IDC, 2006.

Causes of Cost

Cooling is a major component of your power consumption and, by extension, your IT budget. A number of issues drive up power consumption and cooling costs, including the following:

- Increased power consumption as more servers and storage devices are deployed.
- Increased heat density in the racks because of increased computing power in a confined space.

Region	Commercial Power Cost in 2007 (Cents per kWh)	Commercial Power Cost in 2006 (Cents per kWh)
New England	14.79	14.66
Middle Atlantic	13.2	12.81
East North Central	8.62	8.18
West North Central	6.86	6.75
South Atlantic	8.63	8.42
East South Central	7.97	7.97
West South Central	9.37	9.33
Mountain	7.73	7.61
Pacific Contiguous	11.27	11.36
Pacific Noncontiguous	16.94	17.35

TABLE 4-1   Price Per kWh Varies Around The Nation and Is Increasing

- Irregular heat load in the datacenter. This is exacerbated by poor planning for heat management as the topology of the datacenter changes.

- Increasing power costs across the U.S.

- A tendency to overcool datacenters. The "flood-cooling impulse" leads datacenter managers to overcool their datacenters by more than two and a half times what is needed.

Figure 4-1 shows where datacenters are using electricity.

Calculating Your Cooling Needs

In this section, we'll talk about how you can figure out how much cooling your system will require.

All the equipment in your server room generates heat. So does the lighting. And so do the people working there. All these sources of heat contribute to the *heat load* of the server room. Typically this number is expressed in British Thermal Units (BTUs) or kW. One kilowatt is the same as 3412 BTUs.

NOTE *Your server room equipment vendors should be able to tell you how much heat load each piece of equipment generates.*

In order for your air conditioner to cool a room, its output must be greater than the heat load. Before buying any new cooling equipment, it's important to figure out how much you need. To determine the heat load, you must take into consideration a number of factors, not just the heat load of your equipment. The following sections address these additional considerations.

Room Size

The room itself requires cooling. To calculate the cooling needs of the room, use this formula:

```
Room Area BTU = Length (meters(m)) x Width (m) x 337
```

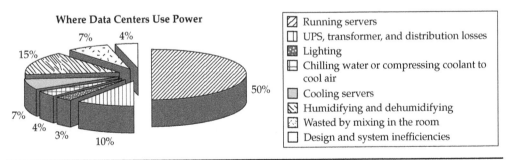

FIGURE 4-1   Datacenters can manage their power use more efficiently.

Windows

Most often, server rooms have no windows. If yours has none, you can skip this calculation. However, if you do have windows, look at these formulas to determine which is most applicable to your datacenter:

```
South Window BTU = South Facing Window Length (m) x Width (m) x 870
North Window BTU = North Facing Window Length (m) x Width (m) x 165
```

If there are no blinds on the windows, multiply the results by 1.5.

NOTE *If you are in the southern hemisphere, swap these formulas. In the northern hemisphere, the heat on south-facing windows is greatest. In the southern hemisphere, the heat on north-facing windows is the greatest.*

Add together the results of these calculations to get your final amount:

```
Windows BTU = South Window(s) BTU + North Window(s) BTU
```

People in the Room

You probably don't have someone permanently stationed in the server room. If people aren't in there, you can skip this section. However, if you do have people located in the server room, the heat load goes up about 400 BTU per person. Here's the formula:

```
Total Occupant BTU = Number of occupants x 400
```

Equipment

Obviously, most of the heat generated is from your equipment. You can find the equipment's power consumption in its documentation or on the vendor websites, if it's not written on a sticker with the serial number.

Don't forget to take into consideration any other equipment that might be in the room (maybe there's a photocopier or other additional equipment). Here's the formula:

```
Equipment BTU = Total wattage for all equipment x 3.5
```

Lighting

Multiply the total wattage for lighting by 4.25, as shown in the following formula:

```
Lighting BTU = Total wattage for all lighting x 4.25
```

Total Cooling Requirement

Now, just add up all these numbers and you'll get the total amount of cooling you'll need for your datacenter, as follows:

```
Total Heat Load = Room Area BTU + Windows BTU + Total Occupant BTU +
Equipment BTU + Lighting BTU
```

You can take this number with you when you go air conditioning shopping. Small air conditioning units have a cooling capacity of between 5000 and 10,000 BTUs. Larger units use a measurement in tons of cooling. One ton of cooling is about the same as 12,000 BTUs.

Reducing Cooling Costs

If you've looked at your datacenter's cooling bill (or have been afraid to), just know there are some ways you can reduce costs. Also, if you find you need more cooling, it might be wiser to deploy equipment that won't chow down a lot of power. Table 4-2 shows how much money different-sized datacenters can save in different parts of the world. It also shows how much pollution can be cut when optimizing cooling.

In this section, we'll talk about some equipment you can use that can save money and help supplement your environment.

Economizers

You can save a lot of money if you are able to put Mother Nature to work for you. In a lot of the country, winter provides you with an opportunity to enhance your cooling system by using the cold outside air to cool things down.

But it isn't as simple as opening a window to accomplish this. To do so, you need to employ what is called an *economizer.* There are two types: air-side economizers and water-side economizers.

Air

An *air-side economizer* regulates the use of outside air for cooling a room or a building. It employs sensors, ducts, and dampers to regulate the amount of cool air brought in.

Datacenter Size (Wattage)	Small (1.5 MW)	Medium (3.5 MW)	Large (8 MW)
Cooling type	Air	Chilled water and air	Chilled water and air
Potential savings	40 percent	30 percent	20 percent
U.S. estimated annual cost savings (@ $0.11/kWh)	$578,000	$1,012,000	$1,542,000
Europe, Middle East, and Africa estimated annual cost savings (@ $0.15/kWh)	$788,000	$1,380,000	$2,102,000
Asia, Pacific, and Japan estimated annual cost savings (@ $0.24/kWh)	$1,261,000	$2,207,000	$3,364,000
Reduction in CO_2 emissions (metric tons per year)	5000	8780	10,000

TABLE 4-2   Cost Savings and Pollution Reduction Based on Cooling Optimization

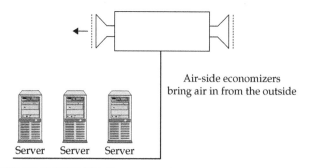

Air-side economizers
bring air in from the outside

Server   Server   Server

FIGURE 4-2   Air-side economizers draw in outside air to cool the datacenter.

The sensors measure air temperature both inside and outside the building. If it notices that the outside air is suitably cold enough to cool the datacenter, it will adjust its dampers to draw in the outside air, making it the main source of cooling.

This cuts or eliminates the need for the air conditioning system's compressors, which provides a big cost savings. This is illustrated in Figure 4-2.

NOTE *Air-side economizers also have exhaust air dampers to prevent the building from becoming overpressurized when outside air is pumped in.*

Not everyone is in love with air-side economizers. Their main beef is over contamination and humidity levels. Because the economizers are drawing air in from outside, pollution can potentially enter the datacenter. A larger concern is the change of humidity in the datacenter.

NOTE *It's not recommended to use an air-side economizer in your datacenter unless an engineering evaluation of the local climate and contamination conditions has been performed.*

If air-side economizers are something your organization wishes to employ, you should consider air filters and supplemental humidification. However, what you spend on filtration and humidification might be more than if you just used your regular air-conditioning system.

Fluid

A *water-side economizer* utilizes evaporative cooling (usually provided by cooling towers) to indirectly produce chilled water to cool a datacenter when outdoor conditions are cool (often at night). This is best for environments with temperatures below 55 degrees Fahrenheit for 3000 or more hours a year.

Using economizers, chilled-water-plant energy consumption can be cut by up to 75 percent. You will also see reductions in maintenance costs, because the fluid-chilled cooling system allows you to drastically reduce—maybe even completely eliminate—the need for chiller operation.

Water-side economizers are especially beneficial, because not only do they save costs, but they don't allow contaminants or altered humidity levels into the datacenter.

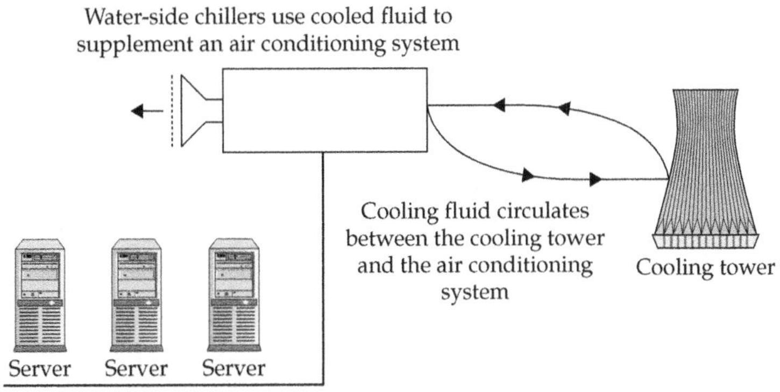

Water-side chillers use cooled fluid to
supplement an air conditioning system

Cooling fluid circulates
between the cooling tower
and the air conditioning
system

Cooling tower

Server   Server   Server

FIGURE 4-3   Water-side economizers cool using a loop connecting to a cooling tower, evaporative cooler, or dry cooler.

Water-side economizers work with a cooling tower, evaporative cooler, or dry cooler to cool down the datacenter. This type of economizer is normally incorporated into a chilled-water or glycol-based cooling system.

Fluid in the cooling system passes through a coil to cool the room, thus eliminating the need for the compressor to operate.

A water-side economizer is illustrated in Figure 4-3.

On-Demand Cooling

On-demand cooling systems are becoming more and more prevalent. These units are brought in to provide temporary cooling when central air is down. They are also widely used in datacenters. There are two types of on-demand cooling systems, very similar in function to economizers:

- **Air to air**   Smaller air-to-air coolers can be wheeled into the room needing cooling. They use flexible ductwork to connect to a window, and then the generated heat is transferred out of the building. They can be plugged into a standard 110-volt wall outlet. Larger units can be mounted on the outside of the building, with cool air being ducted through a window. These units operate on temporary 208-to-230-volt circuits.

- **Water based**   These are much larger units, where a standard garden hose is connected to the device so that water flows in, cools down the equipment, and then is sent through a second hose to run down a drain.

NOTE *Obviously water-based coolers are not the best stopgap for cooling needs. All it takes is one leaky hose and there'll be trouble.*

HP's Solution

Hewlett-Packard offers a cooling technology that it says can cut an IT department's power costs by up to 40 percent. The system, called Dynamic Smart Cooling, uses sensors to control the temperature in specific areas of the datacenter. HP labs were able to reduce the power to cool a datacenter from 45.8 kW using a standard industry setup to 13.5 kW.

Dynamic Smart Cooling is an intelligent solution, and rather than turning your datacenter into a meat locker, the system allows air conditioners—managed by specially designed software—to regulate the cold air delivered to a room based on the needs of specific computers.

Note *HP has also looked to some of its earlier inventions to solve the cooling cost problem. The company modified its inkjet printing technology to create a cooling solution where a device sprays liquid on semiconductor chips to cool them down.*

Dynamic Smart Cooling uses the datacenter's airconditioning system to adapt to changing workloads with sensors attached to the computers. If the system senses that a computer is warming up too much, air conditioners will send more cool air.

Optimizing Airflow

Air exchange is important. To deliver the precise cooling environment, air must be exchanged at a sufficient rate. Normal office environments must change air over twice an hour. In high-density datacenters, air has to be exchanged 50 times an hour. If enough air is not exchanged, cooling air will heat up before it reaches the equipment, and disaster could occur.

Finding the latest and greatest in cooling technology is certainly a useful tactic in reducing your cooling costs. But some good practices can help minimize your costs without you having to buy the newest product.

This section looks at some best practices that can help optimize the airflow around your servers and other networking equipment.

Hot Aisle/Cold Aisle

Equipment is typically designed to draw in air from the front and then blow the exhaust out the rear. As Figure 4-4 shows, this allows equipment to be arranged to create hot aisles and cool aisles.

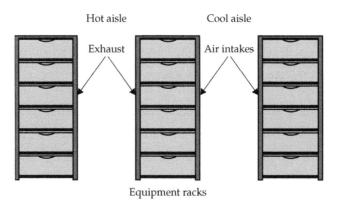

Figure 4-4   Equipment can be configured in a hot-aisle/cool-aisle configuration.

Something you'll notice about Figure 4-4 is that the cool sides of equipment are arranged together, whereas the hot sides of equipment face each other. This allows the equipment to draw in cool air, rather than air that has already been preheated by the rack of equipment in front of it.

The cold aisles have perforated floor tiles to draw cooler air from the raised floor. Floor-mounted cooling is placed at the end of hot aisles, but not parallel to the row of racks. This is because parallel placement can cause the hot exhaust to be drawn across the top of the racks and mixed with the cool air. It also decreases overall energy efficiency.

Raised Floors

Datacenters are conventionally built on a floor that is raised 18 to 36 inches. The higher the floor level, the more air that can be distributed under the floor and the more air that can be used by the cooling system.

But higher isn't always practical. There can be major disruptions to day-to-day operations. Plus, the higher up you build the floor, obviously, the closer you'll be getting to the ceiling. This can be a hindrance not only for rack sizes, but also for the flow of air over the top of equipment.

NOTE *Too much can be too much. To accommodate the cooling needs of 400 watts per square foot, the floor would have to be elevated 5 feet. You can only count on so much from your raised floor before you need to consider supplemental cooling options.*

Cable Management

Developing a good cable management system in conjunction with the hot-aisle/cold-aisle design can equate to more energy efficiency.

Whenever possible, it's best to route your cables under the hot aisle, as shown in Figure 4-5. This reduces the cool air's path to the equipment as it is drawn in through the perforated tiles and into the equipments' cooling systems.

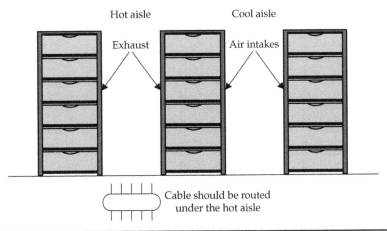

FIGURE 4-5 Route cables along the hot aisle whenever possible to avoid airflow problems in the cool aisle.

Some racks now provide expansion channels that help with cable management and ease heat removal for high-density racks. It may be possible to retrofit existing racks with these channels.

Some organizations are also running cabling above or through racks, rather than under the floors, to reduce the interference with the flow of air from below. Further, some organizations are deploying advanced power strips to bring the power load closer to the rack rather than running so many cables through the datacenter. We've all seen messes of cabling that resemble an enormous blue or grey spaghetti bundle. These bundles act like insulation, trapping heat near the equipment and preventing cool air from passing through.

Vapor Seal

It's also important to ensure you have a good vapor barrier in your datacenter, cutting it off from the rest of the building. If you have a poor vapor barrier, humidity will move into the datacenter during hot months and escape during the winter months.

A good vapor seal reduces the costs to humidify or dehumidify.

Prevent Recirculation of Equipment Exhaust

Your networking gear can get hot enough on its own and doesn't need help from its neighbors—nor does it need to heat up its neighbors. The following are some simple steps you can employ in your datacenter to prevent exhaust from being reabsorbed by other devices. These are illustrated in Figure 4-6.

1. **Hot-aisle/cool aisle**   Employ the hot-aisle/cool-aisle design mentioned earlier in this chapter.

2. **Rigid enclosures**   Build rigid enclosures to keep exhaust heat from being sucked back into the device's cool air intakes.

3. **Flexible strip curtains**   Use flexible strip curtains to block the open air above your racks that have been configured into a hot-aisle/cool-aisle layout.

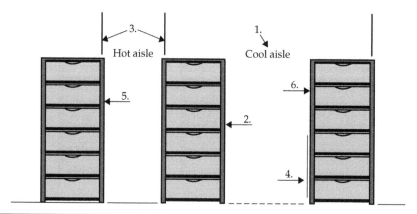

FIGURE 4-6   You can prevent exhaust from overheating your equipment by following some simple steps.

4. **Block unused rack locations with blanks** Equipment typically draws in cool air from the front and exhausts it out the back. Blanking open areas under equipment prevents the exhaust from being drawn back into the device.

5. **Design with cooling in mind** Although most do, some equipment does not draw air in from the front and exhaust it out the back. Some have top-discharge or side-to-side designs. Configure your racks to ensure your equipment doesn't blow into the intake of other equipment.

6. **Select racks with good airflow** Buy racks that don't have an internal structure that would block the smooth flow of air to your equipment.

Supply Air Directly to Heat Sources

Rather than shelling out the money to cool the entire datacenter, you can save some money and just cool down the devices generating heat. These tips can help:

- **Use the correct diffusers** The type of diffuser you would use in an office is not appropriate for a datacenter. Select diffusers that deliver air directly to the equipment that needs cooling.

- **Correctly place supply and returns** Diffusers should be placed right by the equipment to be cooled. They should not be placed so they direct cooling air at heat exhausts, but rather into the air intakes. Supplies and slotted floor tiles should not be placed near returns to prevent a cool air "short circuit."

- **Minimize air leaks** Systems that use a raised floor can lose cool air through cable accesses in hot aisles.

- **Optimize air conditioner placement** In large datacenters, a computational fluid dynamics (CFD) model would be useful. This helps locate the best placement for cooling units. It also helps minimize the distance between air conditioner units and large loads.

- **Use properly sized plenums** Return plenums need to be the right size to allow a lot of air to flow through. Obstructions such as piping, cabling trays, and electrical conduits need to be taken into consideration when plenum space is calculated.

- **Provide enough supply** Under-floor supply plenums must be big enough to allow enough air to service your equipment. Again, take into consideration obstacles such as piping, cabling trays, and electrical conduits.

Fans

Fans also suck up a lot of power, especially when a lot of them are spinning at the same time. Take these tips into consideration to improve fan efficiency:

- **Use a low-pressure drop system** Use low-pressure drop air handlers and ductwork. Make sure there is enough capacity in your under-floor plenums to allow air to flow.

- **Use redundant air handlers during normal operations** It is more efficient to use auxiliary fans at a lower speed than a single fan at high speed. Power usage drops with the square of the velocity. As such, operating two fans at 50 percent capacity uses less power than one fan at full capacity.

Humidity

Datacenter cooling systems must also be able to adapt to exterior temperature and humidity. Because these factors will change depending on where on the globe the datacenter is located—along with the time of year—datacenter air-conditioning systems must be able to adapt to these sorts of changes.

Too much humidity can wreck your datacenter equipment. Too little humidity can wreck your datacenter equipment. Use these tips to help keep your datacenter at the right level:

- **Establish a humidity sensor calibration schedule**   Humidity sensors drift and require frequent calibration—more so than temperature sensors. Also, incorrect humidity sensors are less likely to be noticed than incorrect temperature sensors. As such, establish a frequent test and calibration schedule for your humidity sensors.

- **Allow for sensor redundancy**   Make sure you have enough sensors to keep an eye on your datacenter's humidity level. To ensure a tight control, multiple sensors should be used. At the very least use two, but more are better.

- **Manage humidity with a dedicated unit**   If ventilated air is used (maybe from an air-side economizer), control humidity with a single ventilation air handler.

- **Lock out economizers when necessary**   When using an air-side economizer, minimize the amount of air that's brought in when the dew point is low. This saves money on having to humidify the dry air.

- **Centralize humidity control**   Each datacenter should have its own centralized humidity control system. Multiple systems wind up fighting each other, and the system becomes less efficient.

Adding Cooling

If your datacenter is especially "equipment dense," you'll need to add some extra cooling capacity. The best way to cool your equipment is to make sure the cooling gear is as close as possible to the heat sources. When you decide how to supplement your cooling systems, you should consider what type of system to use (air or fluid based) and what type of design the system will use.

Fluid Considerations

As anyone with a car knows, fluid is a great way to move heat from equipment (in this case, the engine) to keep it cool. As anyone who has ever left their cellular telephone in a pocket as it went through the wash knows, electronics and water don't mix. That's not to say that fluid-based cooling systems have no place in datacenter environments. It just means you've got to use care.

Of course, water isn't the only fluid used for cooling. Though water is normally used in floor-mounted cooling, because of safety concerns, R134a refrigerant is typically used when cooling is used closer to the equipment. This is because refrigerant turns into a gas when it reaches the air, so leakage doesn't pose a threat to your equipment. Table 4-3 lists the advantages and disadvantages of both solutions.

However, it isn't just safety and effectiveness that makes refrigerant a good match for cooling needs. Fluid solutions employ microchannel coils for better efficiency, and a

	Advantages	Disadvantages
Chilled water	• Less expensive • Room sizes don't matter	• Electrical hazard • Less efficient • Fluid treatment may be necessary to prevent fouling • Limited overhead cooling options
Refrigerant	• No electrical hazards • Lower operating costs • Smaller piping requirements • More compact heat exchanges	• Potential compatibility issues with small rooms • More expensive

TABLE 4-3   Advantages and Disadvantages of Water and Refrigerant

low-pressure system results in lower operating costs. It can also provide an energy-efficiency savings of between 25 and 35 percent based on kilowatts of cooling capacity per kW of heat load.

System Design

Because getting close to the heat source is so important, the cooling system's design is important to consider. There are two common designs in datacenters—open and closed.

In a closed design, the electronics and cooling equipment are situated together in a sealed environment. The benefit of this is that it is a high-capacity cooling solution. The downside is that the design isn't as flexible, nor fault-tolerant.

NOTE *Closed systems are good for small solutions, assuming there is adequate ventilation if the system fails.*

In a datacenter environment, however, an open design is preferred, because a closed solution offers little flexibility. For example, if a cooling system fails, the racks are isolated from the room's own cooling opportunities. Inside the enclosure, the server can reach its over-temperature limit in 15 seconds.

With an open architecture, modules can be positioned close to the racks, but are not enclosed, so room air can be a sort of backup if the cooling equipment fails. This makes it much safer for both your organization's data reliability as well as the hardware's physical health.

Not least of all, you have much greater flexibility to configure and reconfigure your datacenter as the system evolves.

Datacenter Design

You can optimize your cooling needs by how you design your datacenter. A number of issues can help you reduce the amount of cooling you need, simply by how you design your datacenter and how cooling is deployed.

This section examines those issues and offers suggestions for overall layout as well as cooling options.

Centralized Control

When designing your cooling plan, it's best to employ a custom centralized air-handling system. This sort of system offers several benefits over the prevalent multiple-distributed-unit system, including the following:

- Better efficiency.

- Can use surplus and redundant capacity.

- Units can work in conjunction with each other, rather than fighting against one another.

- Uses fluid-cooled chiller plants, which are much more efficient than water- and air-cooled datacenters.

- Less maintenance is required.

Design for Your Needs

You wouldn't clomp around in shoes that are two sizes too large or try to squeeze into a pair of underwear that's two sizes too small. We expect things to fit right. Unfortunately, our datacenters' power needs rarely get the exact fit they need. They are usually loaded too light.

Although a certain amount of the dark arts are involved in getting the size right, it is important to get as close as you can with electrical and mechanical systems so that they still operate properly when underloaded, but are still scalable for larger loads.

You can come close to this Zen-like balance if you consider a few issues:

- Upsize the duct, plenum, and piping infrastructure. This reduces operating costs and allows a measure of future-proofing.

- Use variable-speed motor drives on chillers, chilled and condenser water pumps. Also, use cooling tower fans to help with part-load performance. This can be especially helpful when controlled as part of a coordinated cooling system.

- Examine efficient design techniques, such as medium-temperature cooling loops and fluid-side economizers.

- Cooling-tower energy use is typically a small portion of energy consumption. If you upsize cooling towers, you can improve chiller performance and fluid-side economizers. Although this involves a larger cost up front and a larger physical footprint, you'll find savings in operational costs.

Put Everything Together

Efficient cooling isn't just a matter of installing intelligent equipment. Organization-wide considerations must be implemented, including design and decision-making issues. Such issues include:

- Use life cycle cost analysis as part of your decision-making process.

- Involve all key stakeholders to keep the team together on the project. Document and clarify the reasons for key design decisions.

- Set quantifiable goals based on best practices.
- Introduce energy optimization as early as possible in the design phase to keep the project focused and to keep costs minimized.
- Include integrated monitoring, measuring, and controls in facility design.
- Examine and benchmark existing facilities and then track your performance. Look back over the data and look for any opportunities to improve performance.
- Evaluate the potential for onsite power generation.
- Make sure all members of the facility-operations staff get site-specific training, including the identification and proper operation of energy-efficiency features.

As anyone who has tried to string network cabling through an old building knows, planning for the future can save a lot of time, energy, and money. The same philosophy is true of cooling systems—it's a good idea to plan for the future.

Selecting a technology that can scale to future needs is a critical part of your considerations. Because if you do add more power to your system, you'll need to add more cooling.

Most server manufacturers are working on solutions that bring refrigerant-based cooling modulated into the rack to manage heat densities of 30 kW and higher. This will make refrigerant-based systems compatible with the next generation of cooling strategies.

Your cooling system is such a huge portion of your datacenter that it really merits a lot of your attention—not just to reduce your electricity bill, but also to mitigate your carbon emissions. Spending time and effort to ensure you have a well-running cooling system will help not only your organization but also the environment.

It isn't just your machinery that can help reduce your impact on the environment. In the next chapter, we'll talk about some steps that your organization can take on a business level that can mean less money spent and less pollution.

PART

III

What You Can Do

Changing the Way We Work

There is no dearth of information you can refer to in order to make your organization more environmentally responsible. Although the focus of this book is on making your IT activities more environmentally friendly, we'd be remiss if we didn't mention some things that your organization can do at other levels to be more green.

Although this chapter doesn't pretend to be the last word for greening your entire organization, we present some ideas to help implement broader measures in your business.

Rethinking Old Behaviors

Companies do a lot of things simply because that's how they learned to do business. And while trial, error, and time have taught them the best way to do business, that "best" way might not be the most eco-friendly way. What's more, it may not be the most cost-effective way.

In this section, we'll look at some ways your organization can rethink behaviors and turn them into environmentally responsible methods that save money in the process.

Starting at the Top

Before you can make any reasonable progress toward greening your organization, you need everyone to believe that these steps will ultimately help the organization. If they don't see a benefit, there's no incentive for them to get behind your plan.

Naturally, environmental considerations aren't new. And in recent years, being environmentally conscious has been important talk. But the fact of the matter is upper management needs to sign off on greening your IT department, like any major endeavor that affects the entire organization.

This may be easy in some cases. You might find that the organization's CEO wants to initiate eco-friendly measures because his grandkids talked his ear off about it at a recent family picnic. You might find that it's easy because investors are pushing to be environmentally responsible to protect and build their bottom lines.

On the other hand, old thought processes might make it a hard sell. "We've always done it this way and there's no reason to change" is a mentality that you're likely to face when proposing any change.

If you are recommending change to the organization, you need to present management with a well-researched proposal that shows not only benefits to the environment and benefits to the organization, but also fiscal benefits.

Process Reengineering with Green in Mind

A number of business processes can be altered with an eye toward environmental responsibility. One of the places where you might choose to change or alter your business processes is in your supply chain management. Also known as *green sourcing,* using a green supply chain is gaining momentum in the business world.

If you're not already embracing green sourcing, you can make the change by understanding a few issues.

Know Your Needs

This first step is to understand your existing supply chain. You need to study how your organization spends and its consumption patterns. Obviously, you can't make changes to something you don't understand. At this stage, you need to understand the current state of your procurement and how you consume materials.

Make a Plan

Once you understand your supply chain, the next step is to develop a plan. At this stage, you'll create goals and the metrics to track your progress, as shown in Figure 5-1.

For example, some electronics companies want to improve end-of-life management by increasing the lifetime of equipment by making it easier to swap out old components and provide easy upgrade paths. In this case, the electronics companies have multiple initiatives as the result of a single goal.

Internal and External Needs

With a plan in place, you need someone to oversee the project. It isn't sufficient to simply have a plan and expect individuals in your organization to find their piece within the plan. Many companies have chief sustainability officers who coordinate and oversee green efforts. Although this person will have different roles and functions in different organizations, it is important to have someone in place as a single point of accountability.

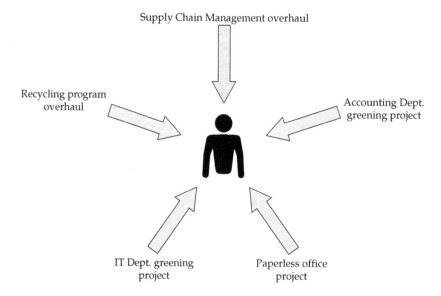

Supply Chain Management overhaul

Recycling program overhaul

Accounting Dept. greening project

IT Dept. greening project

Paperless office project

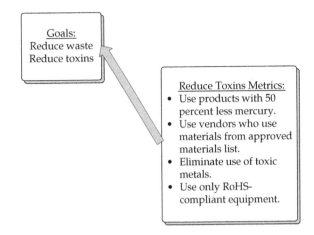

Figure 5-1
Develop a plan based on goals and metrics to measure those goals.

> Goals:
> Reduce waste
> Reduce toxins

> Reduce Toxins Metrics:
> - Use products with 50 percent less mercury.
> - Use vendors who use materials from approved materials list.
> - Eliminate use of toxic metals.
> - Use only RoHS-compliant equipment.

You should also market your progress within your organization and also to your supply chain partners. An important issue is to get people onboard with your efforts. By communicating to everyone why your green efforts are being undertaken, what will be measured, and how you're going to get there, it gives others an understanding of what you're doing and allows them to jump onboard your plan.

Greening Your Procurement and Sourcing

Although sourcing and procurement have the veneer of being all about money, there is more to them than just cost. There are a number of noncost factors to sourcing and procurement, and greening is one of them. When creating requests for proposals, make sure to include a green component as well as clear metrics for their measurement as part of supplier performance management.

You should be as clear and detailed as possible about your wants. For instance, you should forbid harmful chemicals such as the following:

- CFCs
- HCFCs
- Chlorinated solvents
- Cadmium
- Mercury
- Chlorinated or brominated flame retardants

And you should also include language in your agreements that spell out approved and preferred materials, such as long-lasting low-mercury lamps as well as EPEAT and Energy Star–rated equipment.

Know Your Suppliers

When you're evaluating suppliers for their level of environmental responsibility, here are some issues to consider:

- What are the supplier's environmental values? How are they measured and enforced?
- Does the supplier have an environmental management system?

- Who is accountable for environmental performance? Is it just the supplier's environmental staff, or is it all employees?
- Does the supplier comply with federal, state, and local environmental laws?
- Is the supplier willing to understand and work with your environmental goals?
- Has the supplier made efforts to design and manufacture products with the environment in mind?
- How efficient is the supplier in using resources, materials, and energy, as well as recycling and pollution prevention?
- Will the supplier reclaim its products or packaging at the end of their useful lives?

Not every supplier will knock the ball out of the park in answering these questions, although suppliers tend to be pretty black and white when it comes to being green. However, it will give you an indication as to how well that supplier will be in meeting your own green sourcing needs and how well they align with your corporate culture.

Communicate with Your Suppliers

Hit the ground running by setting clear expectations of your supply base during the sourcing process and monitor compliance and progress. This gets you off to a good start and helps smooth out any wrinkles that might appear as you start green sourcing.

Make sure your suppliers know what they need to provide and how they will be measured. This ensures that they are providing what you want and are putting in place the processes to achieve compliance.

What We Expect of Suppliers:
Easily disassembled equipment.
Lead-free solder.
Packing material pickup.
No toxins in products.
Recyclable products that are labeled.

How We'll Measure Suppliers' Compliance:
Product inspection.
Parts listing required.
Disclosure of chemicals used.

Supplier informed of expectations →

Supplier

For example, this can include detailing how suppliers are to recycle discarded materials, that they need to use less-toxic chemicals, and that they create products which are easily disassembled for less waste and easier recycling.

Keep Up to Date with Global Issues

It's important to know what's going on in the global community as far as regulation is concerned. The European Union's Restriction of Hazardous Substances (RoHS) regulations and California's Electronic Waste Recycling Act (EWRA) are likely to impact your supply chain. For instance, because of EWRA, it is prohibited to sell devices in California banned by Europe's RoHS. This includes monitors that contain the heavy metals restricted by RoHS. If you keep up on global regulation issues, you can see how they affect your own supply chain—often for the better.

Keep Up with New Technologies

Green technologies are a moving target, and your industry may be making significant improvements. By keeping up with what's going on in your industry, you can find out where you can make the best changes. You also maintain your competitive edge. Be active in your industry's groups and organizations to keep up with trends.

Start Simply

One of the first steps we suggested was to develop a plan. And although it's important to see the big picture, it's not necessary to overhaul the entire system all at once. You'll go nuts—and it's probably impossible to do, anyway.

Rather, start small. Identify some things you can do simply right away. These get you started, and they serve as springboards to more involved endeavors. Some easy things you can do include negotiating leasing or buy-back options into electronics contracts, as well as ensuring hardware goes back to the manufacturer for recycling. You could also label material types of your products so consumers know how they can recycle them.

Analyzing the Global Impact of Local Actions

We've seen the slogan "Think Globally, Act Locally" on T-shirts and bumper stickers for years. Like so many clichés, at first we got the message, but after seeing it a gazillion times the message turned into an annoyance. Although you see the cliché from time to time, the fact of the matter is that the actions individuals take can mushroom into something that affects the entire planet.

Consider the pyramid shown in Figure 5-2.

At the bottom level of the pyramid is the individual; the top represents the global community. The bottom level represents simple, everyday decisions, such as the decision to recycle a used beer can. As we move up the pyramid, we see that decisions made at a given level help influence decisions made at the next level. Also, the following trends become apparent:

- Individual decisions are replaced by group decisions.
- Decisions become more complex and they encompass a broader range of issues.
- The amount and quality of information needed for decision-making increases.
- Short-term decisions evolve into long-term decisions.

Decisions at both ends of the pyramid influence each other. Everyday choices made at the bottom level ("Will I recycle this can?") are made based on decisions that have been made at the global level ("There's a worldwide trash crisis.").

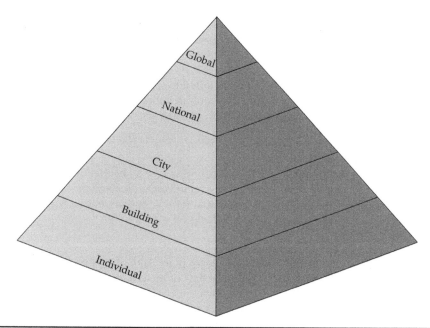

FIGURE 5-2   The decision-making pyramid shows how decisions of an individual can get bigger and bigger.

As you can tell, information generated at the top of the pyramid is policy oriented. Output at the bottom level of the pyramid at action oriented.

Let's take a closer look at how this works, in practice. Table 5-1 illustrates what happens when an issue—in this case, the reduction of CO_2 emissions—is handled at each level of the pyramid.

Steps

So far in this book—and in chapters to come—we've explained how your IT department can conserve energy, but that's not the only place you can make changes. Energy conservation is also a consideration in the non-IT parts of an organization. Keeping green encompasses such issues as water conservation, recycling, and so forth. Let's talk about some of the ways you can be environmentally responsible in the non-IT portions of your organization.

Water

Water use can be a big consideration in your organization. How much of a consideration will vary, depending on how much water you use. For instance, if you're in an office building in a downtown location, you don't have to water the grass. On the other hand, if you are in a campus with lots of lush lawn between your buildings, water usage will be a lot higher.

The following are some tips to keep your water usage under control:

- Document your maintenance and upgrades to fixtures.
- Monitor your water usage. Keep a log of meter reads on a weekly basis so that spikes in usage can be assessed and repairs made in a timely fashion.

Global		
Actions:	International attention is paid to trends in CO_2 concentrations and how international trade is increasing CO_2 concentration. Scenarios are generated to understand the long-term impact of CO_2 concentration. Plans are generated for individual nations to help arrest CO_2 concentration levels.	
Stakeholders:	UN and international organizations, universities, research institutions, and international NGOs.	
National		
Actions:	National policies and programs to reduce CO_2 levels are developed. This is manifested in the form of rules, regulations, research and development, and financial support.	
Stakeholders:	National governmental departments and ministries, universities, research institutions, business and industry associations, and chambers of commerce.	
City		
Actions:	Cities and local governments apply programs developed at the national level to local issues. Goals and objectives are reflected in local ordinances, regulations, and so forth. At the city level, those ordinances are combined with informational campaigns to inform members of the community.	
Stakeholders:	Local governmental agencies, business and industry organizations, local chambers of commerce, financial institutions, NGOs, community groups, and local universities.	
Building		
Actions:	At this level, "real" action takes place. This is where action is taken on programs and ordinances from higher levels. At this level, chosen materials, designs, technology choices, and building usage all play a part in reducing CO_2 levels.	
Stakeholders:	Individuals, clubs, NGOs, and management teams.	
Individual		
Actions:	This level represents the day-to-day use of a building. Individual choices at this level add up to have an impact—for instance, reducing the amount of electricity used, minimizing water usage, recycling waste products, and so forth. These actions can be taken based on regulation by the organization ("Don't throw your cans in the trash—recycle them.") or by an individual's own volition ("I know I should recycle this pop can.").	
Stakeholders:	Individuals, clubs, NGOs, and management teams.	

TABLE 5-1   How the Issue of CO_2 Emissions Is Dealt with at Different Levels of the Pyramid

- Install leak detection and water conservation tools, such as isolated meters and shut-off valves to each appliance or fixture. Rain shut-off devices are especially helpful if you have grass to water.

- Determine flow rates, flush volumes, and daily water use. Put a plan in place to reduce the amount of water that's used.

- Install low-flow fixtures. If you've already got low-flow fixtures, keep up on their maintenance.

If you do have an irrigation system in place, consider these issues to prevent wasted water:

- Inspect your property for leaks on a regular basis. Repair leaks as soon as they're detected.

- Regularly check your irrigation systems (monthly is best) and look for problems. Sprinkler heads routinely break and can go unnoticed for months.

- Adjust watering schedules to fit the needs of the plants. If you water deep and less frequently, plants will develop deep root growth. If you water everyday, plants develop shallower roots.

- Consider getting rid of turf and installing plants.

- Pick weeds early in the season. Grass and weeds are both huge water consumers.

- If you have any tropical plants, be sure they are grouped with plants that have similar watering needs.

- Annuals should be watered on a separate schedule. Their roots are shallower and need more frequent watering, but in lesser amounts.

Recycling

You've likely got some recycling measures in place already. Most companies do, but not every company is as strict as the next one. At some places, recycling simply means throwing soda pop cans into a separate bin. Other companies separate out plastic, different colors of glass, and office paper. Still other places get downright radical about what they recycle. No matter where you are on the recycling continuum, there's likely someplace else you can find to recycle.

If your company is already especially militant about recycling, we're probably not going to tell you anything you don't already know. But if you do need some tips, consider these issues.

Furniture

Think about renting furniture. If you suddenly need new workstations, is it a temporary need? If so, you can easily rent the furniture rather than buy something that might not get used again later. If you do need new furniture or cubicles, think about buying used or refurbished ones.

After the holidays we don't
need them anymore.

We need new workstations
for the holiday season rush.

If we rent them, we don't
need to keep them or figure
out how to get rid of them.

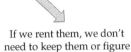

Cooperative Buying

By participating in a cooperative buying program, you help reduce the amount of reusable business waste going into landfills. It also reduces your disposal costs and allows you to buy materials at a low price.

Environmentally Preferable Purchasing Plan

Your company should adopt an environmentally preferable purchasing plan. This establishes environmentally conscious policies for the sorts of materials you buy. Some considerations include the following:

- **Paper**   Buy 35-percent to 100-percent post-consumer recycled paper. It used to be a specialty item that only niche suppliers carried, but now bigger brand-name retailers such as Staples offer paper with up to 100-percent recycled content.

- **Supplies**   Numerous business supplies, such as clipboards, binders, post-its, folders, envelopes, notepads, notebooks, and calendars, can be purchased with different percentages of recycled content. As with paper, many small and online retailers offer a great variety of products. Again, these items can be found at Office Depot and Staples.

- **Paperless**   If you send faxes electronically and scan documents, you won't consume as much paper. Plus, it'll be easier to locate documents you file. We'll talk about going paperless in more detail in Chapter 6.

- **Janitorial**   Just because they're used to clean up our messes doesn't mean that janitorial supplies have to be hazardous. Look for chlorine-free products that have more than 35 percent post-consumer recycled content.

- **Business cards**   Think about wherever paper is used in your organization—even business cards can be bought that are printed on recycled paper.

- **Food products**   If you stock Styrofoam cups, plastic silverware, and the like in your break rooms, think about switching over to buy biodegradable/compostable food service ware.

NOTE *In San Francisco, food vendors are forbidden from using polystyrene foam and must use biodegradable or recyclable materials.*

- **Bags**   Paper or plastic? Ditch the plastic bags and stick with paper bags. Plastic bags are made of petroleum products and do not biodegrade and cannot be recycled.

Energy

We've spent a lot of ink in this book talking about reducing your power consumption—and there's even more discussion in the chapters ahead. But there are some non-IT places where you can also reduce the amount of electricity your organization uses.

Appliances

Your break room likely has various appliances, including refrigerators. When buying refrigerators and other appliances, you should buy models that are Energy Star certified.

Energy Star is the U.S. Environmental Protection Agency's program to promote products that use less power than noncertified products.

NOTE *You can find a list of Energy Star–rated refrigerators via Link 5-1.*

Rebates

You don't have to make all these eco-friendly changes in a vacuum. Chances are, wherever your business is located, you'll be able to get some sort of rebate for changing the type of lighting you use and the like. Failing that, governmental organizations want to help.

For example, the San Francisco Department of the Environment, in partnership with the Pacific Gas and Electric Company, provides free energy audits, reports, technical assistance, and rebates for commercial customers in San Francisco. Your city, county, or province might provide similar services. You just have to ask.

Pollutants

Another place your organization can reduce its environmental impact is through the types of materials it uses. That is, products are available that contain fewer toxins than conventional materials.

Cleaning Products

Most janitorial cleaning products contain ingredients that may cause harm to human health, indoor air quality, and the environment. Some ingredients in janitorial cleaning products can instantly burn the eyes, skin, and lungs. By choosing the least toxic cleaning products for your organization, you lessen your environmental impact, and you also lessen the chance for an employee to be harmed. You can determine which products have low levels of toxins by observing the following:

- Reading the product label and Material Safety Data Sheet (MSDS) can help you make this determination. The MSDSs of many cleaning products that are sold to the general public can be found in the National Institutes of Health's Household Products Database at http://householdproducts.nlm.nih.gov, or via Link 5-2.

- Examine the list of institutional cleaning products that have been certified by Green Seal as meeting its Standard GS-37 for general cleaners and GS-40 for floor-care products. This list is available at www.greenseal.org, or via Link 5-3.

- Read the Janitorial Pollution Prevention website. This public service website has fact sheets on safe and effective cleaning techniques for windows, carpets, restrooms, and other cleaning job. The website can be accessed via Link 5-4.

- Call the manufacturers to ask about any less-toxic alternatives they offer. Many vendors have several product lines, one of which may contain less-harmful ingredients than the others.

Paint

Paint can contain toxic heavy metals, whereas cleaning solvents can consist of toxic and flammable petroleum-based products (such as mineral spirits, toluene, and xylene) that emit volatile organic compounds (VOCs), which can combine with other pollutants to create ozone. Buy and use latex or water-based paints, finishes, and varnishes rather than oil-based paints. Also, buy zero- or low-VOC paints.

Carpet

Toxins are everywhere—even under your feet. When buying new carpet or replacing old installations, choose carpets made with natural fibers, recycled nylon, or low VOCs. VOCs can vaporize and enter the atmosphere, thus contributing to indoor air pollution.

Aerosols

Aerosol mists can trigger asthma and other breathing problems because they contain product and propellant made up of very small droplets that are easily inhaled into the lungs. Up to 40 percent of the contents in an aerosol container can be propellants. The most common propellants are propane, butane, nitrous oxide, and carbon dioxide. Most propellants are petroleum products that are highly flammable. Pump spray bottles are less likely to cause direct health hazards because they are not pressured. They lack propellants, and they deliver the product in larger droplets that are less able to penetrate the lungs.

Fluorescent Lamps

It's better to buy fluorescent lamps because many other types contain mercury or lead. Some fluorescent lamps do contain mercury; therefore, choose energy-efficient fluorescent lamps that contain the lowest amount of mercury content. Also, consider installing motion detectors to light rooms only when people are present, and use timers for other lights to avoid them being left on.

NOTE *Old exit signs should be replaced with LED exit signs or refitted to use LED lamps.*

Paper

If you haven't totally warmed to the idea of a paperless office, then consider buying unbleached paper. The manufacture of office paper and janitorial paper products—including paper towels, toilet paper, napkins, and toilet seat covers—can create hazardous byproducts that are often discharged directly into surface waters such as rivers and the ocean. The use of chlorine-containing bleaching agents to turn paper products bright white can generate a toxic soup of various chlorinated pollutants (including chloroform and chlorinated furans). Look for brands that are unbleached or that are whitened using only oxygen, ozone, hydrogen peroxide, or another chlorine-free process.

Toner Cartridges

Every year, millions of spent toner and inkjet cartridges are thrown away and wind up in landfills or incinerators. Buy locally remanufactured toner and inkjet cartridges, and be sure to recycle your old ones. Remanufacturers inspect empty cartridges for damage and then repair or replace broken parts. They clean the reusable parts and then refill the cartridge with new toner.

Rechargeable Batteries

Each year, over three billion batteries are sold. If batteries leak, they can cause burns to the eyes and skin. But they can also pollute the environment. Batteries can contain:

- Cadmium
- Mercury
- Cobalt
- Copper
- Zinc
- Lead
- Manganese
- Nickel
- Lithium

These heavy metals may leach from landfills, contaminate soil, and pollute surface water and groundwater. If incinerated, these toxic chemicals can be released into the air. Whenever possible, choose products that operate without batteries or use rechargeable batteries.

NOTE *If your organization uses calculators, consider purchasing solar-powered models.*

Nickel-metal hydride (NiMH) and lithium rechargeable batteries are preferable to nickel-cadmium (Ni-Cad) batteries because they are less toxic and can be more easily recharged without losing their power.

NOTE *If you can't find rechargeables, standardize on long-lasting batteries that won't need to be replaced as often.*

Ink

Printing ink can contain such heavy metals as the following:

- Barium
- Cadmium
- Chromium
- Lead

They also can contain alcohol and toxic hydrocarbons. If you dispose of ink improperly, it can contaminate surface water, groundwater, and the soil. Consider using vegetable-based inks instead.

LEED

If you employ green building products in building and remodeling projects, you'll get better quality, a cost savings, better indoor air, and a measure of protection for the environment. If you're building or remodeling, look for suppliers and service providers that use green building products.

The U.S. Green Building Council offers a rating system called the Leadership in Energy and Environmental Design (LEED). With it, a suite of standards for environmentally sustainable construction is supplied.

The project started in 1998, and since its inception LEED has grown to include more than 14,000 projects in the United States and 30 other countries. If an organization meets LEED certification, it is allowed to use the LEED Accredited Professional (AP) acronym after its name, showing that it has passed accreditation.

Because of the inclusion of environmental consideration, LEED creates healthier work environments. It also leads (no pun intended) to higher productivity and improved employee health and comfort. These benefits do come with a cost, however. Green buildings typically cost more to design and construct when compared to conventional buildings. However, these initial costs are mitigated with cost savings over time, not to mention the lessened environmental impact.

LEED certification is granted to buildings based on a 69-point scale, as follows:

- **Certified**   26–32 points
- **Silver**   33–38 points
- **Gold**   39–51 points
- **Platinum**   52–69 points

For more information on LEED, go to the U.S. Green Building Council's website at http://www.usgbc.org, or via Link 5-5.

Teleworkers and Outsourcing

A major way you can reduce the amount of electricity you use and the need for new computers is by simply not doing the work in your building. You still need the work to get done, of course, but you don't need to fill up your office building with workers.

In this section, we'll talk about two methods of accomplishing this task—telecommuting and outsourcing.

Telecommuting

Telecommuting is another good option to help reduce your environmental impact. The biggest hurdle to telecommuting—like the paperless office—is getting people to sign onto it. But this time it isn't workers who might balk at it—a lot of times it is management.

Telecommuting is often wrongly perceived as a vacation and workers not having to do their share of the work. But that isn't the case.

Research organization IDC stated that 8.9 million Americans worked at home at least 3 days a month in 2004. That's only a tiny increase from the 8.7 million people IDC reported as teleworkers in 1999.

Hewitt Associates, a human resources consulting firm, conducted its own survey of 936 large companies. Its results showed that 32 percent of these companies offered telecommuting opportunities in 2004. It was a 1 percent increase over the prior year.

Sun Microsystems operates its own telecommuting program called iWork. With it, workers can work from home, or if they need to they can drive to a flexible work center when they need an office. Around the world, Sun has 115 flexible office locations.

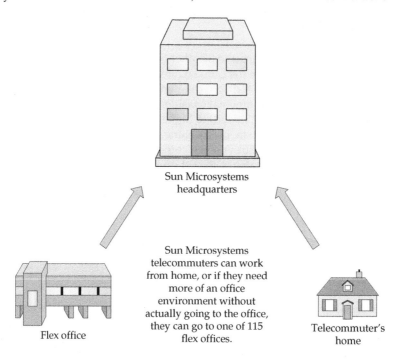

Sun Microsystems
headquarters

Flex office

Sun Microsystems
telecommuters can work
from home, or if they need
more of an office
environment without
actually going to the office,
they can go to one of 115
flex offices.

Telecommuter's
home

NOTE *Sun employees have identification cards with Java encoding. When they insert their card into a workstation, it instantly sets up the user's personal preferences.*

Although this is a nice arrangement for employees, Sun isn't missing out on any cost savings. Sun says this setup has saved the company $255 million over 4 years. It has reduced its cost for real estate by eliminating 7,700 seats. The company also saves money by not having to pay so much for electricity and not having to upgrade computers.

However, telecommuting isn't as simple as sending a worker home with a company-issued VPN client, a username, and password. In order to make it work, companies need to determine which job categories should be eligible; then guidelines and performance goals need to be established. The company also needs to decide what equipment it should provide and develop training for employees and managers.

How to Do It

Setting up a telecommuting program is reasonably straightforward, but there is some work to be done. It's ideal to have these steps in place before sending employees home with laptops.

Assessing and Measuring Performance   Performance standards should be established and should be the same as those for office-based employees who perform the same duties.

You should ensure that telecommuters receive the same training and information as office-based employees. Don't forget—they're still part of your company. Telecommuters should also get the same consideration as their office-based peers for personnel transactions, such as promotions, transfers, and the like.

Work Rules   Just because the employee is working from home doesn't mean that he or she should live by a different set of rules than office-based employees. Will you be able to check in on Dave and make sure he doesn't have his shoes off and have the stereo cranked up? Probably not, but the same rules should apply. Substance abuse and negligence pertaining to work product or hours are important. Although Jeni Johnson may be wearing sandals while she works, she can't start working an hour late and with an open beer bottle on her desk.

Review Requests   Some employees will want to telecommute; others simply want to come to the office. In order to find out who wants to work from home, your human resources staff should consider developing telecommuting guidelines and involve any unions or other employee organizations.

The telecommuting guidelines should include a three-step process:

- **Preapproval**   If an employee wants to telecommute, they fill out a worksheet that the organization can use to evaluate their suitability for telecommuting. Issues to consider in the preapproval worksheet include:
    - Core work hours.
    - Preapproval of the employee's workspace at home.
    - Identification of an alternate work site in case the employee can't work at the first site.
    - Assurance that the employee has the appropriate equipment to safely perform their job without risk of injury. Safety guidelines should also be in place.
- **Approval**   If human resources deems the employee suitable for telecommuting, the employee and organization complete an agreement that spells out the specifics of the telecommuting arrangement.
- **Ongoing monitoring**   The organization should regularly review each telecommuting arrangement to ensure that the criteria originally established continue to be met.

Other issues that the organization needs to be aware of and that the employee should sign off on include:

- The company should pay for a dedicated telephone line for business purposes. It should be understood that the company will review monthly bills. Typically the individual's cell phone becomes their business line while they are at home.

- Responsibility for additional costs related to starting the telecommuting operation (such as installing a broadband Internet connection, a second telephone line, and so forth) needs to be established up front. The organization and employee need to be clear about who is paying for what.

- The employee should have homeowner's insurance general liability coverage and provide a designated person at the agency with evidence of this insurance.

- The employer should conduct regular face-to-face meetings with the staff to bring people together. This could vary from once a week to once a month. For example, you might select to conduct a monthly status meeting at non–rush hour times.

- You also want to be sure employees do not become islands out there. Arm them with instant messaging and possibly videoconferencing capabilities. The technology is there, and costs are very low for a basic system.

- The company should notify the employee that it is their responsibility to notify their insurer about working from home. If there is an additional charge for that coverage, payment needs to be negotiated between the worker and the business.

- The organization needs to have written documentation of what business property is being located at the employee's home.

- If the telecommuter is working on a computer, a plan needs to be in place that spells out what will happen if the computer is down.

Monitoring

Let's say you've got your telecommuters in place and business is moving along nicely. You can't rest on your laurels, however. You have to do some regular monitoring to make sure things are going as you planned.

Some monitoring ideas include:

- Review each telecommuting arrangement at least once a year to make sure the criteria originally established continue to be met.

- Conduct periodic site visits (at least once per year) to evaluate and ensure minimum safety requirements are being met. If there are problems, the telecommuter should correct them per your agreement.

- If site visits are conducted, they should be performed by a qualified safety/ergonomic specialist who can conduct an ergonomic assessment.

- Get annual certificates of insurance coverage from each telecommuting employee.

- In the event of an injury, the business should gather as much specific information as possible. This information will help the worker's compensation adjuster determine whether the injury was work related.

- If a third party experiences damage, the business should gather as much information as possible to determine whether the damage is work related.

Outsourcing

Whereas telecommuting keeps the work in-house—it's just performed by employees at home—outsourcing takes the work out of the company's hands completely and sends it to another company. You aren't moving all of your organization's work to a contractor, and you certainly aren't moving your company's core duties. However, some functions, such as customer service, can be handled by a contractor.

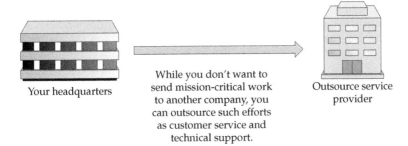

Your headquarters

While you don't want to send mission-critical work to another company, you can outsource such efforts as customer service and technical support.

Outsource service provider

Monetary Savings

Outsourcing can save you a ton of money, or outsourcing can only allow you to break even, at best—it depends on who you listen to. In 2005, professional services firm McKinsey & Co. stated that offshore outsourcing can cut an organization's cost by up to 55 percent. Not shabby. But at the same time, Gartner reported that most customer-service outsourcing will fail and end up costing companies one-third more than keeping the employees in-house.

So who's right and who's wrong? Both. Your success (or failure) at outsourcing will depend on how well you prepare, how well you select an outsource service provider, and how well they'll tackle your project.

But when done right, the cost savings are there.

Lost Jobs

Although you want to be ecologically responsible and save money, you don't want to put people out of jobs. And isn't that all outsourcing is? It's popular to hate outsourcing because it costs Americans their jobs. But maybe not.

According to a study by the Information Technology Association of America (ITAA), outsourcing—wait for it—actually *creates* jobs. In fact, ITAA estimates that by 2010, 337,000 jobs will be created, in addition to those lost to outsourcing—Information Technology Association of America, 2005.

And according to a study conducted by economic analysis firm Global Insight Inc., more jobs are created because outsourcing lowers costs to U.S. companies, thus allowing them to spend money on new workers. Additionally, it increases the efficiency of the U.S. economy, resulting in higher wages.

The ITAA study also estimates that outsourcing will save companies $20.9 billion by 2008.

Environmental Impact

If one of your reasons for outsourcing is to lessen your environmental impact, you need to know that the company handling your outsourcing isn't being environmentally irresponsible. That's a concern for a lot of organizations, and more and more they are asking service providers to follow more stringent environmental standards.

The Brown-Wilson Group, an outsourcing industry consulting firm, says in its report "Black Book of Outsourcing: 2007" that corporations are shifting their environmental concerns to service providers—Brown Wilson Group, 2007.

The report is based on a study of 120,000 outsourcing users. In 2007, 43 percent of companies that were first-time outsourcers included green factors in their decision-making process. Of the entire field of respondents, 88 percent said that environmental issues would influence their decision-making process.

But the decision to push green initiatives isn't wholly a principled one. Brown-Wilson says there is a lot of pressure from investors and consumers for companies to be more environmentally responsible.

At the same time, private companies aren't considering outsourcing at the same rate as publicly traded companies. The study also found that 94 percent of executives in publicly traded companies intend to add green clauses when they renegotiate their agreements. Conversely, only 36 percent of privately owned companies are considering such a move.

The study seems to show that investors are partly responsible for the green move. Is it because they're concerned about the environment? It very well could be. But it could also affect their bottom line. By investing in green companies, investors believe the companies will flourish, thus making their stock go up. But also, socially responsible companies can gain an edge against their competition because of cost reductions, quality improvements, increased profits, and access to new markets. Environmentally responsible companies also face less risk of environmental liability.

How to Outsource

Outsourcing is becoming more and more popular as a way to cut costs. But it isn't just an issue of cutting operational costs that makes it an ecologically friendly way to do business. When you need to add computer and staff capacity for a project, or as part of a growing business, you face the issues of buying equipment, paying for its cost of operation, and so forth. Outsourcing takes that burden off your shoulders and gives it to a company that already has the staff and equipment in place.

In order to outsource a project, you have to understand the issues surrounding the process.

Planning

When you outsource, you become the client. In order for an outsourcing project to be successful, you need to thoroughly explain what you want the outsourcing service provider to accomplish. Before looking for an outsourcing service, you need to understand the following:

- The scope of the work
- The level of effort expected
- The schedule
- The performance goals (used to mark the project's progress)

Establishing project milestones is a good way to develop the project, because they establish deliverables along with deadlines for each deliverable. This will take more work, however, because a feasibility and scoping study must be finished that establishes the full scope of the work, the milestones, and the budget.

Although this sort of study can be costly, there are definitely benefits, such as the following:

- Project requirements and specifications are clearly established before any work begins.
- The project can be reconciled with the budget.
- If it turns out the project is not feasible, it can be cancelled before too much time, money, and effort are committed.

Quite often, projects fail because specifications were not determined before the work began.

Success Strategies

When outsourcing, there are some realities you must embrace—not only to be successful in your endeavor, but also to keep moving ahead productively.

First, don't immediately expect to see cost savings from your outsourcing project. A lot of times, you will have to support duplicate efforts—here and abroad—until the transition is complete.

Realize also that another company is performing the work you've delegated. It's a different company, not an extension of your company. As such, that company might not have the same background your company has. It's best to work with the outsourcing service provider as flexibly as possible.

Mistakes and performance problems are going to happen. There's no way around it. However, if you work some "planned mistakes" into your overall project timeline, you'll be doing yourself a favor. When mistakes do happen, don't lose your cool. You have to be able to correct them in a professional manner.

NOTE *That doesn't mean your outsourcing service provider can drop the ball every step of the way. They need to be accountable and give you what you expect. If you're having repeated problems, it might be time to find a new provider.*

If you are outsourcing a project that involves a call center, many service providers have live call-monitoring capabilities. This allows someone from your organization to listen in—in real time—on the work that is being done. By doing this, you can hear what's going on in your company's name without going overseas to do it. There's also an element of policing. Outsource service providers are less likely to misbehave or do shoddy work when they know they might be listened to.

Payment

Invoicing and payment will vary based on the project, the size of the outsourcing service provider, and the work. Table 5-2 compares the sizes of companies and how billing and payment normally works.

Price will vary, based on the company size and type, the number of Western staff onsite, and whether or not the firm maintains a North American office. However, like buying a car, home electronics, or frozen pizza, picking the least expensive company isn't always the best bet. If you go the cheap route, it's more likely the provider will hire poor-quality staff or that the turnover rate will be high. Ultimately, you get what you pay for.

Outsource Service Provider Size	Billing and Payment Terms
Large	Normally work under advance payment arrangements. They usually require 15 or 30 days' worth of payment in advance.
Mid-size and small	Billing normally done weekly with payment due after a week. Rates are based on production time, which is defined as the time a customer service agent actually spends logged onto the phone system and can take calls. A payroll hour usually provides about 45 minutes of production time.

TABLE 5-2   Payment Terms for Different-Sized Outsourcing Service Providers

Maintenance

Once you have a plan in place, have selected a provider, everyone has been trained, and the program is in motion, you need to keep everything running smoothly—and communication is key to this effort.

Make sure the provider calls you each morning to check in. Even if there's no news to report, you can at least ensure you have consistent information coming in, and you will be able to keep up on arising issues.

Reporting is particularly important, especially if you have metrics that are granular enough to show the work of specific agents. If the metrics look unusual, you can investigate and find out what's going on.

Ensure that the service provider has an action plan in place in case (and when) problems arise.

Finding a Service Provider

In order to find a good service provider, follow these steps. The tips they contain can help you find a good match for your needs.

- **Research, research, research**   Ask companies you know for their recommendations. Nothing sells like a good recommendation. You can also find out about providers that aren't so good, and you'll know to steer clear of them. You can also ask potential providers for client references. You can then talk to these references and find out how effective the companies are.

- **Pursue compatibility**   Find a company that understands your particular needs. Develop a contract that allows you to tweak the agreement as changes occur (they will).

- **Set your standards**   Because your company will be represented by another company outside of your direct control, you need to establish standards by which the other company will behave. List these details in the contract, and check up on the service provider from time to time to make sure they're being followed.

- **Don't get caught with your pants down**   Have a backup plan in place in case the service provider can't carry through on their end of the bargain. If they fail or things fall through, you don't want the fallout to rain on you.

Greening your organization can happen at all sorts of levels. Although this book primarily focuses on your IT department, be sure you don't overlook any other parts of your organization that can be tweaked and fine-tuned.

Earlier in this chapter we talked about the merits of the paperless office. We didn't expand on this topic much here because the next chapter explains it in greater detail, as well as how you can take as much paper out of your office as possible.

Going Paperless

E arly iPhone adopters didn't just get the trendiest gadget of 2007 when they slapped down their money. In many cases, when the first bills arrived to customers they were the size of—forgive the pun—phone books.

It turns out that service provider AT&T sent out phone bills that enumerated each month's charges in such detail that the bills were hundreds of pages long. In some cases, customers got their bills delivered in cardboard boxes. Those mammoth bills were quickly scaled back to more reasonable sizes, but it underscores the appeal of electronic billing and going paperless.

NOTE *One blogger estimated that if Apple reached its goal of having 10 million iPhone users by the end of 2008, it would necessitate 74,535 trees being cut down and turned into paper every year, assuming an average 100-page monthly bill.*

It costs a lot of money to print a bill and mail it (even more if it's 300 pages long and shipped in a cardboard box). But many businesses still use that method, because they simply don't want to change. Paperless billing doesn't just save your organization lots of money—it's environmentally conscious as well. If your organization can go paperless, the change will save trees and money.

Being completely paperless might be a pipe dream. People just like to hold paper. That's why newspapers and magazines—despite having a web presence—are still printed and sold. That's why you're holding this book right now.

This chapter examines the practice of taking your organization in a paperless direction, and explains what you can do to reduce the amount of paper your organization consumes.

Paper Problems

Using so much paper, across the organization, is taking its toll. It's taking its toll on the environment and your bottom line. Let's take a moment to consider just what overuse of paper is doing—both globally and locally.

The Environment

Each year the U.S. alone consumes around 200 million tons of wood products, and this number increases 4 percent each year. The biggest source of wood consumption is paper production. U.S. paper producers consume one billion trees. That's the same as 12,430 square miles of forests each year, resulting in 735 pounds of paper for each American. Although the U.S. has less than 5 percent of the world's population, it consumes 30 percent of the world's paper.

We're not just picking on the Americans here. Worldwide consumption of wood products has risen 64 percent since 1961. Industry expects that amount to double by 2050.

Losing trees and forest land isn't the only problem. The process of deforestation has released about 120 billion tons of carbon dioxide (CO_2) into the atmosphere. Also, 3 million tons of chlorine are used each year to bleach paper. Chlorine is a major source of the carcinogen dioxin, which is regularly dumped into rivers and streams as waste water.

NOTE *Dioxin is bad stuff. It has been known to cause cancer, liver failure, miscarriages, birth defects, and genetic damage in laboratory animals.*

Your Costs

Handling paper can account for 30 percent of your organization's overhead. This number takes into account the average number of hours workers spend on tasks such as filing, distributing, creating, retrieving, and destroying documents.

Further, a report from Gartner indicates that the average document is copied 9 to 11 times at a cost of about US$23. To file a document, it cost US$25. Even worse, the cost to retrieve a misfiled document is US$153—Gartner, 1997.

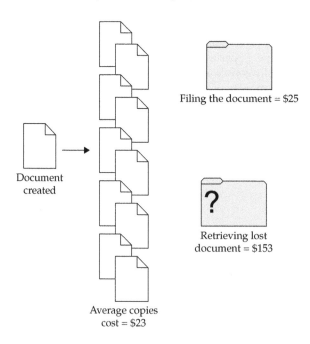

Document created

Filing the document = $25

Retrieving lost document = $153

Average copies cost = $23

Maintaining a paperless office isn't a fanciful notion. You can do it, but there are more mental hurdles than technological.

We've all heard the stories of organizations brought to their corporate knees because important data files were lost. That may have been the case 10 or 20 years ago, but in the twenty-first century, we're all tech savvy enough to follow good backup procedures—plus, equipment is monumentally more reliable. Most companies have backups scheduled to be performed after-hours in a totally unattended way. Further, a new trend is to eliminate backup media entirely (tapes, CDs, DVDs, and so forth) and schedule backups using a commercial online storage service.

Given that thousands of pages of documents can be backed up onto a CD-ROM, can you imagine the savings in backing up a filing cabinet full of paper documents. Although this incurs some initial cost and takes time to do, what would happen if the office caught fire? And this is just copying existing paper. If you adopt a paperless office, you only have to do it once, and then it's all maintenance.

Is it likely your office will catch fire and you'll lose important documents? Probably not. But the chances of the paperwork being lost or misfiled is a real consideration. In fact, 25 percent of all enterprise documents that are misplaced are never found again. And if the document is especially important, you'll spend hundreds of dollars to find it.

NOTE *Also take into consideration paperwork that is sensitive. True, payroll and proprietary company paperwork as well as client information need to be secure, and for years locked offices and filing cabinets have been used to that end. However, restricting access to information maintained online can be easier, and you won't have padlocks hanging off filing cabinets.*

Although the point of this chapter isn't to prompt you to chain yourself to a tree, it is important to realize the environmental effects of moving as much as you can toward a paperless office.

The paperless office brings sundry benefits, not only to your organization, but also to the environment, including the following:

- Lower paper costs
- Less pollution
- Less paper use
- Smaller waste disposal cost
- Lower storage costs
- Less energy use
- Less storage space needed
- Fewer trees cut
- Lower postage costs
- Less pulping
- Easier document handling
- Less waste to be recycled, burned, or sent to a landfill
- Less waste production by the organization
- Less landfill capacity needed

Paper and Your Office

We've talked about the costs of paper—both to the environment and to your pocketbook. But how will your organization benefit from going paperless on a functional level? This section looks at your organization and how getting rid of paper and automating can help.

Practicality

Let's say you've got an appointment with an important client. You need to land the Oberscheimer account. It's huge, and it's critical to your business. As you sit down with Mr. Oberscheimer—a busy man who is getting on a plane in a couple hours—you realize that you don't have an important document that you need. By the time you drive back to the office and return, Mr. Oberscheimer's plane will be somewhere over Kansas. You just lost the Oberscheimer account. You might lose your job.

Now let's reconsider the situation. Again, you're meeting Mr. Oberscheimer, and—again—you don't have that important document. No problem. You take out your laptop, and Mr. Oberscheimer allows you to access his wireless network. You log onto your office server using your corporate VPN connection. In moments, you've got the document on the laptop screen, and mere moments after that, you've secured the Oberscheimer account. In fact, your boss is so thrilled, you're now a partner with the firm. Okay, the "being promoted to partner" part was a bit fanciful, but the rest happens every day around the world.

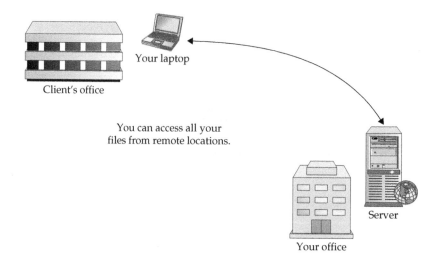

Client's office

Your laptop

You can access all your files from remote locations.

Server

Your office

Although e-mail has removed the need for many interoffice memos, company announcements, and snail mail, there is still an enormous amount of paper changing hands—or being filed—in organizations around the world.

Years ago, the photocopier changed the face of business. And although it would be unheard of for a company not to have a photocopier, those machines are the biggest and most expensive machines in the office. Let's say Mr. Oberscheimer wants a copy of a report.

He probably wouldn't mind getting it e-mailed to him (it would be faster than sending a paper copy, even via a messenger service), and if he wants to print it out, let him pay for it.

NOTE *Mr. Oberscheimer, the visionary that he is, probably has already adopted his own paperless office. As such, he'd want to scan the report and e-file it anyway, so you're actually saving him time and money. No wonder you became a partner.*

Storage

Take a look around your office, and you realize where a lot of paper is hiding. It's in the desk drawers, on the shelves, or tucked away in filing cabinets. It may very well be stashed in a long-term storage location offsite. If you use less paper, you will free up office space (filing cabinets can be removed) and you'll save the expense of buying new filing cabinets.

You can compute how much you spend on paper storage by counting the number of filing cabinets you have. Then, measure how much floor area they occupy. Many filing cabinets have a footprint of 2.5 ft². You might want to double this amount to account for open drawers. Now, multiply that amount by the value of your floor space, and you'll see how much that filing cabinet costs to maintain.

NOTE *Of course, it could be argued that 2.5 ft² of hallway space also costs the same amount. And don't even get starting trying to figure out how much money is wasted by the office joker who squanders company time forwarding off-color e-mails.*

What's inside the filing cabinet is even more expensive. If we assume paper consumes 2000 sheets per foot, and each drawer has 1 foot of file space, then a four-drawer cabinet could contain 16,000 sheets of paper. It's probably only at 75 percent capacity, or 12,000 sheets. That equates to 24 reams of paper. At US$2.50 per ream, you have US$60 worth of paper in that cabinet.

Combining the price for the storage cabinet along with the price of the paper can indicate to you how much it costs to store paperwork. If you store paperwork offsite, you know exactly how much that monthly bill comes to.

Admittedly, the cost may not look that big. However, like so many other elements of Green IT, when you start adding up all these little costs, the total gets to be pretty large.

Destruction

Most paper winds up in the trash, usually within a few years of its first being produced. And for each piece of paper that goes into the trash, you pay with your pocketbook, and the environment pays in deleterious ways. Plus, if you shred sensitive documents, the shredder adds expense in the form of worker time, along with electricity consumed.

NOTE *That price only goes up if you hire someone to take your documents and shred them for you. Offsite shredding costs can be as much as US$500 per ton.*

In the U.S., about 200 million tons of regular solid waste is generated annually, with about 2 percent of that being paper. Landfill prices vary, but US$50 per ton is a typical fee. Landfilling paper costs, therefore, about US$100 million per year.

Going Paperless

Going paperless (or at least reducing the amount of paper you consume) isn't impossible, but you have to approach it with a logical plan in place. This section looks at the business realities of making a no-paper switch. We also look at the technical side of what you need to do to get paper out of your organization's life.

Organizational Realities

The paperless office requires more than buying some scanners. You and others in your organization have to sign on, mentally, to the idea. If you decide to go paperless, there are some realities you'll have to embrace:

- **It won't happen overnight**   You simply cannot expect to make the transition immediately. You can start by scanning existing paperwork and then expand to incoming paperwork. But for some people, even if the document is scanned and filed away electronically, there is still the urge to have a hard copy somewhere onsite.

- **"Paperless" isn't an absolute**   When we say "paperless" what we really mean is *less paper*. You can take a big bite out of the paper problem by scanning all the documents you have filling up filing cabinets. You can direct incoming faxes to be automatically delivered to your computer. But not all of your work can be paperless. Some of your clients or business partners will still want their interactions done via paper. Plus, there will likely be some tax documentation that needs to be maintained as hard copies.

- **You have to sell it**   Not everyone likes change. Marge in human resources has been filing new-hire paperwork the same way for 25 years and she's not about to change her ways—unless you effectively explain the beauty of the new system. Employees have handled paper since their first jobs, and it might be hard to get them to change. The best thing you can do is educate them about the benefits of being paperless, and understand that it'll take some time for everyone to come around. Give it time. Marge will get there.

Once you go paperless (or as paperless as possible), realize that less paper is the tip of the iceberg. You'll save money in the cost of printing, mailing, shipping, and storage. But as you proceed with the system, you'll realize other benefits:

- Less time looking for lost paperwork
- The ability to access most documents in seconds
- The ability to access all your documents from home or satellite offices
- Freed-up real estate in your office as filing cabinets are moved out

Changing Over

Dealing with a world devoid of paper is easy once you get your system down and in place. All you need is to scan your paperwork and save it to your network. A good scanner and a system for storage are the keys to success.

Hardware

The reality of today's information documents is that most of them start out in an electronic format and then are printed. Other than documents that have signatures on them, most are created within spreadsheets, e-mail, word processing, or database applications. The best approach is to try to maintain the electronic format for as long as possible, if not 100 percent of the time. For paper that needs to jump out of the electronic format for a bit, you should aim to get it back into the digital world quickly. The first thing everyone needs is a good scanner. You can buy standalone models, or you can get a printer with built-in scanning capabilities (leverage a printer and photocopier for when your organization has to deal with less enlightened clients and vendors).

You want to keep an eye on the device's scanning page rate and whether it can scan both sides of the page (called *duplex*). You also should consider scanners that include copies of Adobe Acrobat Standard or another PDF creator.

NOTE *Adobe Acrobat Standard is software that allows you to create Portable Document Format (PDF) files. We'll talk more about PDFs and why you should embrace the format later in this section.*

Of course, which feature and model are best for your organization is a matter of your organization's requirements and your budget. Table 6-1 compares some popular scanner models, though the list is far from comprehensive.

NOTE *Although we're not endorsing any particular brand or model of scanner, try and stick with a name you know. The Soduki 5000 may cost just US$49, but there's probably a reason for that. Everyone will appreciate something speedy and functional that performs reliably.*

Scanner	Price	Resolution	Color Depth	Scanner Type	Comments
Xerox DocuMate 252 XDM2525D-WU	$799	600×1200 dpi	48 bit	Fast duplex sheet-fed	Scans 50 images per minute. Includes one-touch scanning.
Fujitsu fi-5120C PA03484-B005	$899	600×600 dpi	24 bit	Duplex	High reliability.
Xerox DocuMate 510 XDM5105D-WU	$289	600×1200 dpi	42 bit	Fast single-pass	Converts scans to PDF at 10 pages per minute. Holds 50 pages in document feeder.
HP Scanjet 8300 L1960AB1H	$449	4800 dpi	48 bit	Flatbed	Optional 100-sheet document holder.

TABLE 6-1   Comparison of Some Scanner Models and Their Features

You might worry about the toll scanned documents will take on your electronic storage. This is, of course, a concern, but it shouldn't be a deal breaker. A scanned PDF file consumes about 250KB per page for black-and-white documents, and 500KB for color. If you stored only black-and-white documents, you'd be able to save 4000 pages per 1GB of drive space.

Software

A good scanner should come with drivers to make it work with whatever computer systems you have in your organization. The driver should allow for the management of the following:

- Resolution
- Color bit depth
- File type
- Default folders

To fully enable your environment, you will need an application that can perform optical character recognition (OCR) on scanned documents, and that will combine the text with the original image in a PDF file. At the Windows desktop level, a very common application is Adobe Acrobat 9 Pro. Your Mac users can use Acrobat or an application such as ReadIris Pro.

PDFs

Why should you standardize on PDF? First of all, there's its sheer prevalence. If you download a document from a website, for instance, more often than not it is in the PDF format. But there are other reasons to consider PDF for your paperless documentation needs:

- **Open format** Adobe has submitted the PDF format to the ISO to have it formally declared a standard.
- **Multiplatform** PDF files are viewable on Windows, Mac, Unix/Linux, and many mobile platforms.
- **Accuracy** Adobe PDF files look just like their paper counterparts. You can also add a layer of digitized text for easy searching.
- **Security** PDFs can be digitally signed and password-protected to ensure only those with the proper security credentials can open the file.
- **Searchable text** Text can be searched within a PDF file for easy information location.

If you've never seen a PDF document before, Figure 6-1 shows what one looks like.

Work Smart

In an organization, it is a good idea to define recommended practices for everyone to follow:

- **Be realistic** Look at your documents and decide which ones you really need. Sure, you should hang on to last year's third quarter report, but do you really need to spend time and effort memorializing a flyer for the company's 1995 summer picnic? Recycle what you don't need.

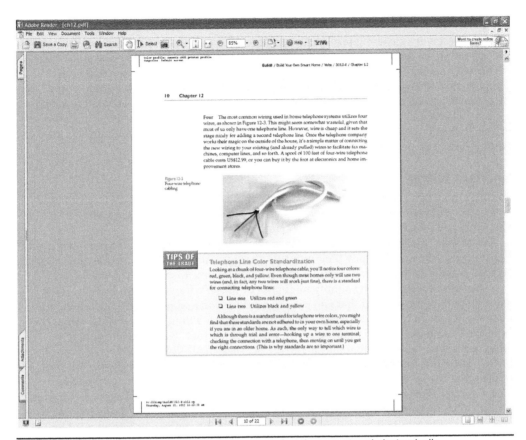

FIGURE 6-1 PDFs retain the look of a paper document, but they are stored electronically.

- **Naming** Each document should be labeled as descriptively as possible as soon as you scan it. It'll be easier to figure out what Third_Quarter_Report_2007.PDF is as compared to RPT10102007.PDF. Naturally, your organization will likely have its own naming conventions for files, but make sure they are descriptive enough so they aren't overly cryptic and confusing.

- **Set up a filing system** Figure out your filing system's logical construction. It needs to be a system that can easily be navigated and doesn't have any odd conventions. Other people will need to use it, too.

- **Shredding and recycling** Once you've scanned your documents, figure out what needs to be shredded, and what needs to be kept. When sensitive documents have been shredded, recycle everything you're getting rid of.

- **Know your limits** Remember what we said earlier about going paperless not being an overnight thing? Here's a perfect example. If you've got thousands of pages to be scanned, you can't do it in one sitting. Set up a system where you (or whoever you designate) makes regular progress on the mountain of paper. Establish a realistic goal, such as 50 pages a day.

Faxing

Of course, receiving incoming faxes is also a source of paper. Even worse, you never know who is going to be sending what, and you never know if it's something you want to keep. There are a number of applications and services to which you can subscribe that will automatically take whatever is being faxed, convert it to an e-mail, and send it to you. Once you get an electronic version of the fax, you can decide whether or not you want to keep it.

Also, what if you're out of the office and a fax that you need comes in? By using a service such as MyFax (www.myfax.com, or Link 6-1) or Maxemail (www.maxemail.com, or Link 6-2), one can check your e-mail remotely and view the fax.

Paperless Billing

More and more companies are offering paperless billing as an option for their customers. For instance, all your customers have to do is log on to a website like the one shown in Figure 6-2, and they can pay their bill each month.

Rather than print and mail monthly statements, companies simply send a reminder e-mail to customers, who can then pay their monthly charges online. If you are not leveraging the Web and e-mail to some degree, consider that it might be time to give it a try.

Complete paperless billing simply might not be feasible for your organization. There may always be some element that you simply need to send as a paper bill. Document process automation firm Esker asked 150 North American billing and invoicing managers about their companies' billing practices. They discovered that 28 percent of customers refuse to accept any invoice that doesn't arrive via snail mail—Esker, 2007.

But it isn't just money and paper that is saved by paperless billing. The Esker study also showed that many of the businesses who adopted paperless billing didn't do so to save money or trees. They just wanted to save time. Many organizations spend a lot less time on the task of billing because they don't have to go through the effort of physically mailing bills.

However, the same Esker study revealed that half of the companies interviewed had not considered paperless billing. The study further revealed that, on average, three employees spend 106 hours per month generating and mailing bills. The time it takes to generate the invoices accounts for 15 percent of that time. The remaining 92 hours are spent on printing, envelope stuffing, addressing, and mailing the bills, as shown next.

Time Spent with Paper-Based Billing

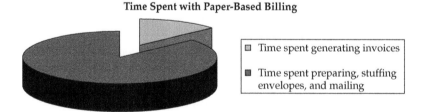

☐ Time spent generating invoices

■ Time spent preparing, stuffing envelopes, and mailing

Another study by Javelin Strategy and Research showed that if every U.S. household paid their bills online, 16.5 million trees a year would be spared. Beyond paper, bills involve envelopes as well as trucks and planes to transport them all over the world.

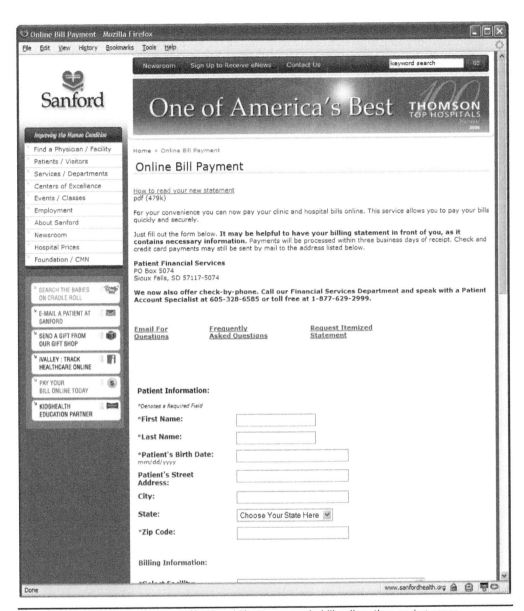

FIGURE 6-2   Many companies now offer the ability to pay one's bill online, thus saving paper.

Handheld Computers vs. the Clipboard

The clipboard has traditionally been associated with working on the move. When a delivery comes to your office, the delivery person has a clipboard. When the doctor comes into the exam room (finally), he's holding a clipboard. When the technician goes out to work on your car, he picks up a clipboard. However, that has been changing over the years.

As industry has been moving to a paperless environment, all those people we associate with clipboards are going high tech. They're replacing those clipboards and piles of paper with personal digital assistants (PDAs) and tablet PCs. Some waitresses don't even write your order down on a pad of paper anymore. They write your order on a PDA, which transmits it straight back to the kitchen.

PDAs

PDAs are small, handheld computers with touch screens that allow you to enter information. They also have memory card slots for data storage, and a wireless connection (usually infrared, Bluetooth, WiFi, or a combination).

PDAs are used in all sorts of fields. For instance, when delivering a package, the delivery driver might ask you to sign for the package on his PDA. Physicians are turning less and less to the clipboard checklist for diagnostic and treatment information. The clipboard and paper checklist has been put onto a PDA, so the doctor simply checks off symptoms and waits for the results to pop up on the PDA screen.

PDAs typically run a version of Microsoft Windows Mobile for Pocket PCs—which is specifically designed for PDAs—or the Palm OS. However, manufacturers may build or purpose a PDA with specific functionality in mind, and make their own proprietary OS for the device.

NOTE *Apple took a stab at the PDA market in the mid-1990s with the Newton. It didn't take root, so to speak, so Apple gave up on it.*

Tablet PCs

Tablet PCs are a hybrid between a laptop and a PDA. Tablet PCs are similar to laptops in size (albeit a bit smaller), and users typically interact with them as they would a PDA—by entering data on a touch-sensitive screen.

Tablets do have keyboards, so they can be used at a desk on someone's lap, but on the move, the keyboard is swiveled underneath the PC and interactions with the device are done on its touch screen.

Microsoft Windows XP or Vista is the OS normally installed on tablet PCs. In fact, when developing Vista, Microsoft came up with a bunch of tools specifically for tablet PC users. Linux can be installed on a tablet PC, in the same way that Linux is installed on any PC.

NOTE *Apple doesn't offer any Mac tablets (yet), although there are some aftermarketers who modify tablet-based equipment to run Mac OS X.*

Unified Communications

Having a paperless office can mean more than just filing away what used to exist on paper and storing it on a computer. Business processes can also change. The way you work can become more streamlined, more productive. A big part of this is in the form of communications.

In recent years, technology bigwigs such as Cisco and IBM have introduced their own visions for a comprehensive communications system in an organization. This system has come under the blanket term *Unified Communications*. In this model, all types of communication—phone, messaging, e-mail, faxes, and so on—are maintained so that they can be sent around the office. This section takes a closer look at one company's strategy and vision—Microsoft Unified Communications.

New Phones

Microsoft has targeted telephones as part of its Unified Communications initiative. Noting that very few people actually know how to transfer a call from their telephones, Microsoft moved ahead with the notion that the problem doesn't lie in the telephones themselves. It's a mental block with the users. As such, Microsoft introduced a suite of business software that will improve office tasks. The new products included in its Unified Communications push include the following:

- Microsoft Office Communications Server 2007
- Microsoft Office Communicator 2007
- Microsoft Office Live Meeting
- A service pack update of Microsoft Exchange Server 2007
- RoundTable—an Ethernet-connected, 360-degree videoconferencing VoIP system

Using the Internet

Unified Communications targets traditional business private branch exchanges (PBXs). These are pieces of telecommunications equipment that serve an entire office. Microsoft notes that when an employee gets a new PBX-based telephone system, it costs the business a week's worth of lost time and US$700. In Microsoft's vision, the less-expensive option is to use the Internet via Voice over IP (VoIP).

Basically, the Unified Communications system treats voice like e-mail. Outlook is configured so that it shows the employee's phone numbers and at which one they can be contacted. When a call (or message) comes through, the employee can decide whether to take the call or to route it to voicemail.

Additionally, Microsoft sees RoundTable as a way to revolutionize conference calling. For example, a conference leader can highlight a specific member or call up a PowerPoint presentation.

Smooth Working

The system also makes it possible to communicate with others using different types of technologies. For example, if you're on the road and you need to check your e-mail, you can call your inbox and have the e-mail read to you, using text-to-speech. You can also check your voicemails and update your calendar, as needed.

The move is an effort to aggregate all the different ways people try to communicate into one, centralized system.

Intranets

You know that human resources manual that's the size of a cinder block? You don't need it. And you certainly don't need a copy on everyone's desk. Just put it on your organization's intranet and employees can access it from their computers. Plus, when you make a change, you need not reprint the book; just send out an e-mail to your employees that the change has been posted to the manual.

Intranets are a great way to reduce the amount of paper that is used in-house. Intranets are a lot like the Internet. But whereas files stored on the public Internet are accessible to anyone, files on your private intranet are only accessible to you and your coworkers.

What to Include

You can put, really, whatever you want on your intranet. As mentioned before, you can post the HR manual. Maybe you have a spot on there where you list the cafeteria's daily specials. The following lists some content you might consider putting on your intranet:

- Often-used documents, templates, and proposals that can help prepare a project
- Frequently asked questions about the organization
- Company bulletin board, where employees can share messages
- CEO blog, to serve as an informational line to the organization
- Staff directory, including personal skills (for example, Sally Johnson plays the banjo)
- Company calendar, with employee birthdays and upcoming events

This is certainly not the limit of what you can put on your intranet, but it gives you an idea of where to start. Whereas the preceding is somewhat benign, there are some more important data issues you should consider before publishing them on the intranet. You also need to think about the following:

- **Security**   Do you plan on publishing sensitive documents on the intranet? If so, you'll likely need to establish password-protected areas of the site. Now's also a good time to figure out who will manage access to that site.

- **Usability**   Is the site easy to manage? We've all seen horribly designed sites that were impossible to navigate. Think about how the site will be designed and how it can be optimized.

- **Publishing rights**   Who will be allowed to post to the intranet and how reliable will the information be?

- **Ownership**   Who is responsible for information on the intranet? Will an approval system be needed before information is posted? How will content be maintained once it is posted? It's recommended that you assign one person to be the intranet coordinator whose task it will be to manage the information on your intranet.

- **Backup plan**   Don't forget to have a backup plan in place. If your system gets hit by a virus or somehow gets damaged or lost, do you have a plan in place that can restore the system?

Building an Intranet

When you've decided to build your organization's intranet, it needs to be composed of specific hardware as well as certain software. Let's look at what you need to build your intranet.

Parts

You'll need the following four components for your intranet, as illustrated in Figure 6-3:

- **Local area network (LAN)**   Your clients need this infrastructure to access the intranet. You can simply use the LAN you've already got in place. If your organization doesn't have a LAN, you can probably chisel company news into a rock and leave it for people to read as they hang their animal skin coats up in the morning.

- **Web server**   An intranet is simply an internal website. To run the website, you need a web server. Chances are, if your organization already has a web presence, you have a web server. But it's more likely that your web server is hosted by your Internet service provider (ISP). No matter. If your website is hosted locally, you can add your intranet pages to it. Otherwise, you'll have to hook up your own web server. The two most popular are Apache and Microsoft Internet Information Server (IIS). Table 6-2 compares the two.

NOTE *If you don't have a web server, this can be corrected by virtualizing it on another server. Or, if you're replacing old servers, you might want to repurpose one or more of them.*

You can outsource your web hosting. This option is less costly and a lot easier. Often, providers supply easy-to-use security and other tools and templates so you can set up a secure intranet quickly.

- **Web browsers on client PCs**   Your clients need a way to read the contents of your intranet, and this is done simply through a web browser, such as Internet Explorer or Firefox. Chances are that you've already got at least one of these installed on your desktops and laptops, so you're ready to go.

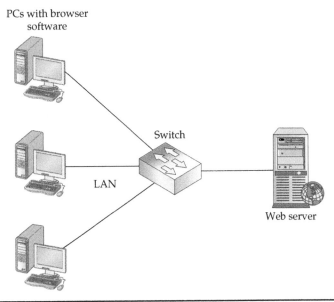

FIGURE 6-3   The components of your intranet are probably already in your organization.

Server	Price	Comments
Apache	Free. You can download it via Link 6-3.	Very popular. As of November 2007, more than 50 percent of the Internet was served via Apache. Also runs on both Windows and Unix/Linux.
Internet Information Server (IIS)	Comes with Windows XP or Vista.	Only runs on Windows machines, which may be more common in many corporate environments.

TABLE 6-2   Comparison of Apache and IIS

- **Web page development software**   Because intranets use the same sorts of files as websites on the Internet, you'll need to put content on the intranet in that format. Unless you want to sit down and hammer out HTML code (which is certainly an option, if you are so inclined), a better way is with an application framework such as Microsoft Sharepoint, or other appropiate tool for your particular requirements.

Installing Apache is a matter of double-clicking an icon, but configuration is more involved. As you might imagine, installation and configuration are beyond the scope of this book. We recommend you check out *IIS 6 Administration*, by Mitch Tulloch if you are interested in the specifics. Figures 6-4 and 6-5 show Apache and IIS in action.

The intranet in this form is great for local users, but if you have people who work from home or are on the road and need to access the intranet, you should establish a means for them to access it and ensure the right security measures are in place.

Likely, if they are connecting to your LAN via a virtual private network or a secure WAN connection, they'll be able to connect to the intranet.

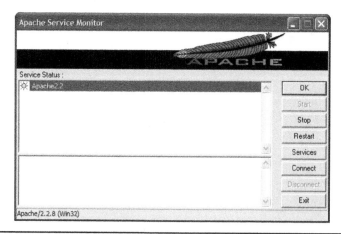

FIGURE 6-4   The Apache web server is a free, open-source web server.

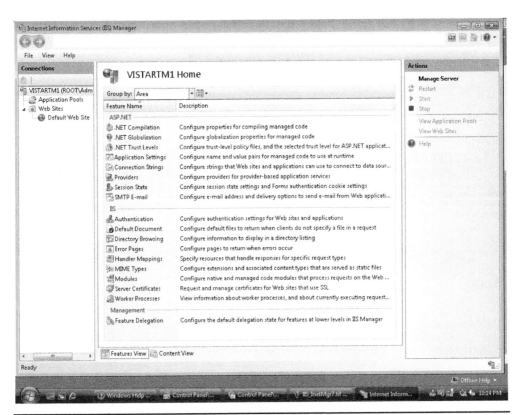

FIGURE 6-5   IIS comes included with Windows and is easy to configure.

Content Management Systems

Websites, including your intranet, are dynamic entities. They have to be, or no one would ever come back to them. As such, you should install a content management system (CMS) to easily add, delete, and update content.

A CMS makes intranet maintenance much easier and can be done by someone with a very limited background with HTML, opening up the role of content management to a wider range of users. Among other things, a CMS facilitates the following:

- Addition of new content
- Removal of old content
- Better organization of the data on the site
- Managing text, articles, documents, files, and other communications
- Managing images and other elements

There are a number of CMSs for both Windows and Linux. Most offer free versions, or you can buy a premium package that offers more functionality. Well-known Windows CMSs include Community Server and DotNetNuke. DotNetNuke is shown in Figure 6-6.

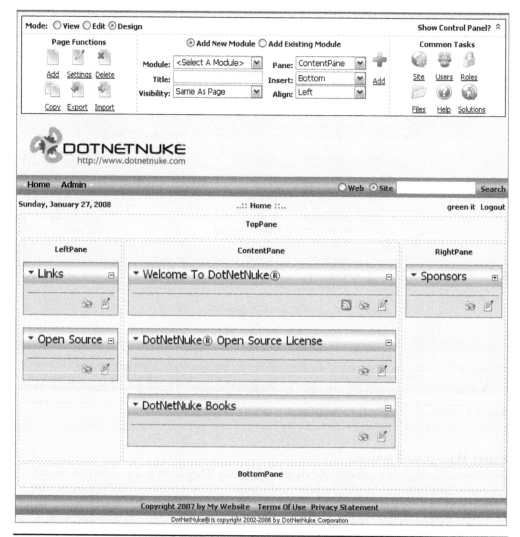

FIGURE 6-6   DotNetNuke is a freeware CMS that allows you to manage your intranet (or other website) in a Windows environment.

NOTE *A more integrated CMS solution for Windows is Microsoft Office SharePoint Server (MOSS). We'll talk about it in more detail in the next section.*

Linux environments play host to a variety of well-known CMS solutions such as Drupal, Joomla, Mambo, Moodle, Post Nuke, and Xoops. Figure 6-7 shows Joomla in action.

Once the site is up, make sure people know about it, and find out whether they think it's useful. Take regular surveys to find out what people find most useful and what helps them to be more informed and efficient.

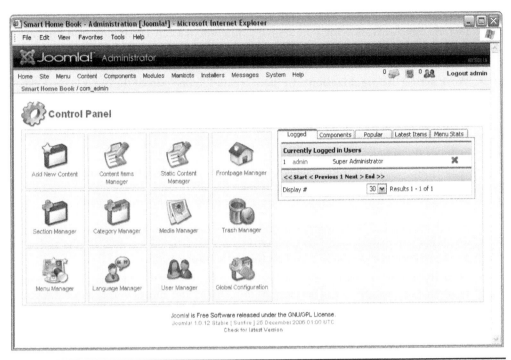

FIGURE 6-7   The Joomla CMS allows you to easily manage the content of your intranet.

Microsoft Office SharePoint Server 2007

A particularly robust and feature-rich CMS application is Microsoft Office SharePoint Server (MOSS). It allows you to take all your organization's information and maintain it in one, centralized location. It is accessed by members of your organization through a web browser.

It supports all intranet, extranet, and web applications in one platform, thus eliminating fragmented and piecemeal systems. Further, it allows you to improve overall productivity by simplifying everyday tasks.

In this section, we'll talk a little about MOSS and how it can benefit your company's intranet. We'll also discuss it from the standpoint of paperless document management.

Features

MOSS allows members of your organization to do their work using Microsoft Office applications, e-mail, or web browsers. Some of the functionality of MOSS includes:

- **The ability to control access**   Just because it's on the intranet doesn't mean it is open for everyone to look at or change. MOSS allows you to establish customized document management policies to control access rights. Access can be managed at a per-item level; you can manage the retention period and expiration actions.

- **Central management**   MOSS allows you to store and manage all your documents and content in one central location. This helps with locating documents. It also allows you to manage how your data is stored: Settings can be modified to add workflow, establish retention policies, and add new content types.

- **Content management**   MOSS includes Master Pages and Page Layouts, which include templates allowing you to give your content a consistent look. You can also publish content from one area to another (for instance, from a collaborative site to your intranet).

- **Work across the organization**   Content created in one part of the organization can be easily integrated into the system and stored in document libraries or web services. Doing so allows you to avoid duplicating effort and making errors from having to manually reenter that data.

Better Business Operations

MOSS not only allows you to store, manage, and view documentation, it also helps with overall, day-to-day business operations. For instance, MOSS allows you to create your own portals that access and display the information you specify. Other features include:

- **Search features**   The Enterprise Search feature searches people, business data, documents, and web pages. This allows more comprehensive search results and allows decisions to be made based on the latest information.

- **Security-minded sharing**   You can get very precise with the information you want to share. For example, Excel Services running on MOSS allows you to share data in real time, but you don't have to share everything. That is, interactive Excel spreadsheets can be viewed in a browser and they can be set up to show just the information you want to share and not any proprietary data.

Collaboration

MOSS also aids with your organization's collaborative efforts. Not only can you collaborate with the person at the desk next to you, but you can work with people at a partner company. Features include the following:

- **The ability to integrate partner data**   You can collect business information from customers and partners and integrate it with your system. This allows you to include their information in searches. It also enhances your working relationship with clients, partners, and suppliers.

- **The ability to work remotely**   You can use Microsoft Outlook to work with MOSS, allowing you to access your organization's data from anywhere.

- **Personalization**   Users can personalize how they interact with MOSS using a tool called MySite.

MySite

The MySite feature of MOSS allows users to create a site so they can store, present, view, and manage content. The sites can be used to present business information about the user, including skills, roles, colleagues, managers, work groups, and so forth.

MySite includes a public view and a private view. Privacy settings allow a user to establish whether their colleagues, manager, or everyone in the organization can see their information. The information that can be viewed includes the following:

- **Workspaces**   This shows workspaces to which a user has access. It saves wasted navigation time.

- **MyLinks**   Shows a list of personal links for the user.
- **Personalization sites**   Content personalized based on a user's role in the organization.
- **Colleague Tracker**   Allows users to track changes in their colleagues' MySites.
- **Outlook e-mail**   Displays a user's e-mail and calendar information from Exchange.
- **Distribution groups**   From the public view, you can see the distribution groups that you belong to. When looking at a colleague's MySite, you can see the distribution groups you have in common.

NOTE   *If your deployment of MOSS has the necessary multilanguage packs and templates installed, users can create their MySite in one of the languages available on the system. This is useful if you're part of a global organization, and users in Norway or China want to develop MySites.*

Electronic Data Interchange (EDI)

It is also becoming more prevalent for organizations to manage their supply chains or deal with vendors and other companies using Electronic Data Interchange (EDI). EDI allows businesses, governmental entities, and other organizations a way to exchange entire documents.

EDI allows the electronic exchange of business documents, such as purchase orders, invoices, ship notices, and over 250 others in a standardized format. Here are some of the benefits to using EDI:

- Significant savings with lower EDI costs
- Increased staff efficiency
- A secure environment
- Increased efficiency through the ability to send and receive any type of file

As Figure 6-8 illustrates, organizations send orders to other companies via EDI, thus speeding up the process over conventionally mailed requests.

FIGURE 6-8   EDI speeds up the process of working with B2B partners.

In this section, we'll look more closely at EDI and talk about why you might want to consider it for your organization.

Nuts and Bolts

EDI uses technologies such as Extensible Markup Language (XML) and the World Wide Web to function. The EDI format is used more for e-commerce transactions.

There are four major sets of EDI standards, each with a specific market:

- The UN/EDIFACT standard is the only international standard and is used largely outside of North America.
- The U.S. standard ANSI ASC X12 (X12) is the largest standard in North America.
- The TRADACOMS standard, developed by the Article Numbering Association (ANA), is the major standard in the UK retail industry.
- The ODETTE standard is used within the European automotive industry.

These standards were first introduced in the mid-1980s and are used to explain formats, character sets, and data elements.

Organizations using EDI can communicate however they want to exchange data. These days, that usually means web- or e-mail-based communications. However, in the past, modems were used to connect to a Value Added Network (VAN) or to connect to a partner directly.

Value Added Networks

A VAN is sort of an electronic post office. It receives transactions, looks at the "To" and "From" information, and routes the messages to their intended recipients. VANs are still widely used, because they provide some additional services, such as retransmitting documents, providing third-party audit services, and providing support.

NOTE *Healthcare clearinghouses provide the same sorts of services as a VAN, but they have more legal restrictions that are present in the healthcare industry.*

Benefits to using a VAN include:

- **Alert system**   VANs can alerts organizations to transmission issues or delivery receipts.
- **Archival storage**   VANs can store critical business data for extended periods of time.
- **Audit trails**   Information including setup, configuration, and document transmission events can be audited.
- **Real-time data delivery**   Data can be delivered in real time, rather than in batches, thus allowing speedier response to transmissions.
- **Reliable and secure transmission**   VANs ensure that a company's data is securely transmitted and is received by the recipient.

Some VANs include Advanced Communication Systems (www.acsvan.com, or Link 6-4), EasyLink Services (www.icc.net, or Link 6-5), and Techdinamics Solutions (www.techdinamics.com, or Link 6-6).

Advantages

The biggest advantage to your organization using EDI is the cost savings. EDI is more efficient than using conventional mail or fax. EDI minimizes data-entry errors, reduces labor costs, and increases the timeliness of transmitted information.

Let's consider what happens in a paper world. Typically, one company generates an order on a computer that is sent to a vendor. When the order gets to the vendor, the mailroom handles it before getting it to the sales department, which then assigns it to a clerk who types the order into the company's own computer system.

This process, illustrated in Figure 6-9, is very slow (you have to print the order, mail it, and wait for it to work its way through the other organization) and prone to errors (the order can be misplaced, the clerk can enter the data wrong, and so on).

By using EDI, the document can be sent computer-to-computer, thus eliminating a lot of the steps where trouble can happen. EDI reduces the time it takes to receive and handle the order from a few days to a few seconds.

This speed not only saves labor hours, it also allows companies to better manage their inventory through speedy replenishment. What's more, the customer can be quickly invoiced, and customer service is enhanced.

Obstacles

Like so many other facets of going paperless, EDI's biggest obstacle isn't the technology, but reengineering human work habits.

Cost is another barrier to EDI. The initial expense of establishing an EDI setup can lead organizations to believe that they're better off filling out forms. The expense comes from implementation, customizing the system, and training employees.

You can make sure EDI is right for your business by figuring out if the initial costs will outweigh any future savings. For instance, a company that receives only a handful of orders every year might not reap the benefits of EDI.

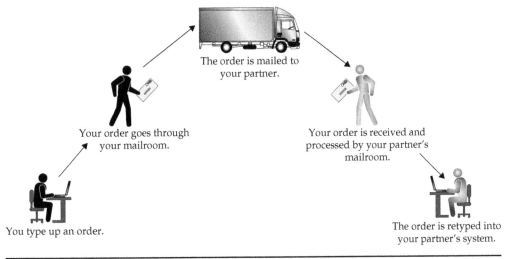

The order is mailed to your partner.

Your order goes through your mailroom.

Your order is received and processed by your partner's mailroom.

You type up an order.

The order is retyped into your partner's system.

Figure 6-9   EDI streamlines traditional, paper-based B2B communications.

That said, it doesn't mean that the company shouldn't adopt EDI—it just means the company doesn't have to set it up within its own organization. You can outsource EDI functions to an EDI service bureau (such as EDI Service Bureau, Inc., via Link 6-7).

Perception is also a problem for EDI. Many think that EDI allows your vendors or business partners to have their hands in your network. There is a perception that suppliers can have open access to their data within your network. This isn't the case.

Although some companies may be hesitant to sign on with EDI, some organizations insist on it—that is, if you care to do business with them. Some smaller companies are required to use EDI if they want to do business with larger trading partners.

Going paperless can seem like a daunting task—and it is. You've used paper all your work life, so it's what you and all your coworkers know. But you don't have to go cold turkey and do it all at once. The best thing to do is to introduce new paperless techniques as they arise. That is, change one business stream at a time.

For instance, maybe next month you'll change your billing to a paperless model. After that has smoothed itself out, look at another business stream—such as that intranet—and get it up and running. By taking the process one step at a time, you'll be sure to make a smooth, easy, effective transition.

The message should be loud and clear by now—going paperless helps your company save money, and it helps the environment. We'll continue to examine how the environment can be helped and how you can be conscientious when it comes to disposing of recyclable material in the next chapter.

Recycling

If and when it comes time to replace your organization's computers, you'll have a number of options—some more environmentally sound than others. Although you likely will want to enlist the aid of a reputable recycler, other options are open to you, such as donating or repurposing those computers. Additionally, no matter what you do to get those boxes out of your offices, you absolutely want to get rid of the information stored on your hard drives.

In this chapter, we'll talk about recycling and its importance. We'll also talk about some alternatives to recycling and explain how you can keep your organization's information safe once you do get rid of your old computers.

Problems

It's no big secret that computers contain harmful toxins, and when they are disposed of improperly, the environment pays the price. But it isn't just the environment that gets hurt when computers are irresponsibly disposed of—in the end, we hurt ourselves. Poisons from computers first affect the people who are stripping them down for precious metals. But after that, the air and groundwater can become contaminated.

It's also no big secret that a lot of end-of-life computers wind up in China and Africa. But they're half a world away, so it's their problem, right? In this section, we'll take a closer look at just how big a problem e-waste has become for China and Africa. We'll also talk about the toxins that are in computers that make responsible recycling so important.

China

The tales of e-waste in China have made headlines in recent years. It's no surprise that the stories have been newsworthy, but it is a surprise that we hadn't heard them earlier.

America ships to China up to 80 percent of its e-waste. In addition to the U.S., Canada, Japan, and South Korea send their e-waste to Guiyu, China. In 2006, the U.S. exported enough e-waste to cover a football field and rise a mile into the sky. Most of the waste winds up in the small port city of Guiyu. It's a town 4 hours from Hong Kong that is home to 5500 "recyclers." Guiyu's location is shown in Figure 7-1.

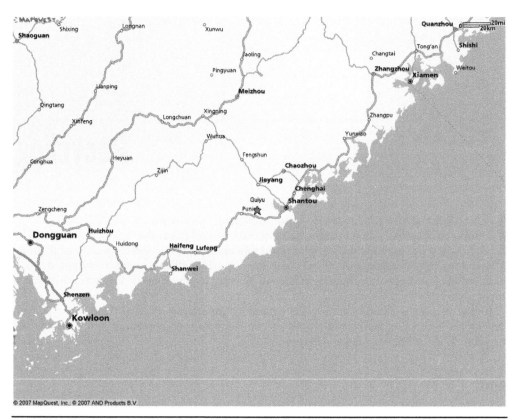

Figure 7-1   Guiyu is located in southeast China and is the world's largest destination for e-waste.

E-waste recycling is big business in Guiyu. It is responsible for the employment of 80 percent of the town's families—more than 30,000 people. On average, workers make between US$1 and US$3 per day.

To reclaim copper, gold, and other materials from the 15 million tons of e-waste in Guiyu, workers dip motherboards into acid baths, grind plastic casings from monitors, and grill components over open coal fires. Guiyu has some of the largest dioxin levels on the planet.

NOTE *Eighty-two percent of children in the Guiyu region under 6 years old in the area have lead poisoning.*

After disassembly, one ton of computer scrap yields more gold than 17 tons of gold ore. Circuit boards can be 40 times richer in copper than copper ore. Guiyu started taking scrapped computers in 1995. In 2001, the Basel Action Network made a video about the city and its e-waste issues, but by 2008 very little has changed.

Africa

A similar problem is playing itself out in Africa. In the Ikeja Computer Village, near Lagos, Nigeria, thousands of vendors are packed into the market, where all kinds of electronics can be purchased. Up for sale are computers, fax machines, cellular telephones, and other devices that have been repaired. Lagos' location is shown in Figure 7-2.

This all sounds like imported e-waste is being turned around and reused in a positive manner, but the truth is that as much as 75 percent of the electronics shipped to the Computer Village are irreparable, says the Computer and Allied Product Dealers Association of Nigeria, a local industry group.

Although Nigeria has a good repair market, it lacks a system to safely deal with e-waste. Most of it winds up in landfills and unofficial dumps. As such, toxins seep into the earth. And when plastic cases are burned, they churn carcinogenic dioxins and polyaromatic hydrocarbons (PAHs) into the air.

It is estimated that 500 shipping containers filled with used electronic equipment pass through Lagos each month. Each container can be packed with a load equal to:

- 800 computer monitors
- 800 CPUs
- 350 large television sets

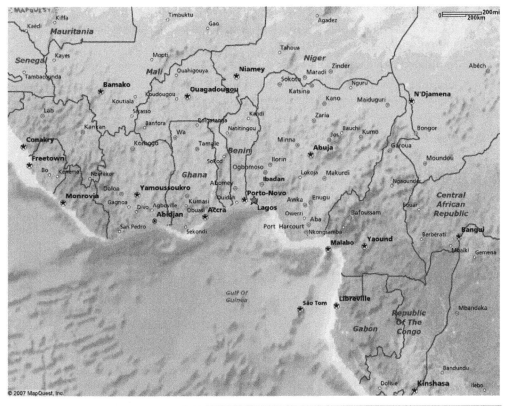

FIGURE 7-2 The port town of Lagos is Africa's second most populous city and a major destination for e-waste.

Local officials estimate that between 25 and 75 percent of this material is irreparable. So, even assuming the low end of this range, Lagos landfills could be home to 100,000 computers and 44,000 television sets per month.

African importers don't mind dumping useless materials into landfills; with the few items they can remanufacture and sell, they still turn a tidy profit. For example, a working Pentium III computer sells for about US$130 and a working 27-inch television sells for US$50. Also, any working components can be sold separately.

NOTE *Sometimes an unknowing exporter might put a Cisco router worth $15,000 into a shipping container filled with mixed electronics. Those are known as "lottery tickets."*

Materials

Computers contain a lot of components and a lot of toxic materials. Effective recycling and disposal is important because you want to prevent the following hazardous materials from getting into the environment:

- **Lead**   Used in glass in TV and PC cathode ray tubes as well as solder and interconnects. Older CRTs typically contain on average 4 lbs of lead (sometimes as much as 7 lbs), whereas newer CRTs contain closer to 2 lbs of lead.

- **Mercury**   Used in small amounts in bulbs to backlight flat-panel computer monitors and notebook displays.

- **Brominated flame retardants**   Used in plastic cases and cables for fire retardancy.

- **Cadmium**   Was used in Ni-Cad rechargeable batteries for laptops and other portables. Newer batteries (nickel-metal hydride and lithium ion) do not contain cadmium.

- **PVC**   Used in wire and cable sheathing.

Means of Disposal

Obviously (but unfortunately not so obvious to some), you can't just throw your computers in the dumpster, slam down the lid, and call it a day. As highlighted in Chapter 2, different areas have different requirements for the disposal of end-of-life technology. Recycling is one way to get rid of old devices, but there are other strategies when dealing with old equipment. This section talks about what you can do with all the computers you need to get rid of.

Recycling

Computer recycling involves breaking down the computer to recover metals, plastic, and glass for reuse. It also aids in keeping hazardous materials from tainting the environment. Computer recycling is complex, because there are over 1000 different materials in a computer. As such, computers are one of the most complex things to recycle.

Computer recyclers are normally large companies or government programs. They need to handle high volumes of recycling materials to make their business profitable. They look for components containing precious metals, such as gold, silver, and platinum.

Often, companies don't get rid of their end-of-life equipment. Instead, they fill up closets and whatever open space they can find to store them. Some reasons not to recycle old equipment include:

- Not knowing how to properly dispose of equipment.
- The slim chance the equipment might be used in the future.
- The possibility that the equipment can be given to another organization.

If you are in a similar situation and just don't know what to do with old technology (whether to recycle or donate), Earth911.org can help. This resource helps you locate local sources for recycling, donating, or disposing of end-of-life equipment.

Another resource is the EPA's eCycling program, which helps put your business in touch with recycling for your electronics. The eCycling website is located at www.greenitinfo .com/links under Link 7-1.

Most computer recyclers remarket working parts and entire computers because they are able to recognize higher profits than through shredding and smelting to recover materials.

Table 7-1 lists some of the biggest recycling companies and their websites where you can go for more information.

Company	Website	Comments
Noranda/MicroMetallics Corporation	Link 7-2	Emphasizes its accountability in computer recycling.
		Has three recycling facilities, in Ontario, Tennessee, and California.
Waste Management	Link 7-3	America's largest recycler.
		Member of Sony's Take Back recycling program.
IBM Credit Corporation	Link 7-4 (Select Asset Recovery Solutions from the left navigation menu.)	Offers online buyback for up to 250 computers.
		Offers a disk overwrite service to protect data.
Metech International	Link 7-5	Recycling sites in Massachusetts and California capable of handling 50 tons of recycling per day.
		Also operates sites in Thailand and Malaysia.
		Employs accountability in disposal of material.
UNICOR Federal Prison Industries	Link 7-6	U.S. government recycling organization employing inmates.
		Offers nationwide coverage.

TABLE 7-1   Some Major Recyclers

Refurbishing

Whereas recyclers use means to completely dispose of computers, computer refurbishers recondition discarded computers to get them in working order. This work is most often done by commercial refurbishers such as Dell Refurbished, IBM Refurbished, and Amandi Services. There are also noncommercial refurbishers, which are usually nonprofits or school programs.

When a refurbisher receives discarded computers, it tests them, extracts useable parts from computers that are not repairable, and then fixes the ones that can be fixed. Generally speaking, one working computer can be built from two or three discarded machines. This is illustrated in Figure 7-3. Nonworking computers are sent to a recycler.

An important part of refurbishing is wiping, or simply reformatting hard drives to remove existing data and installing the appropriate operating system. It costs about US$105 to refurbish a computer. These costs include labor, parts, and e-waste disposal.

The field is broken into two parts—noncommercial refurbishers and commercial refurbishers.

Noncommercial Refurbishing

This field is composed mostly of nonprofit and school-based programs doing computer training. This market turns around reused computers and provides them to low-income families. More than 70 percent of noncommercial computer reuse is sent to schools.

CompuMentor—an organization that helps provide PCs and other technology to low-income individuals—estimates that there are as many as 500 programs in the U.S., with an average capacity of 200 computers per year.

Larger programs—such as Computers for Schools Canada; Per Scholas in New York; and Students Recycling Used Technology in Portland, Phoenix, Georgia, and Silicon Valley—provide 10,000 or more computers each year.

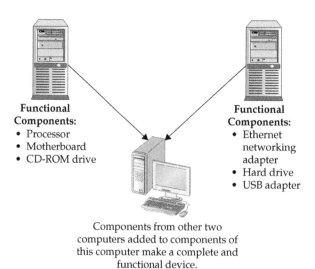

Functional Components:
- Processor
- Motherboard
- CD-ROM drive

Functional Components:
- Ethernet networking adapter
- Hard drive
- USB adapter

Components from other two computers added to components of this computer make a complete and functional device.

Figure 7-3   Generally speaking, it takes the components of three computers to make one, functional computer.

Commercial Refurbishing

You may want to take matters into your own hands and sell your computers (either individually or in lots and with or without the hard drives) on eBay. Of course, this will necessitate assignment of resources to manage the process, but it's certainly an option. However, most major computer companies have their own divisions for repurposing computers—companies such as HP Financial Services and IBM Global Asset Recovery Services.

There are also hybrids of the noncommercial and commercial programs out there. RECONNECT (www.reconnectpartnership.com, or Link 7-7) is a partnership between Dell and Goodwill Industries. Computers can be brought into Goodwill locations, Dell will refurbish them, and then the repurposed computers are sold with the proceeds going to Goodwill Industries.

Make the Decision

Whether you choose to recycle or reuse is a decision you have to make to keep all your end-of-life PCs from filling every cabinet, closet, nook, and cranny in your organization. In order to figure out what you're going to do with the computers and monitors, you have to define clear objectives for what you want done with the equipment and what the final place will be for them.

Do you want your equipment in the resale marketplace? Do you want the equipment demanufactured into raw materials to be marketed as recyclables? If so, you should consider finding a reseller or demanufacturer.

If you want the systems destroyed, you should consider a recycler.

Are you interested in providing a community service by donating equipment? Do you want a tax deduction for your contribution? If so, you might consider donating or repurposing your equipment.

NOTE *Make sure the organization is a not-for-profit corporation as defined by the Internal Revenue Service's 501(c) tax exempt status.*

If you have decided on donating computers for reuse, you should think twice—just to make sure it's still a good idea. First, you need to think about the age of the computers. If they are too old (more than 5 years) they may not be able to run the same software that other computers do.

Also, will the recipient be able to use the equipment or refurbish it for use? If it is too old, it might not be economical for the recipient to pay to bring the machines up to working order.

Finally, make sure any sensitive personal or business information has been removed from the computers.

NOTE *We talk about decommissioning hard drives later in this chapter.*

Life Cycle

Deciding what to do with your computers when you're done with them shouldn't be a consideration when the delivery truck pulls up with new machines. Rather, planning for the end is something you should have done when you thought about buying them.

Establishing a system's life cycle gives Information Resource managers a tool to control budgets and respond to management with a business case for the new machines, their operation, and how you will ultimately phase them out of the organization.

From Cradle to Grave

Let's take a closer look at what is involved in the product life cycle, from the very beginning to the very end.

A product life cycle takes all parts of the computer's life into consideration. Figure 7-4 shows the phases of a product's life cycle.

Terms

At the outset of a life cycle, you must determine what your overall objective will be through the development of a new system. That is, what capabilities and objectives will be served by the new system? For example, if you are going to be replacing your organization's computers with new ones, identify why they need to be replaced. Are they not performing up to your standards? Are they failing?

Feasibility Study

The next step is a feasibility study, which asks whether the concept for a new system is achievable and realistic in terms of money, time, and the end result. As an outcome of the study, you may find that all you need to do is update components of your existing system rather than completely replace it. This saves you money, and it also prevents a computer from having to be recycled.

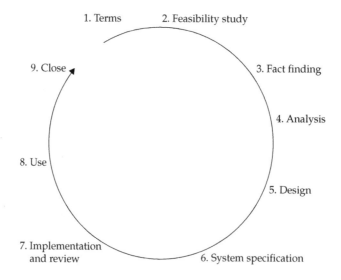

The Systems Development Life Cycle

FIGURE 7-4   A product's life cycle takes all phases of a product's existence into consideration.

Fact Finding

Take a look at your existing system and establish how it is being used. Monitor your staff and ask them how they use the system. It's a good idea to watch them so you can get a realistic idea of how they use the system. Often, people will not be completely forthcoming with their answers because they might be embarrassed about the parts of the system they have trouble using.

Analysis

At this stage, you get the chance to be a kid in a candy store. Think up your ideal system, taking into consideration the needs identified in the "Terms" section. Don't limit yourself by anticipating budgetary limitations. Design your system the way you would if you had a blank check.

Design

Now come back to reality and, using the model you made in the previous section, start building your real model. Use whatever elements you can from the "Analysis" section. At this stage, you produce a document that describes the system, but it need not contain specific brands or models of hardware or software.

System Specification

Now that you have general hardware and software packages in mind, it's time to figure out which specific products will be purchased. At this stage, you choose exact models, brands, and identify suppliers.

Implementation and Review

Set up the new system, train your staff to use it, and then monitor it for initial problems. Make any changes necessary to the system to improve performance. Once the new system is working as you want to it, you can get rid of the components of the old system.

Use

Use the new system for day-to-day operations. Be sure to maintain and update it as needed. Part of usage is tuning your system for optimal functionality, so be sure to figure ongoing maintenance and monitoring into your life cycle plan.

Close

In this stage you put the system in its final resting place (at least final as far as your organization is concerned). You can close the system and migrate data to a more modern system. At this stage, you decide what you will do with your data and think about how the machines will be disposed of.

Life

The life of your system is a fuzzy thing. You want to keep it around for several years to justify its acquisition, but the fact of the matter is its usefulness will end at some point. A system's life is based on three factors. Whichever of these factors arises first will determine how long the system's life actually is:

- **Useful life**   This expresses the equipment's lifetime, in which eventually the equipment wears out and it is not feasible to repair it anymore.

- **Technological life** A system may become impractical to maintain even though it can still be repaired and maintained. For example, it might not be possible to find the right type of memory chips for the system because they are no longer made. Another way to look at this is obsolescence.

- **Economic life** A system might still be functional, but it costs too much to use. It might also be that newer systems can be purchased that have lower operating costs so that the payback period of making that purchase is short.

A system's life is based on economic
and technological factors.

It might not be possible to precisely predict the lifetime of a system up front, but you can estimate it by taking these factors into consideration.

Cost

Of course, overall cost is an important factor when evaluating your system's life cycle. But if you find a computer that costs US$2000 to buy, realize that you aren't just spending $2000 per box. You also have to pay for the electricity to power it. You also have to consider maintenance costs, and the like. So when figuring out cost, you must include a number of factors:

- **Initial purchase price** The typical balance IT managers face here is deciding whether to pay a higher upfront purchase price in the hope that lower operating costs can be realized. There are also issues of how much money can be spent on the upfront purchase price.

- **Energy costs** The power it takes to run your machines can be a significant part of overall costs. The more "high performance" a computer is, the more likely it will need additional cooling, which also adds to the overall power cost.

- **Maintenance** If you buy especially inexpensive computers, you may find yourself paying more in maintenance costs. Cheap computers are great at first, but when hard drives fail and NICs don't work properly, you'll spend money fixing these computers.

- **Replacement**   If you're planning on an especially long life cycle for your computers, realize that some computers will simply fail and some you will want to replace, just for the sake of their role in your organization. You may also need to replace certain components, either through mechanical failure or just as part of your organization's needs. Plan for replacing components or even entire computers.

Whereas the preceding are costs you can expect for the physical machines, there are other costs associated with your system that you should also add into your cost estimates. These indirect costs include the following:

- **Interest**   Maybe the largest indirect cost to your system is the interest you pay on borrowing money to make the initial purchase. As such, you should figure your interest costs into any life cycle cost considerations.

- **Administrative costs**   These costs will vary from organization to organization, system to system. And they're likely to be somewhat of a moving target as well as somewhat fuzzy. These include costs for arranging and administering service agreements, tracking equipment with property tags, and so forth.

- **Staffing**   Depending on your system, you may find that you need more (or in some cases fewer) people to run it. That might mean you need to adjust the size of your IT staff. Plan the impact of those salaries into your life cycle cost estimates.

- **Downtime**   If the system is down—either on purpose for updates or because of unreliability—those costs manifest themselves in the form of reduced productivity. Certainly, you can't pre-quantify how often the system will go down, but if you plan regular updates and maintenance, you should be able to predict how often you'll have to take the system down and what that impact will be on the overall organization's productivity.

Buy or Lease

There's no overall "right answer" when deciding whether to buy or lease your equipment. The decision will depend on your organization, what you're expecting of the equipment, and what you want of a computer purchase deal.

Leasing

There are a number of benefits to leasing your equipment. Benefits include:

- **Keeping your equipment up to date**   Because computers become obsolete quickly, you pass the financial burden of their obsolescence on to the leasing company. Let's say you've got a 3-year lease on your sales department's computers. Once that lease expires, the computers go away and you can find a new deal.

- **Predictable monthly expenses**   You'll always know what you're spending on your machines, because you've already hammered out a deal and you know what you're paying.

- **Low (or no) upfront costs**   Most leases don't require an upfront payment. So if your organization has trouble with cash flow, likely you'll be able to avoid a down payment.

- **Staying competitive** If it's important that you are technologically equal (or better) than your competitors, leasing allows you an option to get the latest and greatest equipment with regular rollover.

But leasing isn't all perfect. Let's talk about the downsides of leasing. Cons include:

- **Paying more, overall** Leasing is more expensive than outright buying. For instance, if you spend $2000 for one computer upfront, you would pay $2880 if that same computer was leased for $80 per month for 3 years. Plus, when the lease is over, you give the computer back. If you had bought it, you'd still own it.
- **A deal is a deal** With a lease, you still have to pay for the equipment even if you don't use it anymore. If your business changes or leased equipment is no longer needed, you're still obligated to make the monthly payments.

NOTE *If you do decide to lease, work out an early-out clause in your contract. You'll still have to pay something, but you can lessen the sting. Also, you may be able to purchase a "technology refresh", where you can upgrade your equipment as some point in the lease agreement.*

Buying Buying equipment also comes with its own set of pros and cons. Pros include:

- **Ease in comparison to leasing** Rather than mess with agreements and having to return equipment at a certain date, when you buy your equipment, you go out, you buy it, and it's yours. Lease terms can also be tricky to negotiate, and you might end up getting unfavorable terms or spending too much.
- **Maintenance is up to you** Leases usually require you to follow a maintenance schedule established by the leasing company. When you own the computers, you can decide when to defragement hard drives, install operating system updates, and so forth.
- **Tax deductibility** If you buy the computers, you can write off the price from your taxes. If you lease, you can only write off the monthly cost.

There are also negatives to buying equipment:

- **High initial outlay** If you buy your computers, you'll have to spend that money up front. You may have to use a lot of your credit lines to make the purchase or dip considerably into the company coffers. That money could have been used to build the business through marketing, advertising, or something else.
- **You're stuck with it** With a lease, when the lease term is over and the machines go back to the lease company, disposal becomes the company's problem, not yours. However, when you own the computers, you have to figure out how to recycle or repurpose the machines.

Green Design

An important area you should keep in mind in your life cycle considerations is designing your system with environmentally responsible use, retirement, and disposal. When designing your system, keep these thoughts in mind:

- **Design for repair**   Some equipment is not designed so that it can be repaired (at least not easily) and is simply seen as disposable. Include as many elements as possible that can be repaired.

- **Design for upgradability**   This goes hand-in-hand with the notion of being reparable. Build systems that can be upgraded, rather than having to replace entire components when needed.

- **Design to minimize power consumption**   As mentioned before, the less power you use, the less money you'll spend and the less electricity that will have to be generated. Your ledger wins; the environment wins.

- **Design for recycling or a clean disposal**   This means designing systems with material types that are easily recycled or can easily find a second life when you're done with them. It can also mean including elements that are less toxic, such as using RoHS-compliant equipment or EPEAT-rated equipment.

In essence, including green considerations into the life cycle process involves considering the end of the system's life when performing the initial design.

Recycling Companies

If you've decide to go the recycling route, you should bear in mind certain considerations when making a selection. Naturally, you want to save money, but you also want to go with a recycler who is environmentally responsible (not all are—a lot of that stuff in China came from unscrupulous recyclers). You also want to find a company that is accountable and maintains good records about what they did with your old machines. In this section, we talk about factors to consider when selecting a recycler.

Finding the Best One

The quality of electronic recyclers will vary from company to company. Not all companies are created equally. There is an implied sense of honor and responsibility just by being in the electronics recycling industry, but this isn't always the case.

Remember the resurfacing monitors in that halcyon Minnesota lake? The college that owned them tried to do the responsible thing and have them recycled. It was the recycler who did the bad deed.

Although investigators looked into who the culprit was who dumped the computers in the lake, one thing was plain and clear from the ID tags on the backs of the monitors—they belonged to a Twin Cities college. It was a PR headache for the college, and one that you can avoid by selecting the right company to dispose of your end-of-life equipment.

The EPA recommends selecting recyclers who do the following:

- Maximize reuse, refurbishment, and recycling over disposal and incineration.

- Take precautions to reduce emissions and exposures to workers and the environment.

- Provide special handling of components that may contain substances of concern.

- Ensure that exported electronic products are being sent for legitimate reuse, recycling, or refurbishment.

- Ensure that downstream recycling, refurbishing, and disposal facilities follow management practices that are consistent with the guidelines.

Checklist

The EPA utilizes a checklist for federal agencies to help evaluate potential recyclers. The checklist is a good tool for your company. It can also help you evaluate the following:

- **Collectors and haulers**   Those who collect end-of-life electronics and generally work under contract with another business.
- **Repair shops**   Those who repair computers for resale and remove operational components for the highest level of reuse.
- **Electronics demanufacturers**   Those who take electronics apart for reusable components and also for scrap value.
- **Private asset recovery operations**   Those who specialize in providing the highest return on discarded computer equipment. They usually work with large-scale businesses.

Here are some questions to ask when considering a recycler:

- Can the electronics recycler give a general description of its business? This type of information may include point of contact, number of employees, years in business, and ownership history.
- Does the electronics recycler accept the products you want recycled?
- Does the electronics recycler service your geographic area and type of organization?
- Can the electronics recycler clearly describe its fees for various types of equipment?
- Can the electronics recycler offer additional services that you may require? Additional services may include onsite collection support, transportation support, product reuse or refurbishment, hard-drive erasure/destruction, product tracking, and recycling guarantee or certificate.
- Can the electronics recycler identify its federal, state, and local environmental agency contacts?
- Can the electronics recycler provide information on its compliance history? This type of information should include recent criminal (past 5 years) or civil (past 3 years) violations, and how they were, or are, being addressed.
- Does the electronics recycler have environmental and/or health and safety management systems/plans in place? Management systems and/or plans may include environmental management system (EMS), environmental risk management plan, hazardous materials management plan, emergency prevention, preparedness, and response plan.
- Can the electronics recycler provide a description of its processes? An electronics recycler should be able to provide an overview of its procedures for demanufacturing, reuse/resale/donation, secure destruction, disposal and waste handling, product manufacturing, and storage.
- Can the electronics recycler provide a description of what it does with the electronic equipment it receives? An electronics recycler can utilize a variety of processing methods, including brokering (matching buyers and sellers), resale of whole units,

remanufacturing, demanufacturing, material recovery (physical separation to capture plastics, metals, glass, and so on), material processing (shredding and grinding), and donation (school systems, nonprofit organizations, and so on).

- Can the electronics recycler provide the names and/or locations of the downstream businesses to which it sends equipment or components?
- Does the recycler export equipment outside the U.S.?
- Does the electronics recycler audit its end-markets either via audit, questionnaire, or other measures?
- Does the electronics recycler send materials for disposal in landfills or for incineration?
- Can the electronics recycler supply you with documentation or certification of final disposition?
- Does the electronics recycler maintain appropriate insurance/assurance? Types of insurance/assurance may include general liability insurance, environmental liability, insurance, and financial assurance (for example, bonding).
- Will the electronics recycler allow you to verify this information through an onsite evaluation?

The EPA has more information about managing electronics recycling and refurbishment via Link 7-8. Although the site is geared for governmental agencies, your organization would certainly benefit from the information it provides.

Certifications

You should also take a potential recycler's industry certifications into consideration. Certifications include the following:

- Institute of Scrap Recycling Industry's (ISRI) Recycling Industry Operating Standards (RIOS) certification
- International Association of Electronic Recyclers (IAER) certification
- International Organization for Standards (ISO) ISO 14001 certification

Certification achievement is totally voluntary, but it is a good sign of the recycler's commitment to quality service. On the other hand, if a recycler doesn't have any of these certifications, it doesn't mean they won't provide quality service. However, because it takes a lot of work to earn these certifications, you can almost be guaranteed that the recycler disposes of materials in an appropriate manner.

Hard Drive Recycling

You've probably spent a lot of time and money ensuring that your network is secure. You have firewalls, antivirus software, and strong password use—among other measures—all in place to ensure that no one gets access to your company and its confidential information. But that sensitive information you've tried so hard to protect can be up for grabs once your computers leave your company, destined to be recycled or repurposed.

Although you may be expecting the attack to come from hackers and viruses, a 2007 study by Gartner shows that 90 percent of all security breaches occurred because of user missteps. That is, users brought the damage on because of their own actions (or lack of action).

Hard-drive decommissioning is the act of removing data from the hard drive before it is sent for recycling or repurposing. Unfortunately, this is often done incorrectly and, especially if you're sending hundreds or thousands of computers out of your organization, it can be costly. On the flipside, data in the wrong hands can be even costlier. The cost can be measured in lost company information, trade secrets, and the like, as well as potential damage to your company's reputation should the company be required to disclose the loss under one of the numerous data breach laws in effect around the world. To top it off, loss of certain types of data could be a civil and/or criminal liability for company officers.

Yes, criminal and civil action is a possibility because of the enactment of recent laws to protect individuals' health and financial information. This section examines what you can do to keep your organizations' hard drives from giving up their secrets.

Consequences

Breached data can bring public relations, legal, and business repercussions. Data confidentiality is highly regulated by the U.S. Government. For example, the healthcare industry has Health Insurance Portability and Accountability Act (HIPAA) guidelines in place that put rules on confidential personal data. If that data gets out, the organization that lost it faces strict penalties. U.S. businesses and their employees and partners suffered huge losses after financial misdeeds by officers at Enron and Tyco International. As such, the Sarbanes-Oxley legislation places rules on financial data.

In the past, it was just a good idea to keep data secure. Now it's the law. As a result of these laws, it isn't just a customer or client who suffers if data is leaked. Now, companies can face huge financial penalties. Even more sobering, company officers and directors can face prison time.

Table 7-2 illustrates potential penalties if the laws are violated.

How to Clean a Hard Drive

Often, when selling an old computer, returning it after a lease, or recycling it, you simply reformat the drive or delete the files. When this is done, users tend to think that the data is gone, but it's not.

By going through a reformat or deleting files, one tends to think that the data is gone—after all, "format" sounds like the process means business, and you even hear the hard drive buckling down and making some serious sounds.

	Sarbanes-Oxley	Fair and Accurate Credit Transactions Act of 2003 (FACTA)	HIPPA
Directors and Officers	$1,000,000		
Institution	$5,000,000	$11,000	$50,000 to $250,000
Prison	20 years		1 to 10 years

TABLE 7-2   Potential Penalties If Confidential Data Is Not Protected

But the truth of the matter is that even though the data can't be seen on the computer once it has been formatted, that only means it can't seen by the operating system. Quick formatting just writes to a portion of the disk, but most of the old data is still there and is readily accessible using fairly common recovery tools. Even disks that have been completely formatted can be partially or completely recovered.

You can safely decommission your old hard drives using several methods. Let's talk about the pros and cons of each one.

Deleting

Deleting data is the most common way for a user to remove information from the hard drive. The problem is that nothing is actually deleted. When a file is deleted, the file system's pointer to that file is removed, but that doesn't remove the file itself. The only way the file will be completely removed, using this method, is if data overwrites the area where the file resided.

The data remains on the hard drive, as shown in Figure 7-5, and it can be recovered with the right software.

Overwriting

Software overwriting is a method in which the hard drive is completely written over with random data three times. The U.S. Dept. of Defense (DoD) actually requires drives to be written over three times because there may be problems with the following:

- Ineffectiveness of the overwrite procedures
- Equipment failure, such as a misalignment of read/write heads
- Inability to overwrite bad sectors of tracks of data in inter-record gaps

Software overwriting is illustrated in Figure 7-6.

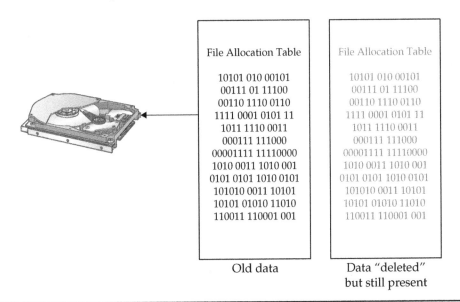

File Allocation Table	File Allocation Table
10101 010 00101	10101 010 00101
00111 01 11100	00111 01 11100
00110 1110 0110	00110 1110 0110
1111 0001 0101 11	1111 0001 0101 11
1011 1110 0011	1011 1110 0011
000111 111000	000111 111000
00001111 11110000	00001111 11110000
1010 0011 1010 001	1010 0011 1010 001
0101 0101 1010 0101	0101 0101 1010 0101
101010 0011 10101	101010 0011 10101
10101 01010 11010	10101 01010 11010
110011 110001 001	110011 110001 001
Old data	Data "deleted" but still present

Figure 7-5   Deleting a file doesn't actually remove it from the drive; this simply tells the computer that that portion of the hard drive is available to be written to.

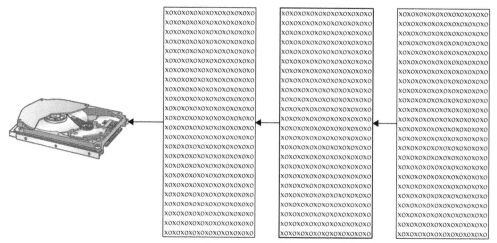

Software overwriting writes gibberish onto the hard drive three times.

FIGURE 7-6   Overwriting a hard drive with random data enables preexisting data to be completely removed.

This is an appealing solution because there are plenty of applications you can buy to do this; plus it can be done in-house. Additionally, overwritten drives can be used again. They can be used within your organization or you can sell them.

On the other hand, software overwriting is a time-consuming process. It can take several hours to wipe one drive. This can cause a loss of productivity, especially in an organization that is overwriting hundreds or even thousands of hard drives.

NOTE   *Sometimes cost can also be an issue. Some software requires a separate licensing fee for each hard drive that's being overwritten.*

Degaussing

If you remember VHS videocassettes, you may also remember the warning labels on them to keep them away from magnets. There was a good reason for this—a powerful enough magnetic force could erase a videocassette. This is also known as *degaussing*.

Degaussing uses a machine that produces a strong electromagnetic field and destroys the information stored on a hard drive. Degaussing was done in the past with weaker magnets; however, the magnetically shielded hard drives of today call for a stronger electromagnetic field.

Although the zap from the electromagnet is quick, it also destroys other components of the hard drive, leaving them inoperable. As such, they cannot be reused and you don't know for sure if all the data has been erased.

You also have to take care when using a degaussing machine. While wiping one hard drive, you run the risk of destroying other machines that might be in the area.

Degaussing is typically outsourced. Third-party companies buy the degaussing equipment and perform the work, but this can lead to chain-of-custody issues.

Mechanical Shredding

Mechanical shredding is what it sounds like. Old hard drives are fed into a shredder and they're torn into a gazillion pieces. As with degaussing machines, you probably wouldn't buy one, but would rather outsource your drives to a shredder.

The benefit is obvious—someone would need tweezers, a microscope, glue, and a lot of patience to get the hard drive back together.

The downside is similar to outsourcing to a degausser—chain-of-custody issues.

Secure Erase

So is there anything you can do that won't let your data come back to haunt you? Yes. A technology called Secure Erase was introduced in 2001. ATA and SATA drives contain the technology to erase the data contained on them. But if this is such a great thing, why haven't you used it? That's because it has been disabled by most motherboard BIOSs probably because of concerns that a user might accidentally destroy data.

NOTE *There is no way to recover from Secure Erase. Really. There's no way to recover from Secure Erase.*

In fact, the National Security Agency and the National Institute for Standards and Testing have given Secure Erase a higher security rating than block overwriting software.

And remember how we warned about liability if financial and health data were ever leaked? Secure Erase is approved to erase that data.

You can employ Secure Erase by downloading a Secure Erase utility that Dr. Gordon Hughes (from the University of California at San Diego's Center for Magnetic Recording Research) helped develop. You can find more information and a download at Link 7-9.

To use it, follow these steps:

1. You need to know how to create a DOS boot disk and load the extracted HDDerase.exe onto the bootable floppy disk.

2. Boot the computer from the floppy.

3. Make sure the boot priority setting is currently applied in your system's BIOS.

4. Type **hdderase** at the system prompt.

5. All ATA hard drives connected to the system will be displayed.

6. Make sure the jumpers on the hard disk are correctly configured—that is, don't set the jumpers to CS (cable select). They should be set to "master" or "slave."

7. Complete the utility.

NOTE *It is likely that your computer does not have a floppy drive. If that is the case, burn HDDerase.exe to a CD-ROM and boot from there.*

Obviously, Secure Erase takes some technical know-how, but it is a less-expensive method and takes less time. You also don't have to worry about chain-of-custody issues.

Requirement	Software Solutions	Degaussing	Shredder	Third-party Providers	Secure Erase
Destroys data beyond forensic recovery	No	Maybe	Maybe	Maybe	Yes
Control of the process	Yes	Maybe	No	No	Yes
Certification and audit trail	No	No	No	Yes	No
Easy to install and use	No	No	No	No	No
Reformat for reuse	Yes	No	No	No	Yes

Table 7-3   Pros and Cons of Hard Drive Erasure

Which Method?

Each method presented so far has its pros and its cons. Some are speedy, some are thorough, and some are inexpensive. But also some are slow, some are unreliable, and some put your organization in the kind of danger you want to avoid.

You'll need to weigh the pros and cons depending on your organization's needs and what you are prepared to do to protect your data. Table 7-3 compares the methods we've talked about.

Although you run the risk of losing control over your hard drives when you outsource their decommissioning, that doesn't mean you shouldn't do it. Many companies pride themselves on their security and discretion.

When you consider a third-party to decommission drives, you need to be confident you are picking a company that will do what it's being hired to do in an effective and reliable manner. After all, what your company does today could be twisted around and used against you in the future.

You should pick a vendor based on your confidence in that vendor, the vendor's technical capabilities, its organizational integrity, and its staying power over the long haul.

Companies such as IBM Global Financing's Asset Recovery Solutions not only can sanitize your hard drives, but can also provide remarketing services so you can sell your decommissioned drives.

CDs and DVDs

The introduction of CDs in 1983 heralded a new standard for music media. Music could now be released on 120 mm × 1.5 mm plastic and aluminum discs, rather than on 12-inch record albums. The sound was perfect, and you didn't have to worry about the CDs wearing out or getting easily scratched.

Note *We can debate whether or not the sound from a CD is better than that from a record album, but that's a discussion for another place.*

It didn't take long before computer data was stored on CDs—lots of data, in fact. Soon, it was possible to write to CDs, and they became an attractive medium for removable data storage and archiving. By the mid-1990s, DVDs made their appearance and—while initially a vehicle for movies—soon found use with computers.

However, like other fantastic developments—including the automobile, computer, and cellular phone—there is an environmental downside to the CD's presence. The big seller for CDs and DVDs is their size. These things were designed to be small. The real problem concerns recycling. If we all just had a few CDs or DVDs, it wouldn't be such a big issue. However, when you consider that Americans dump an average of 45 tons of CDs and DVDs each year, you can see the environmental problem (Worldwatch Institute, 2008).

According to the Worldwatch Institute:

- In 2000, more than 700 compact disc factories were operating worldwide.
- In 1983, when CDs were first introduced in the United States, 800,000 discs were sold. By 1990, this number had grown to close to 1 billion.
- The European market for music CDs has expanded rapidly, with almost 2.9 billion compact discs produced in Western Europe in 1998.
- Each month, more than 45 tons of CDs become obsolete—outdated, useless, or unwanted.
- Each year, more than 55 million boxes of software go to landfills and incinerators, and people throw away millions of music CDs.

Bad News

There's good news and bad news in the world of CD and DVD disposal. Being the optimists we are, let's get the bad news out of the way.

CDs and DVDs are made from different kinds of lacquers, aluminum, and sometimes gold. Most of their composition is made up by polycarbonate plastic, which doesn't readily break down and will be around for hundreds of years.

Further, sending CDs and DVDs to a landfill is a bad idea, because in addition to being around for a long time, they can release Bisphenol A. Burning discs is another poor choice, because they release toxic fumes.

Good News

There is good news. Many recyclers accept CDs and DVDs. The components can be recycled into everything from automobile parts to office equipment.

Recycling is available, but it's not as easy as putting your organization's CDs and DVDs out with the glass bottles. Specialized recyclers will take the discs to reclaim the high-quality plastic. Some CDs and DVDs contain 20 milligrams of gold, which is another commodity that can be rescued.

The use of these recyclers is usually free, but you have to pay to ship your CDs and DVDs to them. The security of your data cannot be guaranteed, so your best bet is to cut the CDs and DVDs in half with a pair of shears before releasing them from your custody.

NOTE *Recyclers don't care in what condition the CDs arrive. They're just going to shred them anyway, so don't bother with packing material. Also, be sure to send in physically damaged discs as well.*

It doesn't make sense to mail in a disc at a time (although you could). A better idea is to set up a bin in the corner of the office, and once it fills up with CDs and DVDs, ship it to a recycler.

The following are some places to start in your CD and DVD recycling efforts:

- **North America**   Link 7-9 and Link 7-10
- **United Kingdom**   Link 7-11 and Link 7-12
- **Australia**   Link 7-13 and Link 7-14

More good news: Companies and individuals *are* recycling. One recycler in San Jose, California processes a million CDs each month. In its second year in business, the company recycled 20 million CDs. A lot of those CDs came from software companies looking to get rid of surplus inventory.

Change Your Mindset

You can lessen the amount of discs your organization uses by following some simple tips:

- Use rewriteable DVD/CD media.
- Find out if the information you're looking for on disc is available over the Internet. If it is, you may not need to buy the disc.
- Keeping your discs out of direct sunlight and away from heat and water will prolong their life.
- Minor scratches can be fixed by rubbing a mild abrasive (such as toothpaste) on the disc surface in a circular motion from the center to the outside.

Consumers take advantage of the shiny discs by doing things such as turning them into dresses, disco balls, drink coasters, and reflectors for bicycle seats. However, you're not likely to task someone in your organization with turning all your old CDs into disco balls. Chances are, they'd just go in the trash, adding to that 45 million ton count.

David vs. America Online

You may remember a few years back opening your mailbox to find membership discs from America Online (AOL). You may also remember seeing those discs in your Sunday newspaper, on boxes of cereal, and near grocery store checkout lines.

Well, the chickens have come home to roost. Now, all those discs (it is estimated that more than a billion were made) are out there somewhere. Some are in people's basements, some are in storage, but a lot of them wound up in landfills.

NOTE *Believe it or not, some people actually collect the AOL discs. Depending on what image was silkscreened on the top, collectors actively seek the discs that are missing from their compilations and trade with like-minded collectors.*

However, a couple of IT workers from Berkeley, California decided to send a message to AOL. In 2001, they set a goal of collecting one million of those installation discs and then shipping them to AOL. For a time, they even had a website (www.nomoreaolcds.com)

where they actively sought people to send them their AOL discs. When one million discs had been collected, the duo intended to ship them to AOL (they estimated it would take 45 moving trucks).

As of 2007, they had collected 400,000 discs before the project was shut down.

This was sort of a radical initiative, but it underscores the need for companies to be more responsible with their CD and DVD creation and distribution. The discs take between five and ten seconds to create, but they remain with us for hundreds of years.

Recycling your computers isn't a small task. You need to do more than just call a company to take the boxes away. You need to spend time thinking about which company is best suited for your needs and how you will prepare for your computers' ultimate disposal.

When you decide to upgrade or buy new equipment, some considerations can help you save money, electricity, and the environment. In the next chapter, we'll talk about the components of your users' computers and how they can be made greener.

PART III

Hardware Considerations

A huge expense for your organization comes in the form of hardware. You want the equipment that meets your business's goals and functions, but you also want to pay as little as you can. As we've talked about already, it isn't just the machines themselves that cost money. The power that goes into them adds to the cost.

This chapter looks at different ways you can select computers for your organization that use less power. This means you'll spend less money in the long run and will cause less damage to the environment.

Remember, too, as you read: The power savings may seem small in some cases, but that's only for one machine. When you realize those costs across hundreds or thousands of computers in your organization, you'll see some real savings.

Certification Programs

These days, it isn't difficult to find hardware that is energy efficient. In the past, you had to really buckle down, read labels, and understand the ins and outs of power consumption to make a thoughtful decision. Today, you can certainly compare the attributes of different computers and components if you want, but you don't have to because a number of certification programs take care of the hard work for you. You can just look at a product and—depending on what level of certification it has—know that you'll save money.

This section looks at some common certification programs and explains how you can use them to your benefit.

EPEAT

We talked about the Electronic Product Environmental Assessment Tool (EPEAT) in Chapter 2. There aren't a lot of machines out there that have been EPEAT certified; however, because this is a mandate for U.S. government procurement—and because the government buys a lot of computers each year—look for manufacturers to kick up their production of EPEAT-certified machines.

EPEAT evaluates electronic products according to three tiers of environmental performance: bronze, silver, and gold.

The complete set of performance criteria includes 23 required criteria and 28 optional criteria in eight categories. To be registered as EPEAT certified, products must meet all the required criteria. Products may then achieve a higher-level EPEAT rating by meeting additional, optional criteria.

The three levels of EPEAT certification establish how well a given device meets the EPEAT requirements. Table 8-1 compares the EPEAT environmental tiers.

EPEAT maintains a listing of certified devices on its website. For example, Figure 8-1 shows a sample listing of gold-rated laptop computers.

You can find out which devices are currently EPEAT certified by visiting the EPEAT website at www.epeat.net, or by following Link 8-1.

RoHS

European businesses are already required to be environmentally responsible because of Restriction of Hazardous Substances (RoHS) laws. That certification doesn't simply apply to products sold in the European Union. Plenty of RoHS-certified devices are offered all over the world. It's easy to tell whether equipment is RoHS compliant because companies tend to advertise the fact when their equipment is RoHS compliant.

NOTE *If your business is located in California, you are already well aware of the RoHS laws. As of January 2007, businesses in California are forbidden to buy any hardware that is banned under European RoHS law.*

Further, if you are ordering a lot of computers from a manufacturer, you can be sure to tell the manufacturer you want your computers to be RoHS compliant. For example, Toshiba will build computers that are lead-free and meet other RoHS guidelines.

NOTE *You can read more about RoHS in Chapter 2.*

Certification Level	Requirements
Bronze	Product meets all required criteria.
Silver	Product meets all required criteria plus at least 50 percent of the optional criteria that apply to the product type being registered.
Gold	Product meets all required criteria plus at least 75 percent of the optional criteria that apply to the product type being registered.

TABLE 8-1 The Three Levels of EPEAT Certification

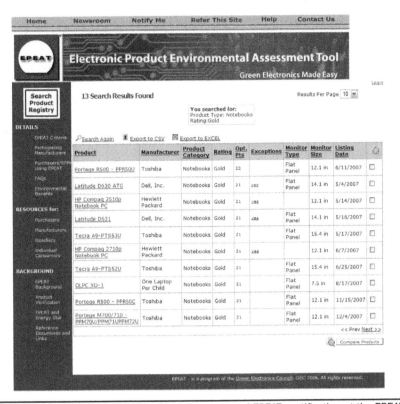

FIGURE 8-1 You can see which electronic devices have earned EPEAT certification at the EPEAT website.

Energy Star

EPEAT and RoHS are certainly important certifications, and they're becoming more prevalent, but the biggest and most well-known program for certifying energy-efficient electronics in the United States is the Environmental Protection Agency's (EPA's) Energy Star program. Like EPEAT, hardware must meet specific standards in order to be Energy Star certified. In this case, however, those standards are based on power consumption.

In this section, we'll take a closer look at what it takes to be Energy Star certified and what that means for computers, monitors, and other devices.

Computers

Computers have been certified under the Energy Star program for years. In 2007, the EPA made Energy Star certification even more stringent. The EPA estimates that by toughening certification standards, the new computer specification will save consumers and businesses more than US$1.8 billion in energy costs over the next 5 years and prevent greenhouse gas emissions equal to the annual emissions of 2.7 million vehicles.

In order for a computer to be Energy Star certified, it must meet the requirements outlined in Table 8-2.

You can find your cost savings from using Energy Star–rated computers by using the savings calculator at the Energy Star website which you can access through Link 8-2.

This tool is shown in Figure 8-2. To find specific models of Energy Star-rated computers, use the finder tool at Link 8-3. Some sample output is shown in Figure 8-3. To find specific laptops, follow Link 8-3.

Product Type	Tier 1 Requirements
Desktops, integrated computers, desktop-derived servers and gaming consoles	Standby (Off Mode): <= 2.0 W Sleep Mode: <= 4.0 W Idle State: Category A: <= 50.0 W Category B: <= 65.0 W Category C: <= 95.0 W
Notebooks and tablets	Standby (Off Mode): <= 1.0 W Sleep Mode: <= 1.7 W Idle State: Category A: <= 14.0 W Category B: <= 22.0 W
Workstations	TEC Power (P_{TEC}): <= 0.35 × [P_{Max} + (# HDDs × 5)] W **Note:** Where P_{max} is the maximum power drawn by the system, # HDDs is the number of installed hard drives in the system.
Efficient power supply requirements	Internal power supplies: 80 percent minimum efficiency at 20 percent, 50 percent, and 100 percent of rated output and minimum Power Factor 0.9. External power supplies: Either Energy Star qualified or meet the no-load and active mode efficiency levels provided in the Energy Star External Power Supply (EPS) specification.

TABLE 8-2   Tier 1 Energy Efficiency Requirements Effective July 20, 2007

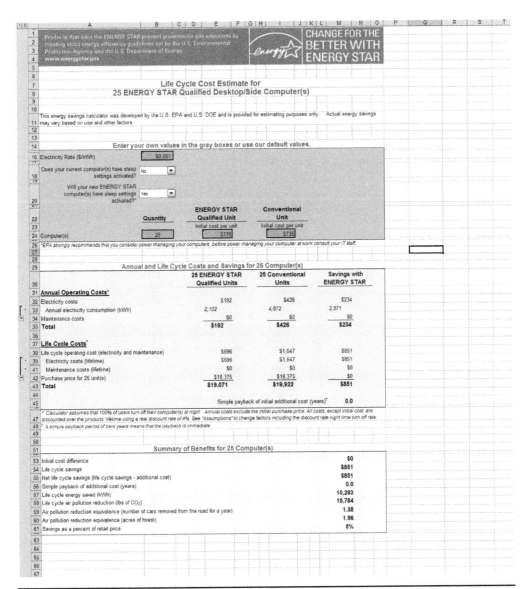

FIGURE 8-2 You can calculate your savings using an Excel-based tool provided by the EPA.

Monitors

When you're selecting monitors, a great place to start is by examining models that are
Energy Star qualified. These monitors use 20 to 60 percent less electricity than monitors that
aren't Energy Star certified.

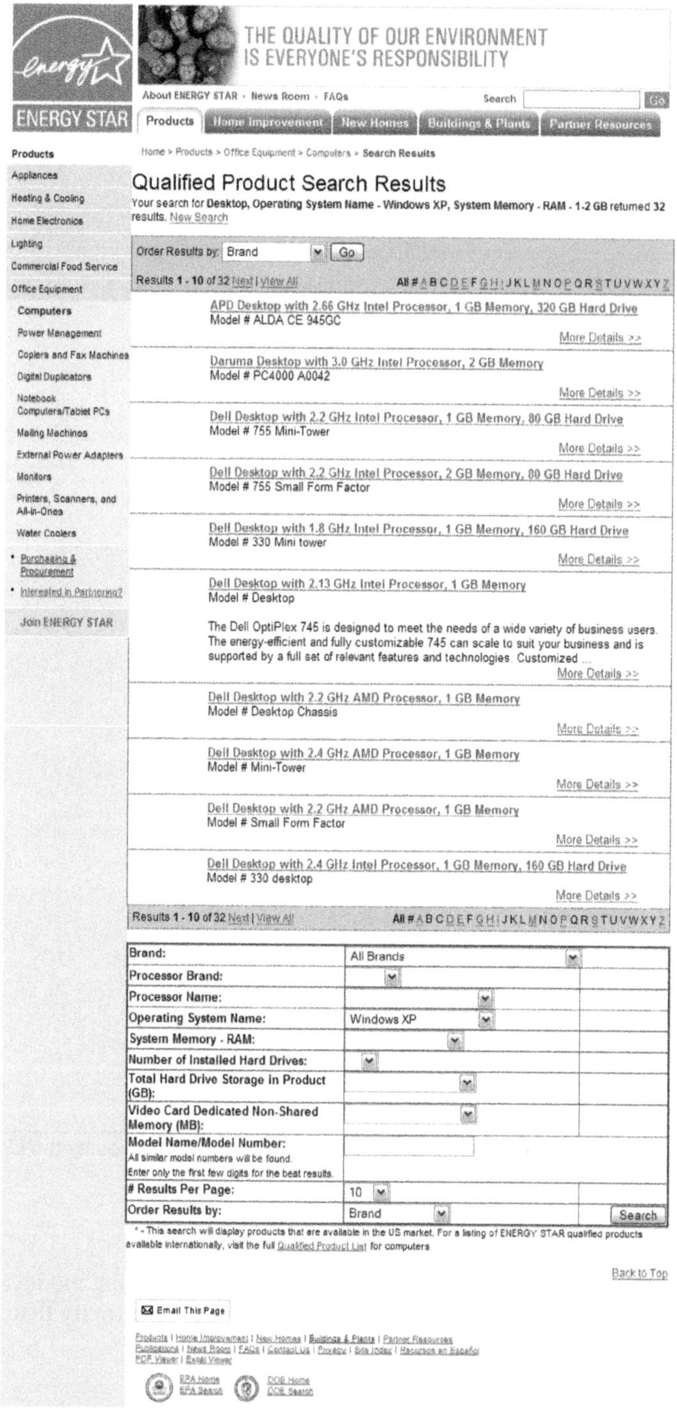

FIGURE 8-3   You can find specific Energy Star–compliant devices at the Energy Star website.

For example, if a monitor currently uses 199 kWh per year and you find a monitor that uses 105 kWh per year, your savings (based on 8.5 cents per kWh) is US$8 per year. That is not a huge amount of money—your lunch probably costs more. But if you multiply that by the number of monitors in your organization, you'll quickly realize the savings.

The Energy Star website contains a more thorough tool than our rough estimate. It is a Microsoft Excel tool that can help you calculate your cost savings. The tool is shown in Figure 8-4. It can be downloaded via Link 8-5.

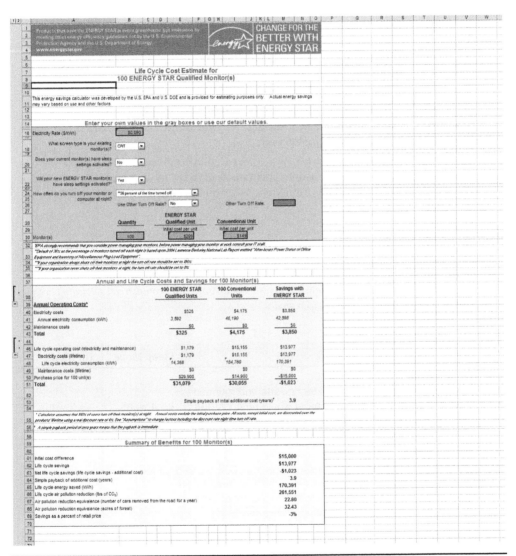

FIGURE 8-4   You can determine how much cost savings you'll realize by using the calculator provided by Energy Star.

In order to achieve an Energy Star certification, monitors must meet the following criteria:

- In On mode, the maximum allowed power varies based on the computer monitor's resolution.

- In Sleep mode, computer monitor models must consume 2 watts or less.

- In Off mode, computer monitor models must consume 1 watt or less.

The exact specifications for Energy Star's tiering measurements are listed in Table 8-3. To find out whether a monitor you are considering is Energy Star certified, you can visit the vendor's website. Or, you can search products via Link 8-6.

Your business will save money by using Energy Star–certified monitors. Consider the following issues:

- **Electricity usage cut in half**   You'll save US$25 to US$75 per PC each year.

- **Cooling loads reduced**   You'll also save US$5 to US$10 per PC per year in office cooling costs. That number increases to US$10 to US$25 in warm climates.

- **Reduction in peak load demand charges**   If your utility charges extra during peak demand times, this amount is lessened.

- **Faster boot times**   Waiting for computers to boot is eliminated. Because the computers are already technically "on," you don't have to wait for them to boot up. They simply need to awaken from low-power mode, which is much faster than a bootup.

NOTE   *Of course, there are some costs associated with adopting Energy Star settings. However, these costs are minor compared to your overall savings. You may incur costs when computers are being updated if they are asleep. That is, they may not get the automatic updates, so staff will have to attempt to reinstall the updates. However, open-source and commercial software packages are available that can help manage sleep modes.*

	On Mode	**Sleep Mode**	**Off Mode**
Tier 1 maximum allowable power consumption (effective January 1, 2005)	$Y = 38X + 30$ (Y is expressed in watts and rounded up to the nearest whole number, and X is the number of megapixels in decimal form.)	<= 4 watts	<= 2 watts
Tier 2 maximum allowable power consumption (effective January 1, 2006)	If $X < 1$ megapixel, then $Y = 23$ If $X > 1$ megapixel, then $Y = 28X$ (Y is expressed in watts and rounded up to the nearest whole number, and X is the number of megapixels in decimal form.)	<= 2 watts	<= 1 watt

TABLE 8-3   Energy Star Power Tiers

You should also be mindful of computers that need to be accessed from outside the organization. For instance, if a user needs to use Remote Desktop (we'll talk about that a little later in this chapter), then only set the power management feature on the monitors, not the CPU.

To maximize power savings, the EPA recommends setting computers to enter system standby or hibernate after 30 to 60 minutes of inactivity. To save even more, set monitors to enter sleep mode after 5 to 20 minutes of inactivity. The lower the setting, the more energy you save. In your organization, you would likely manage this via a user policy setting that is mass-distributed to your users. Also, when users try to awaken their computers, they'd be met with a password, to ensure security.

NOTE *On laptops, be sure to activate these settings in the AC power profile, not just the DC (battery power) profile.*

Printers, Scanners, All-in-Ones

Again, it is advantageous to your organization to seek out Energy Star–rated peripherals such as printers, scanners, and all-in-one devices. Like computers and monitors, these devices don't cost any more than noncertified models, but they do use less energy.

For a laser printer to earn the Energy Star certification, it must:

- Use at least 25 percent less energy than regular printers.
- Be able to print on both sides of a page, thus saving paper.
- Run cooler and last longer, thus reducing the cost of air conditioning and maintenance.

In order to find a qualified printer, scanner, or all-in-one, use the product finder tool via Link 8-7.

Thin Clients

When considering client computers, you should also think about the advantages of using thin clients. These computers rely on the server for processing activities and are used mainly for input and output between the server. With the vast improvements in networking speed and the large shift in computers being used more as communication devices as opposed to processing devices, thin clients can make a lot of sense.

Fat clients are the PCs that normally sit on your users' desks. These machines do most of the processing and then transfer the results of the data to the server. Thin clients usually run web browsers or remote desktop software.

Advantages to using thin clients include the following:

- **Lower administration costs** Thin clients are largely managed at the server, and there's less opportunity for hardware failure. Also, because the entire system is managed centrally, there's less chance of virus or other malware infection.
- **Security** Because no data is actually stored on the thin client, the chance for physical data theft is drastically reduced.

- **Lower hardware costs**   Thin clients tend to be less expensive than fat clients because they do not contain disk drives, application memory, and high-power processors. They also have longer lives before needing upgrading or becoming obsolete.

- **Efficiency**   In a fat client, the CPU is idle most of the time. With a thin client, memory can be shared. If multiple users are using the same application, it only needs to be loaded into the server's RAM once. In a fat-client scenario, each workstation must have its own copy of the application in memory.

- **Lower energy consumption**   Thin clients use a lot less energy than fat clients. This reduces the amount of energy consumed, which equates to less heat generation, thus reducing the price of air conditioning.

- **Easy hardware failure management**   If a thin client fails, it is easier to replace than a fat client. If a thin client fails, the unit is simply swapped out. There is no need to try and recover files and transfer them from the old, broken machine to a replacement.

- **Hostile environments**   Because thin clients don't have moving parts, they can be used in dusty environments and other harsh locales, such as manufacturing floors. Because they lack moving parts, there's no worry over fans clogging and overheating the computer.

- **Ease of upgrade**   If your system needs more computing power, it's easier to add another blade server to increase system resources to the level you need rather than having to upgrade individual clients. This results in less downtime, and you don't have to worry about disposal of replaced equipment.

- **Less noise**   Because there are no fans in the thin clients, no noise is generated.

- **Less disposed equipment**   Thin clients can remain in service longer than fat clients, so they aren't disposed of as often. Also, because there are no hard drives or DVD-ROM drives, there are fewer components to discard when they reach the end of life.

Servers

There are different ways you can use servers in your green workplace. Through consolidation and virtualization, you can remove unnecessary machines from your workplace, but you can also use servers for new functions. In this section, we'll talk about the different types and functions of servers.

Blade Servers

As noted earlier in this book, the main appeal of blade servers is that they increase your organization's datacenter capabilities, without adding to its size. In this section, we'll talk about what you should look for if you are specifically looking for blades.

Benefits
Before we talk about specifics for selecting models, let's examine why blades are so useful to your organization. Some benefits include:

- **Less space needed**   Blades take up 35 to 45 percent less space than tower or rack-mounted servers.

- **Reduced power consumption** By consolidating power supplies into the blade chassis, you reduce the power supplies needed and you benefit from an overall reduction of power use.

- **Lower management cost** When you consolidate your servers, deployment, management, and administration are simplified and improved. This, of course, also manifests itself in cost savings and less headache for the IT staff.

- **Simplified cabling** Rack-mounted servers were a good way to consolidate hardware in fewer locations than tower servers. However, they also had a lot of cabling involved. Blade servers reduce cabling requirements by 70 percent. Why is this a big deal? Fewer cables means better airflow, which means lower cooling costs.

Features

When choosing a blade server, you have to think about what you're going to use it for. For instance, if you are going to be performing complex calculations with a lot of data, you'll need a server that's pretty powerful.

Unfortunately, some companies buy bigger servers than they need, so they're spending money on processing power they're not using. The benefit of a blade system is that you can easily update the system if you discover you need more power. It's better to plan for future growth than to pay up front for power you don't need.

Table 8-4 lists some types of servers, what they do, and some sample uses.

Features, expansion, build quality, and processing density are all factors to consider when choosing a blade server.

Consolidation

For some functions, you may not even need to purchase new servers—you can just repurpose existing machines to serve those needs in your organization. Most organizations have several small servers that each perform the function of a single legacy application that cannot be removed because it is still used by some processes. These servers are excellent candidates for consolidation.

Server Type	Functionality	Usage
Single-function blade server	Bare-bones CPUs, sometimes with onboard storage or porting, and they run single applications.	Ideal for academic or office environments where blades can be assigned individual tasks, including web hosting, e-mail, and scheduling software.
Blade PCs	The central core of a thin-client setup. This server provides the processing and storage capacity for clients, which is then accessed by thin clients.	General office applications.
Enterprise-level blade server	Maximum power set in a small space. These systems generally use multiple racks and require compatibility with legacy systems, networks, and software.	These are most often used by digital production studios, high-level stockbrokers, and financial corporations.

TABLE 8-4 Different Types of Blade Servers

If you consolidate the servers onto a single platform, you save the entire energy consumption of the original server and its cooling costs, and you also have better manageability.

Consolidation wasn't practical 5 years ago, but now virtualization has made it a reality. Virtualization is the practice of software creating the instance of a PC on a server. This way, multiple virtual servers can exist on one machine.

Then you load the virtual server, install whatever operating system and applications you want, and run it side-by-side with other virtualized servers.

If this sounds like an option for your organization, we'll explain virtualization—and show you how to do it—in Chapter 12.

Products

Many companies offer blades. IBM, Hewlett-Packard, and Dell all have their own offerings with their own features and capabilities.

For example, in January 2008, Dell revealed its M-Series PowerEdge blade servers, which consume 19 percent less power and achieve 25 percent better performance per watt than some of their competitors.

NOTE *Dell also offers lead-free servers for customers who want to green up their IT departments.*

Hardware Considerations

Obviously, we can't unequivocally tell you, "Buy [such and such] computer and monitor for all your organization's workstations." That's also the case for servers, printers, and every electronic device in your business. The reason is simple—one size doesn't fit all. The devices that are best for your organization aren't best for someone else's. That being said, there are some guiding principles you should follow to find the hardware that will have the least impact on the environment.

There are several factors to consider—from overall design (can it be easily upgraded?) to manufacturing to ultimate disposal. In this section, we'll talk about what you should look for when buying new hardware.

Planned Obsolescence

In the previous chapter, we talked about end-of-life hardware. And part of your systems development life cycle was planning for the end. This is also known as *planned obsolescence*—realizing up front that at some day in the future, your shiny new equipment won't serve you anymore.

When looking at new hardware, also think about how you will dispose of it and consider buying hardware that can be kept around longer than normal. The following are some considerations:

- Lease and buy-back programs provide a good way to get rid of your computers if you plan on installing new ones. In addition to formal leasing companies, you can also find leasing programs through Dell and Gateway. Some manufacturers take back your old machines.

- Use hardware and operating systems that are readily upgradeable.

- Make sure spare parts, service, and support will be available in a few years. This is normally defined in "years available after production."
- Make sure the memory is easily expandable.

Packaging

Although packaging and shipping aren't a concern for the overall operation and functionality of your system, they are a consideration when trying to lessen one's environmental impact, not to mention the cost of disposing of that material. A lot of times, computer equipment comes in packaging that cannot be reused or recycled. Multiple-material packaging makes recycling difficult, and nonrecyclable materials (such as polystyrene) abound.

NOTE *Paper manuals add to the problem. There may just be one paper manual included with a PC, but if you're buying hundreds or thousands of new computers, those new manuals stack up. Add to that the fact that they're largely unused. Users will sit down and start working without ever cracking that user manual.*

The following are some tips you can employ when having new computers shipped to you:

- Ask for multiple computers to be packaged together for shipping, rather than being boxed individually.
- Require recycled-content materials and recyclable packaging.
- Require material types to be identified. Recyclers need to know material types, so require labeling to show what type of plastic is used.
- Require manufacturers or shippers to take back packaging for reuse or recycling.
- Ask for online manuals and preinstalled programs.

Toxins

You know by now just how toxic computers can be when their useful lives are over. You can manage how much toxic material is used by looking for hardware that has been created following these guidelines:

- Look for manufacturers who use low levels of toxic chemicals.

NOTE *The State of Massachusetts recently awarded points to bidders who avoided toxic chemicals in the manufacturing and assembly of computers.*

- Look for manufacturers who use lead-free solder.
- Look for manufacturers who use low-mercury and long-life lamps in flat-panel displays.
- Batteries should be removable, rechargeable, and recyclable.

Other Factors

Some other issues need to be present when considering hardware. They may seem like little things, but these little things can become big headaches that can ultimately lead to your getting rid of a computer before it needs to be disposed of.

If you're looking at overall responsibility in manufacturing, think about issues such as these:

- Are machines and parts designed so that they can be assembled and disassembled with universally available tools?

- Require that metal casings be readily recyclable. Metal casings are recyclable. Plastic casings require flame retardants and are not recyclable.

- Require recycled-content computers.

- When possible, use remanufactured or refurbished equipment—it's less expensive and saves another box from a landfill.

- Look for manufacturers who do what they can to lessen their products' toxicity in adhesives, labels, coatings, finishes, fasteners, and metallic paint.

- Machines should be Energy Star compliant for overall energy use as well as sleep modes. Require that Energy Star is active upon delivery.

- Require online or electronic documentation.

- Choose printers and copiers that use remanufactured toner cartridges.

- Think about air quality when selecting printers. Environment Canada requires a desktop printer's ozone concentration not to exceed .04mg/m3. Dust concentration cannot exceed .24mg/m3.

Remote Desktop

You can also make life easier for workers who are on the road or occasionally have to work from home or a remote site. They can access their office computers, if they're using Windows, via Remote Desktop.

But it isn't just out-of-the-office workers who can benefit from Remote Desktop—people inside your organization can also use it. It can be used for the following purposes:

- **To power thin clients** If you buy thin clients, Remote Desktop can be used to connect your thin clients to the server.

- **To extend the life of existing machines** Rather than getting rid of old machines, you can turn them into thin clients and run applications from the server.

Remote Desktop is a feature that was initially rolled out with Windows XP. It allows the user to access their computer—as the name suggests—remotely. Suppose a user needs to access their computer from home or from another computer on the company network; Remote Desktop allows the user to access everything on the remote computer—including files, applications, and network connections. Remote Desktop not only allows the user to access the remote computer's files, but the desktop appears exactly as it does on the remote machine.

There are two components to a Remote Desktop connection:

- **Server** The remote computer to which you will be connecting. It could be your office desktop computer or a special computer set up for road warriors to access when they're out and about.

- **Client** The computer you will use to form your connection with the server. It could be a PC at home, a road warrior's laptop, or even a coworker's PC in a neighboring cubicle.

Using Remote Desktop

Before you can use Remote Desktop, it's necessary to prepare your server and client computers. It's also a really good idea to test your connection to make sure everything is working the way you want it to. After all, once you're away from the server, the computer cannot be accessed to perform any tweaks or fine-tuning.

Remote Desktop Server

When configuring a Remote Desktop server, you will be indicating which user accounts will be authorized access. These user accounts must have passwords. If the computer the client will be accessing does not normally utilize a password, you will have to create one for Remote Desktop.

When you configure your server for Remote Desktop, you enter the user account name when Windows Vista asks for the object name in the Select Users dialog box. To configure a Remote Desktop server, follow these steps:

1. Select Start | Control Panel | System And Maintenance.

2. Click the Allow remote access icon from the System portion of the dialog box.

3. In the Remote Desktop portion of the dialog box are two selections you can make, based on your connection and security needs (see Figure 8-5):

    - Allow connections from computers running any version of Remote Desktop (less secure)

    - Allow connections only from computers running Remote Desktop with Network Level Authentication (more secure).

    Network Level Authentication (NLA) is a new form of authentication that completes user authentication before a remote connection is made. This is a more secure method of authentication and can protect the remote computer from attacks and malware.

    The best choice is to select the second radio button, allowing connections only with NLA-enabled computers. However, if your connecting computers don't have NLA, or you just don't know whether they do, you should select the first radio button.

NOTE *How do you know if your computer is using NLA? Open the Remote Desktop Connection tool, click the small icon at the top-left corner of the dialog box, and then click About. We'll explain how to open the Remote Desktop Connection tool in the next section.*

---

4. Click the Select Users button. This calls up the Remote Desktop Users dialog box in which you will add users who will be allowed to remotely access this computer. Administrative accounts are automatically given access.

5. Click Add. This calls up the Select Users dialog box, as shown in Figure 8-6. User accounts have three identifying components: object type, location, and name.

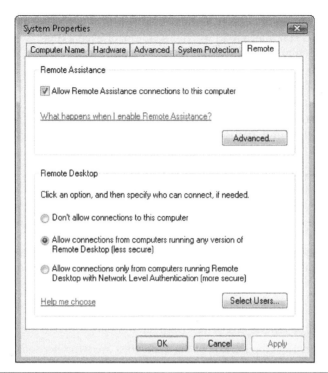

FIGURE 8-5 Selecting what type of users can access your computer will alter the security settings.

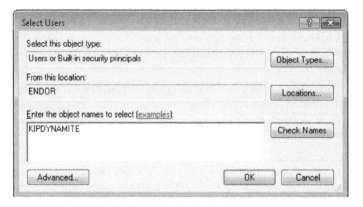

FIGURE 8-6 Adding a user to the Remote Desktop server indicates who can access the computer.

6. If you want to locate a user account from the Remote Desktop server, make sure the "Select this object type" option is set to Users. Then type an account name in the "Enter the object names to select" box. If you wish to enter a user from another computer on an Active Directory–based LAN, click the Locations button and select the domain. Then enter the user account name.

7. Click Check Names. This gives Windows Vista a chance to enter the name in the *computername\username* format.

8. Click OK. The user you just indicated will be added to the list of users permitted to remotely access your Remote Desktop server. To add more users, repeat steps 6 through 8.

9. Click OK twice to exit all the dialog boxes.

10. Finally, if your Remote Desktop server is protected by a firewall, make sure the firewall allows remote connection traffic.

Remote Desktop Client

The Remote Desktop Connection tool is installed by default and is located by accessing Start | All Programs | Accessories | Remote Desktop Connection. Figure 8-7 shows what the tool looks like when you first start it.

We're talking specifically about Windows Vista and Remote Desktop, but Remote Desktop doesn't just work with Windows Vista. The tool was introduced in Windows XP, but if you have older versions of Windows that need to connect remotely, Microsoft provides a tool that can be used on Windows 95, Windows 98, Windows 98 Second Edition, Windows Me, Windows NT 4.0, and Windows 2000. The Remote Desktop client is a 3.4MB file that you can download via Link 8-8. When installed, this client allows older versions of Windows to connect to a Windows Vista Remote Desktop server.

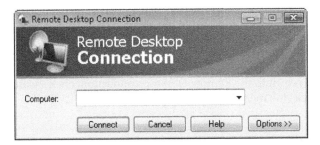

FIGURE 8-7   The Remote Desktop Connection tool is used to connect to the server.

Establishing a Connection

Once your Remote Desktop server and client have been configured, you should test the connection to make sure it works the way you want. The first step is to ensure that the Remote Desktop server is turned on and you're connected to the network.

If someone is logged on locally, the client trying to access the server will see a message telling them that the local user must first disconnect. Simultaneously, at the remote computer the user will see a message allowing them to prevent the Remote Desktop session from taking place. If the user fails to respond to the request after a certain amount of time, Windows assumes the user is away, and they are automatically logged out.

Next, start the Remote Desktop client using these steps:

1. Select Start | All Programs | Accessories | Remote Desktop Connection.

2. From the Computer drop-down list, pick the name of the server computer or enter its IP address. If the drop-down list does not contain any computer names, click Browse For More to see the available computers in your domain or workgroup. This list will only show computers that have been enabled for Remote Desktop.

NOTE *If you don't know a computer's IP address, you can find it by selecting Start | My Network Places and then clicking View Network Connections. Right-click your LAN or Internet connection, choose Status, and then click the Support tab.*

3. Click Connect.

4. When Remote Desktop is done forming its connection with the remote computer, you'll see a Windows Vista–style splash screen. The screen contains icons for the users who have been authorized to remotely access the computer. Click your icon and then enter your password.

5. Click OK.

Once connected, the client will see what the server's desktop looks like, and they can use it as if they were sitting at that computer. The main difference, however, is at the top of the screen, where a special toolbar can be used to minimize, maximize, or close the Remote Desktop view. For example, if you wish to work on your client computer, you click the minimize button. To return to the Remote Desktop connection, click the maximize button. The pushpin icon locks the menu in place.

In Practice

In the real world, how does all of this equate into dollars and cents? Let's consider the example of Aperture Science, Inc. The company has 5000 clients and 1000 servers. Let's take a look at how changing over hardware can consume less power, as well as less money.

Aperture Science, Inc. isn't going to switch everyone over all at once. It's just not realistic. The company has decided to phase in the project over 5 years, as well as to virtualize as much as possible, so it will be consolidating its 1000 servers into 720 servers. Additionally, the company is turning half of its clients into thin clients.

So each year, the company is sending 1000 PCs and 200 servers to be repurposed or recycled. Those machines will be replaced by 500 PCs, 500 thin clients, and 144 blade servers—all Energy Star rated.

The old fat clients cost US$61,800 to power over 3 years. By switching over to new machines, the company will spend US$1650 to power the thin clients and US$13,900 to power servers, for a total of US$15,550, or a total savings of 75 percent.

The servers will be a different story. Efficiencies will vary by server, but let's consider a conservative estimate of a 25-percent power savings per blade. Aperture Science, Inc. stands to save a lot of money with the new blade servers. In the past, each server consumed 280 W. The new blade servers will consume 218 W. That doesn't sound like a massive difference, but remember, the company is reducing about 25 percent of the total servers, from 1,000 to 720. Over the span of 3 years, Aperture Science, Inc. will save US$120,825 in power costs.

Not only is the company saving money on power consumed, it's also saving money in cooling (about US$60,300). What's more, the amount of datacenter space it needs for its servers will drop from 1200 square feet to 540 square feet.

Additionally, the company will see cost savings in software licensing fees, and management costs are going to be greatly reduced. Savings will come in many guises. Some will be easy to compute, others will be more fuzzy. Table 8-5 enumerates the cost savings as well as shows some savings that will differ across organizations depending on their needs and utilization.

Description	Savings Estimate	Comments
Moving from rack-mounted servers to blades	25 percent	Generally speaking, a company can reduce about 25 percent of its server farm by switching to blades.
Floor space for blade servers vs. rack-mounted servers	45 percent	Blade servers will take up a little more than half the space of existing rack servers.
Powering blade servers vs. rack-mounted servers	25 percent	Rack-mounted servers consume about 280 W, whereas blades consume 218 W.
Thin-client power consumption vs. fat-client consumption	85 percent	Thin clients (with a monitor) consume as little as 24 W, whereas fat clients (with a monitor) consume 170 W.
Energy Star–rated monitors vs. conventional monitors	92 percent	Energy Star monitors save power because of hardware considerations and also software settings.
Energy Star–rated computers vs. conventional computers	55 percent	Energy Star computers save power because of hardware considerations and also software settings.
Organizational savings	Varies	Organizations will save money in such areas as software license fees, management, repair, cooling, and so forth.

TABLE 8-5 Electricity and Money Can Be Saved in Several Ways

Hardware is a major investment for your organization. Not only do you have to consider your mission-critical applications, but if you are considering lessening your environmental impact, you have another layer of issues to consider. However, going green is not impossible. In fact, many large companies are doing just that. In the next two chapters, we'll look at a few of the companies who not only have gone green in their datacenters, but have made the commitment to reduce their carbon footprint across the entire company.

IV
PART

Case Studies

CHAPTER

Technology Businesses

Although the focus of this book is on the impacts of technology on the environment, we don't mean to paint technology companies as evil entities, intent on wrecking the planet. Quite the contrary. The fact of the matter is that many technology companies are leading the charge toward environmentally responsible, cost-conscious equipment.

In this chapter, we'll look at three companies that are being socially responsible—Dell, Hewlett-Packard, and Rackspace. These companies are leading the way in the area of development, product life cycle, and recycling.

This chapter serves two purposes. First, it allows us to look at companies that are trying to minimize their ecological impact. Although there are certainly those out there who would still condemn Dell and Hewlett-Packard for producing the levels of greenhouse gases that they do, the fact of the matter is that these companies are making significant efforts to cause less harm to the environment.

The other purpose of this chapter is to show you the sorts of efforts these companies are making, and possibly give you some inspiration to make changes in your own operations. Can you ever do as much as Dell, Hewlett-Packard, or Rackspace? Sure. Why not? By looking at what these companies (and others) are doing, you can look at your own organization and see where changes can be made.

We'll start with a look at the company with the biggest green efforts, Dell. We'll talk about what puts Dell at the top of the heap and how it is lessening its impact on the planet. After talking about Dell, we'll switch gears to one of the oldest technology companies whose green efforts go back almost two decades. In the end, we'll round things out with a look at Rackspace, a company that offers green solutions to its customers while striving toward its own environmental goals.

Dell

Remember the Dell Dude? He hawked computers around 2000 with his catchphrase, "Dude, you're getting a Dell." If you do remember, then Dell certainly got its money's worth in its advertising campaign. Five years after the Dell Dude was retired, people still remember him.

NOTE *The Dell Dude actually had a name. The character's name was Steven.*

But what Dell really wants you to know—and remember—is its commitment to the environment.

Dell—started in the founder's college dorm room in 1984—is a US$59 billion computer company that builds, sells, and supports computers, peripherals, and other technology products.

In 2007, Dell set its sights on being the greenest technology company on the planet. This is not just a laudable goal for Dell, it is also something that will cause a healthy competition from its rivals. As more technology companies try to lessen their impact, everyone wins.

Dell has embraced the notion of being green in three areas:

- Environmentally friendly materials
- Energy efficiency
- Recycling and recovery of end-of-life products

In June 2007, Dell launched a number of zero-carbon initiatives:

- Reducing its carbon intensity, or greenhouse gas emissions, by 15 percent by 2012
- Requiring suppliers to report carbon emissions data during quarterly business reviews
- Partnering with customers to build the "greenest PC on the planet"
- Offsetting carbon with its "Plant a Tree for Me" program

NOTE *Dell also coined the term "The Re-Generation." This refers to people of all ages, all around the world, who want to make a difference in improving the planet's environment.*

In this section, we'll take a closer look at what Dell's doing to be so green. However, we are not here to give a plug for Dell. We simply hope you will find some of what Dell has done applicable to your organization.

Recycling Programs

Dell offers a number of recycling opportunities to its customers. Even though they have been advocates of recycling, as legislation becomes more pronounced for mandating product recycling, Dell is ratcheting up its efforts.

Dell was the first technology company to establish a product recycling goal in 2004 and then completed its global consumer recycling program in 2006. In July 2007, Dell announced that it had exceeded its targets in working toward its multiyear goal of recovering more than 275 million pounds of computer equipment by 2009. In 2006, Dell announced it has recovered 78 million pounds of used equipment from customers, a 93 percent increase over 2005. It was also 12.4 percent of the equipment that Dell sold just 7 years before.

Dell favors the producer-responsibility approach to recycling, which requires the producers to take responsibility for end-of-life equipment. There are three ways that Dell recovers old computers.

Nonprofit Partnerships

Dell has partnered with organizations such as Goodwill Industries and the National Cristina Foundation to match consumer donations. Further, if a consumer brings a computer to be recycled into a Goodwill store, Dell will pick it up, refurbish it, sell it, and give those profits to Goodwill.

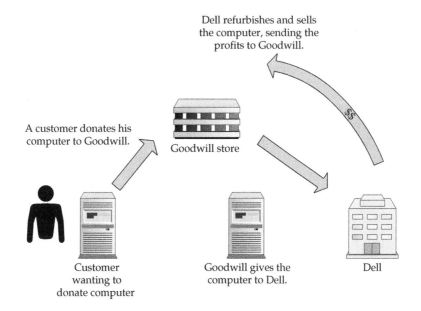

Dell refurbishes and sells the computer, sending the profits to Goodwill.

A customer donates his computer to Goodwill.

Goodwill store

Customer wanting to donate computer

Goodwill gives the computer to Dell.

Dell

NOTE Dell also commissions third-party audits of all of its recycling partners and it has a no-export policy. Dell will only process recovered equipment in countries where facilities and processes have been audited and that do not export waste to third-world nations.

Businesses

Getting rid of the family computer is straightforward enough. Load it into the minivan, drive it to a responsible recycler, and be done with it. But what do you do when you have hundreds or thousands of computers?

Dell helps organizations remove old IT equipment as well as offers a number of different services to handle the removal, including erasing the hard drives. Using Dell's program, your organization can elect to recycle or sell the old equipment. Dell will accept equipment including desktops, notebooks, servers, storage devices, networking equipment, monitors, printers, and computer peripherals such as keyboards and mice.

Dell is embracing the life cycle concept for electronics. No longer does the relationship end after the gear is sold. Dell offers organizations two options to dispose of old equipment:

- **Value recovery**   Whatever value Dell is able to recover from your old equipment will be given back to your organization.
- **Recycling**   Used equipment that has no resale value is recycled.

In either case, Dell's service includes transportation, equipment disposition, and data destruction.

Data destruction is offered at different levels:

- **Level 2** Three-pass read/write using Norton G Disk or equivalent
- **Level 3** Seven-pass read/write using Norton G Disk or equivalent
- **Level 4** Physical disk destruction

If you are interested in knowing what's going on with your recycled equipment, Dell offers equipment disposition reports so you know right where the equipment ended up.

Customer Programs

Whereas businesses have to pay Dell for its recycling and repurposing services, consumers get free recycling. Dell will recycle any Dell machine ever built for free. If you have another brand of computer and buy a Dell, the company will dispose of your old machine for free.

The process is fairly straightforward. You can bring equipment in to be disposed, or you can arrange with Dell to have it picked up, though some small fees apply.

If you have late-model equipment, it may be eligible for a cash rebate voucher that can be used on any Dell product.

Dell gives the following estimates for computers that may still have some value:

- A desktop PC with an 833MHz Intel Pentium III CPU, 128MB memory, a 20GB hard disk drive, a CD drive, and no monitor is valued at around $50.
- A desktop PC with a 1.3GHz Intel Pentium IV CPU, 256MB memory, a 30GB hard disk drive, a CD drive, and 17-inch display is valued at around $110.

NOTE *For more information on recycling old hardware, flip back to Chapter 7.*

Datacenter

Dell has built its datacenter efforts around efficiency and using more environmentally friendly products.

Dell builds its Energy Smart datacenters as follows:

- By engineering products for energy efficiency
- By optimizing datacenters for specific customers
- By partnering with other industry members to drive change

NOTE *We'll talk more about datacenters in Chapter 11.*

Technology

Dell's PowerEdge line of servers were engineered to balance energy efficiency, performance, and cost. Efficiency has been enhanced through a number of technological improvements, including temperature-sensitive fan technology, more efficient power supplies, smaller form-factor hard drives, and low-voltage processor options.

The 40-watt Dual-Core Intel Xeon processor models consume up to 40 percent less energy than a standard dual-core processor running at the same frequency.

NOTE *Dell is also working with Microsoft and VMware to provide optimized virtualization solutions. We cover server virtualization more in Chapter 12.*

Combining power-consumption savings with reductions in cooling and power costs, the Dell datacenter solution can save businesses hundreds of dollars per server every year. Large datacenters can save more than US$1 million each year.

Dell offers a calculator on its website (see www.greenitinfo.com/links and click Link 9-1) that can help you compare server models and features. It also shows you the lessened environmental impact of a given model along with the cost savings, as Figure 9-1 shows.

Compared to standard configurations, using PowerEdge Energy Smart servers means:

- For every four servers, you can run a fifth at no additional energy cost.
- You can fit four more 2U servers per rack without adjusting the power specs.
- For every four racks, you can add one complete rack at no additional energy cost.

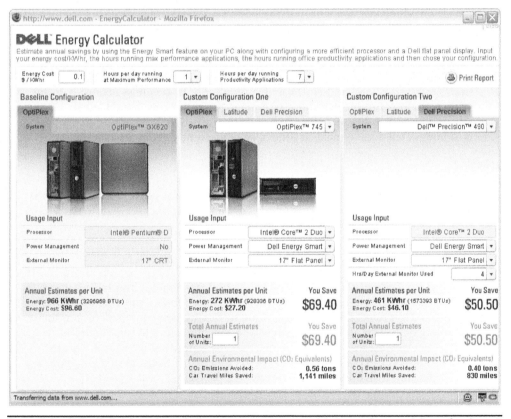

FIGURE 9-1 At the Dell datacenter website, you can compare models to see how much less of an impact a given server will have, along with the cost savings you can expect.

Professional Services

The Dell Datacenter Environmental Assessment (DCEA) helps customers determine the power consumption and cooling requirements for current and future deployments. This helps Dell's customers understand how to cool their datacenter as cost-effectively as possible.

The company also offers its Datacenter Capacity Planner, which helps businesses find the right size for their rack deployments and utilize the latest technology and density advancements.

Partnerships

Dell also utilizes partnerships with other companies to improve datacenter efficiencies. The company uses its Dell Power and Thermal Lab in Austin, Texas to study and address cooling issues that arise as datacenter densities increase.

The lab, which is 875 square feet, allows engineers to simulate the following:

- Various heating loads
- Model customer server loads
- Varying cooling capacities

The facility even has a smoke generator that can be used to study recirculating air patterns.

Dell is also working with various industry bodies to develop standards to help quantify the impact of energy efficiency of the datacenter. In the absence of standards, it's hard to quantify the impact of technology decisions.

Green Initiatives

Dell's efforts to be green are evident through a number of its business activities. From ecologically conscious products to the way it manages its supply chain, Dell focuses on environmental responsibility at every level of its organization. Let's take a closer look at the sorts of things Dell does to make as little of an environmental impact as it can.

Packaging

When we think of environmental responsibility, we immediately think about reduced toxins in the devices or we think of recycling programs. Although these are important issues that must be tended to, there are other places where environmental impact needs to be considered. An area we may not think of is packaging.

NOTE *Packaging waste accounts for more than 30 percent of U.S. solid waste.*

Dell has made efforts to reduce the sheer amount of packaging it uses to ship its products. The company starts by making its products more robust so that less packing material is needed to protect them. For organizations buying large numbers of computers, Dell offers multipacks. This allows shipments to be consolidated into smaller units.

This effort doesn't just result in a reduced impact on landfills. Like so many green issues, there is a savings to your bottom line. If you buy one of Dell's multipacks, you save on shipping costs and then on the cost to recycle that packaging.

NOTE *Because of Dell's efforts to reduce packaging costs in 2005, the amount of plastic foam and wood materials was reduced by 5258 tons. Dell's goal was 5000 tons.*

Manufacturing

Dell's supply chain is kept lean and mean. With a very tight inventory management philosophy, Dell builds its computers largely to order. This allows Dell to offer a larger catalog of product, while not necessarily having all that equipment preconfigured and waiting for a buyer.

Designing for the Environment

Dell has met the requirements of the European Union's restriction on the use of hazardous substances (the RoHS directive) globally. Dell changed its chemical use policy by committing to eliminate the use of brominated flame retardants and polyvinyl chloride from product designs by 2009.

Though Dell is a tech company, it still uses paper. To reduce impact there, Dell developed its Forest Products Stewardship program. Dell's marketing publications use on average 50 percent recycled content paper, meeting its 2009 goals 3 years early.

NOTE *For more information about RoHS and other official directives for environmentally friendly electronics, flip back to Chapter 2.*

Energy Smart

Dell has its own certification for eco-friendly equipment—Energy Smart. Dell Energy Smart combines energy-optimized hardware and software, energy-optimized professional services, and partnerships with regulatory bodies and standards organizations to help drive future innovation around energy-efficient products.

Dell's Energy Smart workstations, desktops, and notebooks can reduce power consumption by as much as 78 percent. That reduction, as we've said before, helps the environment as well as your bottom line.

Figure 9-2 shows the Energy Smart calculator.

As an example of Energy Smart savings, a server may cost about $100 more up front; however, it can save $200 each year in energy costs. Information about Dell's Energy Smart program can be found at Link 9-2.

Transportation

It isn't just what goes on behind Dell's front door that is making an impact. The company has also retooled its transportation operations to cut costs. Dell has undertaken several measures to lessen its greenhouse gas emissions:

- **SmartWay initiative** Carriers are encouraged to follow the Environmental Protection Agency's (EPA's) SmartWay initiative, in which shippers and transportation companies work in concert to develop the most efficient methods to save fuel and reduce emissions.

- **Head's up to customers** When a product is shipped to a customer, Dell sends out a notification so that the customer will be available to receive it. This reduces the number of times the delivery van has to drive to a customer.

- **Consolidated shipping** Dell instituted its less than truckload (LTL) Direct program to reduce the number of miles driven. Trailers were refitted with metal beams so that products could be double stacked. Airbags were positioned in the trailer to cushion the load.

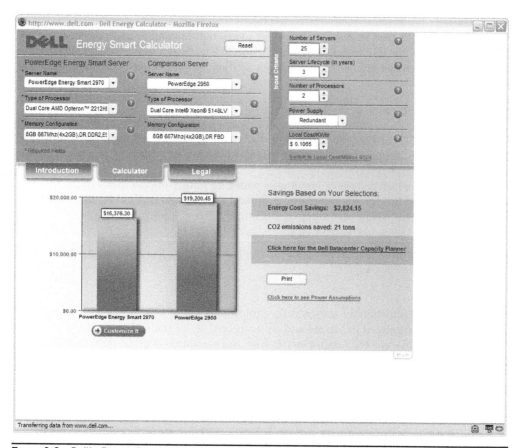

FIGURE 9-2   Dell's Energy Smart calculator can help illustrate how much money you'll save and what your environmental impact will be.

Supply Chain

Along with other electronics industry members, Dell helped develop the Electronic Industry Code of Conduct (EICC) to create a standardized industry code of conduct. Within the EICC, rather than punish noncompliance, the goal is to improve citizenship and operational efficiencies throughout the world.

NOTE   *The EICC's website address is www.eicc.info and can also be found at Link 9-3.*

Dell also uses it business process improvement (BPI) program to help suppliers improve their operations. In the program, Dell and its suppliers work together to mitigate problems, such as manufacturing quality, delivery, and cost. The EICC and BPI programs are important because they give Dell an opportunity to be a good corporate citizen and show partners where they can improve their own operations, from an environmental perspective.

Dell also requires that its suppliers report their greenhouse gas emissions. If a supplier doesn't report emissions data, it can affect the business it does with Dell. The amount of business done with a supplier can be affected by how well it is keeping a lid on greenhouse gas emissions. But Dell isn't being heavy-handed about it. If a supplier wants help in reducing emissions, Dell will work with it.

Facilities

Although Dell is trying to lessen its carbon footprint, it still makes a mark. Dell's biggest source of impact is from electricity consumption. In 2007, Dell's U.S. electricity usage accounted for 97.8 percent of its carbon emission.

To reduce the amount of electricity it uses, Dell has implemented several changes, including:

- A power management program that turns off machines when not in use. That saved 13 million kWh of electricity, which equates to 8500 tons of CO_2 and US$1.8 million in savings.
- Renovated lighting in its Texas facilities. This gave the company a 9 percent reduction in power consumption.

However, facilities considerations aren't just about electricity usage. Dell has set a goal to have all facilities certified through the Leadership in Energy and Environmental Design (LEED) green building rating system. Those same standards will be applied to new buildings and remodeling projects.

Customer Interaction

Dell wants to keep its customers close to its efforts in being environmentally aware. It does this through a number of programs in which the customer can be actively involved with Dell to help reduce toxins and carbon emissions.

Education

Dell's enviro-responsibility doesn't take place in a vacuum. The company actively communicates with customers and other stakeholders. Dell has a number of customer communications programs, the idea being to educate them about energy efficiency as well as other environmental issues, such as climate change and pollution.

That educational process starts when a computer is purchased online. When a customer configures a computer, the website walks them through the process, helping them make responsible choices. If a customer is interested in configuring their computer environmentally, the site can provide better suggestions with power management enabled by default.

Servers can be compared, side by side, so that in addition to model features, you can see how much electricity a given server uses, and how much your cost savings would be over a 6-month period.

Dell reports that it has seen increased visits to its website for its Environmental Data Sheets and online energy calculators. When customers review a data sheet, it gives Dell a chance to make a pitch for EPEAT-rated equipment, and then show the EPEAT rating, energy consumption, and other information about the product's materials.

Calculators can also show customers how their power management settings and monitor choices will result in environmental impact. This is communicated as CO_2 emissions and energy savings.

"Plant a Tree for Me"

Your computer is still going to use electricity, and it will still make some sort of impact on the environment. In an effort to offset the CO_2 emissions generated by a new Dell computer, the company has started its "Plant a Tree for Me" program.

The program—a joint effort among Dell, The Conservation Fund, and Carbonfund.org—allows customers to donate a fee that will be used to plant a tree. The idea is that the tree will allow consumers to offset the carbon emissions that their Dell computer will use over a 3-year time period.

Customers can donate US$2 for a notebook and US$6 for a desktop. All of those funds go toward planting trees and reforestation efforts.

An extension of the "Plant a Tree for Me" project is "Plant a Forest for Me." This is a corporate extension of the program where millions of trees are planted in sustainably managed areas. Many companies—such as Staples and Ask.com—have committed to participate in the program to offset some of their carbon impact by purchasing trees.

Hewlett-Packard

In the previous section, we talked about Dell. Not even 25 years old, the company started in its founder's dorm room has made it a mission to be the tops when it comes to environmental responsibility. But while that young whippersnapper Dell has been at this green thing for just a few years, Hewlett-Packard (HP) has been doing the heavy lifting for half a century.

A jaded onlooker might consider the HP of today and say, "Oh, it's just jumping on the bandwagon," but they'd be wrong. HP has been a leader when it comes to social issues, from philanthropy to labor issues to the environment.

This section covers HP and what it does for the Green IT cause. We'll look at the company's recycling programs and its business practices. But before we get to that, let's take a look at HP's rich history of doing the right thing.

History

HP has a long commitment to environmental responsibility and has been a few degrees ahead of the curve for a long time. True, it didn't start recycling efforts and energy conservation efforts from the get go, but in a lot of cases it was the first company to have started such initiatives.

Table 9-1 shows a timeline summary of HP's environmental efforts.

HP's eco-friendly business practices don't seem to be slowing down, either. The company has set a goal to reduce its overall global energy use by 20 percent by 2010. To get below 2005 levels, HP plans to introduce energy-efficient products and services to customers and institute energy-efficient operating practices in its global facilities.

The goal fits in with the company's global environmental strategy that addresses three levels of business: products, internal operations, and supply chain management. Recent changes that HP sees helping the company reach that goal include:

- The introduction of select HP desktop business PCs that offer 80 percent efficient power supplies and were the first to meet the U.S. Environmental Protection Agency's new Energy Star 4.0 requirements. The new power supplies are 33 percent more efficient than their predecessors.

Year	Achievement
1957	Citizenship company objective established by Bill Hewlett and Dave Packard.
1970	Glen Affleck is named to the newly created post of environment control coordinator for HP.
1971	HP starts recycling of computer printouts and computer punch cards.
1973	HP establishes environmental policy to continually monitor its operations to reduce pollution.
1975	HP establishes Energy Conservation Guidelines to encourage employees to conserve energy and reduce costs.
1976	HP starts van pools in the California Bay Area.
1977	Seventy-three carpool locators are organized to assist employees in California.
1987	Computer product recycling is launched internally.
1988	HP Hazardous Waste Minimization Council is formed to develop a corporatewide strategy.
1989	Polyvinyl chloride (PVC) is removed from HP's DeskJet packaging.
1990	Chlorine-bleached white boxes for the DeskJet are replaced with natural, more environmentally responsible brown boxes.
1991	HP establishes the Planet Partner LaserJet print cartridge recycling program.
1992	HP becomes one of the first U.S. Environmental Protection Agency's (EPA) Energy Star partners. HP launches the Design for Environment program with a focus on energy efficiency, material use, and design for recycling.
1993	HP stops the use of ozone-depleting substances in its manufacturing operations worldwide, 2 years ahead of an international ban.
1994	HP publishes its first annual environmental report. HP's first packaging management system is created and includes environmental guidelines to decrease the environmental impact of its product packaging. HP becomes one of the first companies worldwide to encourage telecommuting by formalizing its telecommuting policy. HP Labs starts work on smart cooling technology for datacenters.
1996	HP eliminates the use of all ethylene glycol ethers in manufacturing. HP joins the U.S. Environmental Protection Agency (EPA) PFC (perfluorocarbons) Reduction Climate Partnership to reduce specified PFC emissions by 10 percent from 1995 levels by the end of 2010.
1997	HP establishes the Planet Partners inkjet print cartridge recycling program. HP opens its first recycling facility in Roseville, California, becoming the only major computer manufacturer to operate its own recycling facility.
1998	A small group of HP employees form the HP Sustainability Network, a group interested in sustainability at work and at home.

TABLE 9-1   HP's Long History of Environmental Efforts (*Continued*)

PART IV

Year	Achievement
1999	Thirty-millionth LaserJet cartridge is recycled through the Planet Partners recycling program.
	HP inkjet printer is the first on the market to achieve German eco-label Blue Angel certification, 3 years earlier than any competitor.
	HP DeskJet 970 offers first inkjet duplexer producing two-sided printing capability and the opportunity to reduce paper consumption.
2000	HP is one of the first global businesses to achieve companywide ISO 14001 certification of its worldwide manufacturing operations.
2001	HP opens a second U.S. recycling facility in Nashville, Tennessee.
2002	HP publishes its first combined Social and Environmental Responsibility Report.
	HP releases its Supply Chain Code of Conduct, which extends the company's ability to manage suppliers' conformance to social and environmental standards.
2003	In the 12 years of Planet Partners operations, more than 176 million pounds (80 million kilograms) of HP LaserJet and inkjet print cartridge materials have been returned and recycled worldwide.
	HP recycled plastic is included in the first hardware product replacing virgin plastic with material obtained from end-of-life HP products.
	HP announces a "smart" cooling solution for datacenters that dramatically reduces energy use and saves customers money.
2004	HP ranks eighth overall in the Accountability Rating, the first global index that evaluates how well the world's 100 largest companies account for their impacts on society and the environment. HP is the only U.S. company ranked in the top ten.
	HP co-develops the Electronic Industry Code of Conduct to promote industry standards for socially responsible business practices across global supply chains.
	HP has recycled more than 750 million pounds (340 million kilograms) of hardware and HP print cartridges globally to date.
2005	HP begins a free hardware recycling service in the European Union in advance of the EU Waste Electrical and Electronic Equipment (WEEE) Directive.
	HP ships its first fully EU RoHS (Restriction of Hazardous Substances)–compliant products.
2006	HP has recycled more than 920 million pounds (417 million kilograms) of hardware and HP print cartridges globally.
	HP launches the Focused Improvement Supplier Initiative in China and the Central European Supplier Responsibility project, two capability-building projects to help suppliers build management skills for social and environmental responsibility.
	HP and the World Wildlife Fund (WWF) announce a joint initiative to reduce HP's greenhouse gas emissions from its worldwide operations.
	HP reduces onsite greenhouse gas emissions by 31 percent from 2005 levels, surpassing its goal.

TABLE 9-1   HP's Long History of Environmental Efforts (*Continued*)

Year	Achievement
2007	HP marks the 20th anniversary of its recycling programs.
	HP announces several energy-efficient products and services:
	• Dynamic Smart Cooling
	• C-Class blade servers with embedded thermal logic
	• Desktop business PCs that offer 80-percent-efficient power supplies; these products meet the new Energy Star 4.0 requirements
	• Extended Halo Studios
	• HP BladeSystems
	HP sets a goal to reduce its global energy use by 20 percent of 2005 levels by 2010.
	HP donates $2 million to the World Wildlife Fund (WWF) to advance the science and education of climate change.
	Polyvinyl chloride (PVC) is removed from all HP packaging designs.
	HP meets the goal of recycling 1 billion pounds of electronics and HP print cartridges 6 months early. HP has a new goal of recovering a cumulative 2 billion pounds of electronics and print cartridges by the end of 2010, doubling the annual recovery rate.

TABLE 9-1 HP's Long History of Environmental Efforts (*Continued*)

- Dynamic Smart Cooling, which is designed to deliver 20 to 45 percent savings in cooling costs for datacenters.
- Redesigned print cartridge packaging for North America. The new process was expected to reduce greenhouse gas emissions by 37 million pounds in 2007.

Recycling Programs

As you saw in Table 9-1, HP's recycling efforts go back to 1971. Though the company started with recycling computer printouts, over the years its efforts have evolved to include inkjet cartridges, computers, and most other devices. Programs are geared at customers and businesses, and they give several options for customers who want to get rid of old equipment.

Since 1987 the company has been recycling technology products and currently offers recycling services in 45 countries.

HP uses company-approved recycling vendors to handle product that cannot be reused. Recyclers dismantle equipment and process materials to extract as much value as possible.

NOTE *In Europe, HP was key in the creation of the European Recycling Platform and Nordic Electronics Recycling Association. This helped the company comply with European Union producer responsibility recycling legislation.*

Recycling vendors must meet HP's supplier code of conduct and global recycling standards. These standards require vendors to handle and process equipment so that toxins are not released into the environment. It also prohibits the export of whole equipment or recovered materials without the company's consent.

NOTE *HP monitors compliance through site audits.*

Customer Programs

HP has a number of ways that customers can return their old products for recycling. In some cases, the customer might realize some cost savings off a new HP product, but whether the customer gets some savings or not, they get to recycle the machine knowing that it is being done in an environmentally responsible way.

Trade-In HP is also cutting down the amount of thrown-away computers by allowing customers to trade in used equipment. They can either get a check from HP or apply the amount the equipment is worth to a new HP purchase.

To get a quote, HP just needs information about the device, including product type, manufacturer, model, condition, and the consumer's ZIP Code. Then, HP will provide a prepaid shipping label for the item. You can get a quote from HP by using the tool at Link 9-4. This is shown in Figure 9-3.

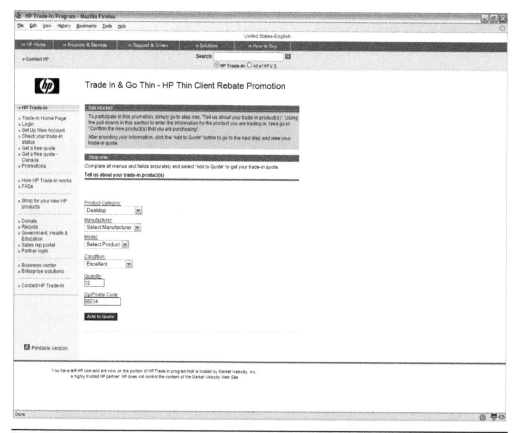

FIGURE 9-3 Customers can get a quote on their trade-in at the HP website.

For businesses or other organizations that want to trade in more than 50 machines, have multiple locations, or have an extended rollout period, HP has a custom quote tool, as shown in Figure 9-4. This tool is located at Link 9-5.

Wal-Mart Partnership   In 2007, HP and Wal-Mart teamed up to offer a free recycling program for purchasers of the HP DeskJet F4140 All-in-One printer. The idea was (besides moving product) to recognize the efforts of consumers who purchase all-in-one products, which reduce the amount of devices one purchases and therefore has to power and ultimately get rid of.

Customers who purchased the DeskJet printer could go to the HP or Wal-Mart website, print a prepaid mailing label, box up old electronic equipment, and then ship it to one of HP's U.S. recycling facilities.

Reuse

HP offers its own reuse programs (HP Renew and Asset Recovery Services) that help extend the life of computer equipment and reduce the environmental impacts of their disposal.

The programs also make it possible for customers to purchase pre-owned equipment that has been returned to HP. Additionally, HP can build computers to a customer's specific needs, using refurbished equipment.

Though it sounds like customers are getting old, mediocre equipment, the programs offer remanufactured equipment that is as little as 6 months old. The program is available worldwide.

Remanufactured equipment comes from various sources:

- Customer returns
- Cancelled orders
- Products damaged in shipping
- Trade-ins
- Buy-backs
- Loaned equipment
- Leased equipment

The products are refurbished, reboxed, and resold, usually with an HP warranty. The company sells products from most of its product lines, including printers, personal computers, and monitors.

NOTE *HP has even remarketed entire datacenters.*

If HP deems that a returned product cannot be refurbished, it is sold through brokers into the reuse market.

Donate

For customers who don't want to see their computers recycled and want to do something responsible with them, HP has also partnered with the National Christina Foundation to facilitate the donation of used or unwanted technology equipment.

PART IV

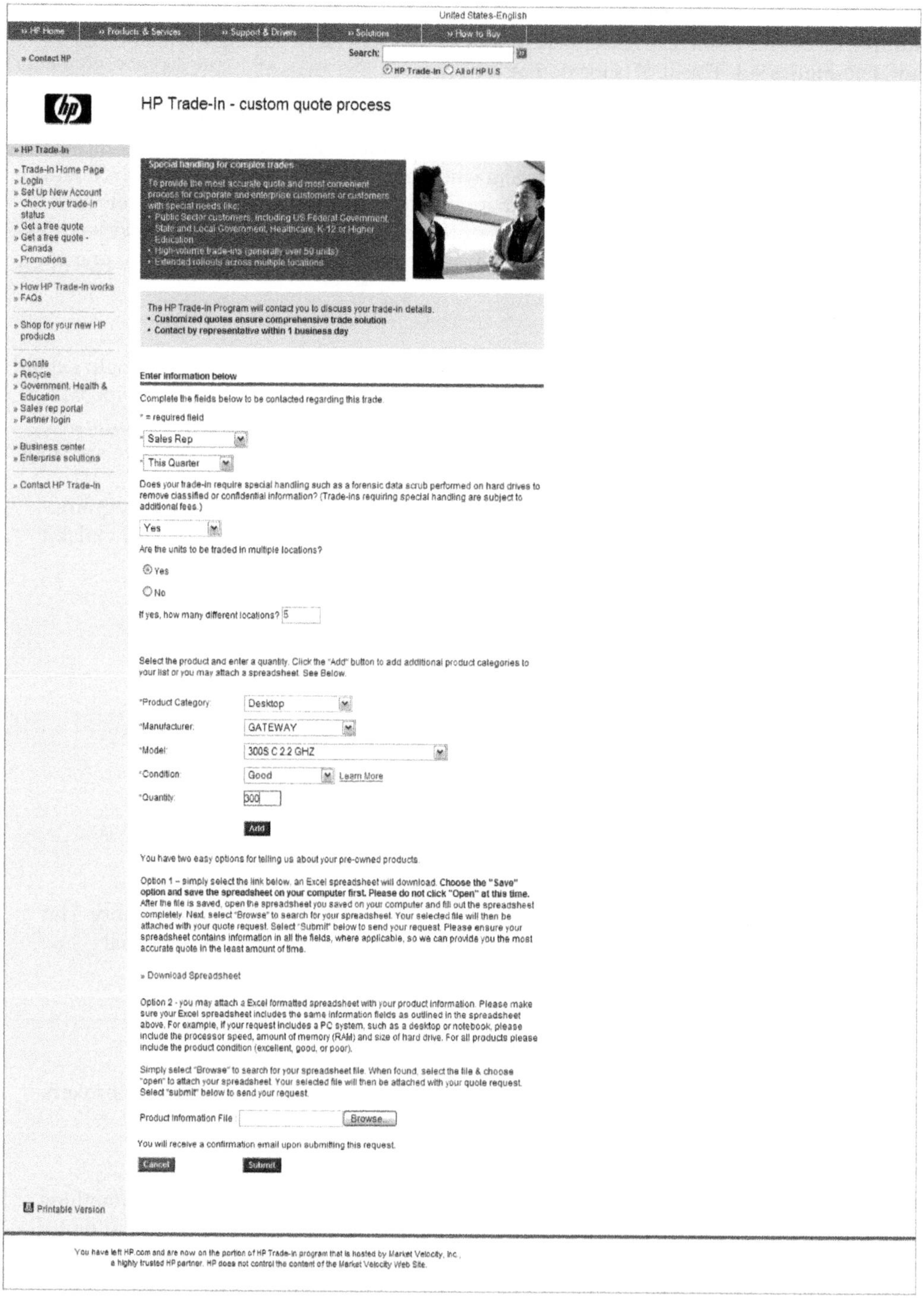

FIGURE 9-4 If your organization wants to trade in a lot of computers, HP offers a custom quote tool at its website.

The national Cristina Foundation provides computer technology and solutions to give people with disabilities, students at risk, and economically disadvantaged persons the opportunity, through training, to lead more independent and productive lives.

HP will accept PCs, notebooks, Intel-based servers, printers, scanners, monitors, copiers, plotters, projectors, digital cameras, PDAs, networking equipment, and data storage devices by most manufacturers.

Ink and Toner

HP is as well known for its printers as it is for its computers. When you think about the enormity of HP's printer efforts, you realize that those printers don't work in a vacuum—they need ink and toner cartridges. Another place HP is looking to be environmentally responsible is by producing inkjet cartridges made of recycled used cartridges, water bottles, and other plastics.

Between 2005 and 2007, the company manufactured 200 million inkjet cartridges with recycled content. By converting old HP cartridges into new ones, the company says it has diverted about 8.8 million pounds of recyclable plastic from landfills. The company's new recycling process allows them to produce ink cartridges made up of 70 to 100 percent recycled content. In 2006, HP used in excess of 5 million pounds of recycled plastic in manufacturing inkjet cartridges. The company plans to double that amount.

HP acquires ink cartridges returned though its Planet Partners product recycling program, which allows consumers to return HP products to the company for free.

Business Operations

HP has a number of initiatives that help it be environmentally responsible. Processes are going on at all levels of the company to ensure that it is lessening its carbon footprint.

Design for Environment

HP has integrated environmental considerations into its product designs, taking into account such issues as energy efficiency, provisions for reuse, and recycling. HP introduces new materials to meet customer expectations, to capitalize on emerging technologies, and to substitute for materials of concern.

HP minimizes materials, utilizes recycled and recyclable materials when possible, and reduces packaging size and weight to improve transportation fuel efficiency.

Figure 9-5 highlights the features of HP's attention to environmental detail at different levels of its product life cycle.

Transportation is a key part of HP's environmental considerations. With customers around the world, a lot can be done in the realm of logistics that can make a huge dent on the environment—or make much less of one. HP's logistics initiatives, such as efficient planning and alternative pallets, help reduce the amount of energy the company consumes.

Most of HP's products are assembled in Asia, but sold in Europe and the Americas. Product is typically shipped from Asia to regional distribution centers for delivery to their final destinations by truck or rail. Air transport is used for lighter products, such as cameras, and when speedy delivery is necessary. Servers are normally built in the region where they are sold.

Although HP relies on fossil fuels for ships, trucks, and aircraft, its Design for Logistics program streamlines the efficiency throughout HP and decreases the energy use per pound of product transported.

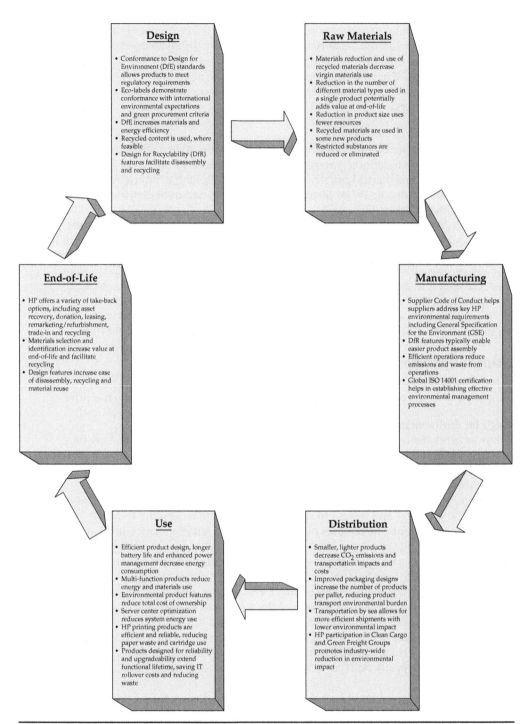

Figure 9-5 Each level of HP's product life cycle is committed to environmental responsibility.

HP also tries to ship product by sea, rather than air, whenever possible. This results in less CO_2 emissions. As Figure 9-6 shows, each ton of freight sent by air results in 0.6 kg of CO_2 emissions, compared to 0.003 kg for sea transport.

Transportation is the number-one source of pollution on the planet. HP is trying to reduce its impact by shipping as much freight as possible by sea. Although you may not have the need to ship product by sea, there's still good sense in examining your own shipping needs and consolidating them as much as possible. For instance, instead of shipping three quarter-filled trucks with product, wait until you can put those three shipments into one truck. Obviously you want to send product as expeditiously as possible, but try and determine whether you can make your own processes more efficient. With gas prices as high as they are, not only will you be reducing environmental harm, you'll also be saving some money—maybe a lot.

Supply Chain Management

An enormously complex part of HP's business is in its supply chain management. The company supports the IT industry's largest, most complex supply chain. It deals with governments, other big businesses, all the way down to the corner drug store.

HP spends more than US$50 billion each year in materials, components, manufacturing, and distribution. HP has made a commitment to be a positive force in the communities where it operates. Investing in supply chain social and environmental responsibility (SER) and supplier diversity helps HP achieve its global citizenship goals.

Social and Environmental Responsibility (SER)   HP has made a commitment to protect international human rights wherever it can, and the company is especially dedicated to making a positive effect on the workers who manufacture its products. That commitment is reflected in HP's Human Rights policy and through its SER program.

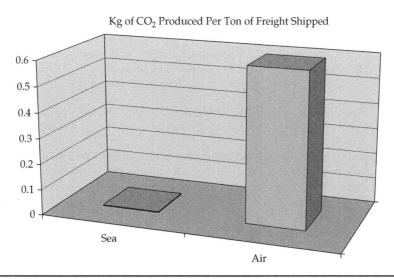

FIGURE 9-6   Shipping freight by sea results in a 200-times reduction of CO_2 generated.

HP has made commitments to the following:

- Integrating supplier SER into its sourcing operations
- Protecting worker rights
- Improving suppliers' working conditions and health and safety
- Reducing suppliers' environmental footprint
- Collaborating with nongovernmental organizations (NGOs) and stakeholders to validate, inform, and improve HP's efforts
- Participating in industrywide initiatives to leverage its efforts across the electronics sector

In 2002, HP established its Supply Chain Social and Environmental Responsibility Policy and its Supplier Code of Conduct. The goal of these programs is to extend HP's social and environmental policies to its supply chain.

In 2004, HP was part of the group that developed the EICC, which helps foster responsible practices in labor, human rights, health and safety, the environment, and ethics across the electronic industry's global supply chain.

Supplier Diversity   Another component of HP's supply chain is an element of diversity. HP says it embraces a diverse supply chain because this will bring in fresh ideas, innovative products and processes, and make a contribution to the economic strength of the communities in which HP operates. In the U.S., HP's supplier diversity program is aimed at businesses that are minority-owned, women-owned, and veteran-owned.

The program is expanding in Europe, and it will require establishing new regional definitions of diversity that reflect local society and culture. HP is working with local governments to do that.

Product Innovations

HP has made products for years that meet Energy Star, RoHS, and other guidelines, but it isn't just the machines that sit on your staff's desks that HP concerns itself with. The company is also looking at what it can do to help keep energy costs down in the datacenter.

Datacenter

HP has focused some of its environmental efforts on the datacenter, specifically developing technologies and tools that can help organizations achieve better energy efficiency and cost savings.

HP performs datacenter assessments using high-tech modeling technologies. This shows where efficiencies can be realized and how cooling can be optimized. An option HP offers is 3-D Thermal Zone Mapping, which shows a multicolored thermal map of the entire datacenter. Data from that model is used by the customer to organize the datacenter for best efficiency and savings.

With this data, the customer can do the following:

- Understand the thermal characteristics of their datacenter.
- Identify overlapping regions of cooling capacity. This is ideal because high-density and/or mission-critical equipment could be located there for optimal cooling.

- Analyze "what-if" scenarios, including room layout or infrastructure changes as well as cooling capacity changes or failures.
- Ensure that a proper cooling solution has been achieved by addressing areas of overprovisioning and smoothing out isolated hotspots.

Dynamic Smart Cooling

We talked about it a bit in Chapter 4, but HP's Dynamic Smart Cooling bears inclusion here. The system is designed to deliver 20- to 45-percent savings in cooling energy costs, or allow additional equipment to be added to the datacenter while keeping costs steady.

The system uses an intelligent control node to continually adjust air conditioning settings based on real-time air temperature measurements, which are based on feedback from sensors positioned on IT racks.

HP is implementing this program in its six new consolidated datacenters in three geographic zones of the U.S.

Rackspace

Rackspace, a Houston, Texas–based IT hosting company, realizes that it can't be all things to all people. While the company wants its customers to take advantage of the computational power in its servers, it also wants to be a responsible company. To do both, Rackspace allows its customers to meet in the middle.

When buying a server, customers can select either one with basic specs, or they can choose a server that has been built with green IT in mind. A visit to their website (www.rackspace.com, also Link 9-6) shows how you can buy a preconfigured, greener option. A basic model and its greener counterpart are shown in Figures 9-7 and 9-8, respectively.

But that isn't to suggest that the servers are the greenest options on the planet. They are just better than regularly configured servers.

"We're trying to find a sweet spot between performance and being green," says Rackspace CIO John Enright. "We tried to find the best mixture of components. You can get high performance, but then you lack efficiency. As you go further down, you get more efficiency, but less performance."

Rackspace is also seeing a surge in customer demand for consolidation. As such, they're offering VMware on their servers and virtual machines on those servers.

Embracing a New Idea

Rackspace ventured into the realm of efficiency because their United Kingdom and European datacenters were mandated to be more efficient. While adhering to European Union laws, Rackspace decided to implement better efficiency company-wide.

"Green awareness has certainly been up recently, but two years ago when we started, there really was none," said Enright.

Soon, customers were asking for greener solutions.

"It took on a life of its own," remembered Enright.

At one point, Rackspace hosted a "Green Day," which allowed vendors to come in and talk about the environmental benefits of their products. The next step was to survey their customers and find out if they would be willing to pay extra for more efficient equipment. It turns out that they would.

FIGURE 9-7   Customers can buy "regular" server configurations.

Rackspace also offers a unique feature on its website, as shown in Figure 9-9.

While on-line chat in and of itself is not unique, it is unique what Rackspace is doing with the conversations. When a chat session is concluded, it is archived and data-mined to study information about green usage and preferences.

"We're seeing a lot of interest in green IT," said Enright. "There's nobody saying, 'It's a terrible idea.'"

Green IT Up

Since introducing more efficient servers, Rackspace has decided to take environmental responsibility as a core business value.

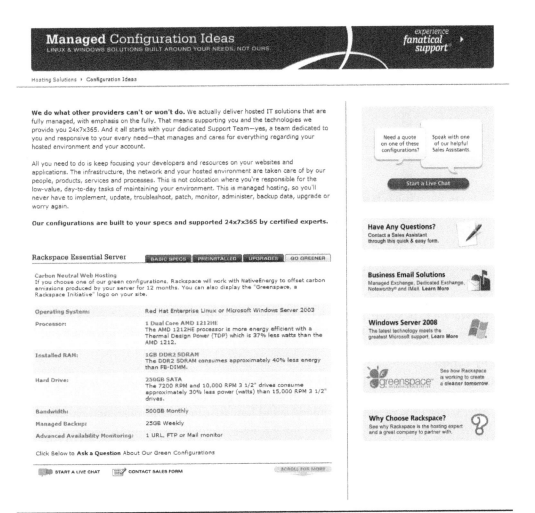

FIGURE 9-8 Rackspace allows a "Go Greener" option that allows customers to buy servers that are more ecologically friendly.

"We've thought about a lot of things," said Enright. "Like how to buy renewable energy."

For instance, its United Kingdom location uses 100 percent renewable energy. They are trying to find renewable energy resources in the United States. They also offer an offset program called "Native Energy." The program offers funding green projects on their behalf.

But while carbon offsets are Rackspace's solution now, they are looking for a better way to use renewable energy.

"One complaint about carbon offset is the question often arises, 'Are you sure it's funding green energy?'" observed Enright.

While still using carbon offsets, the company is looking for the next step beyond.

Additionally, Rackspace is building a new datacenter in San Antonio and they are taking the opportunity to make it as environmentally friendly as possible. But, like their servers, they can't go to the extreme. There is a balance to be struck.

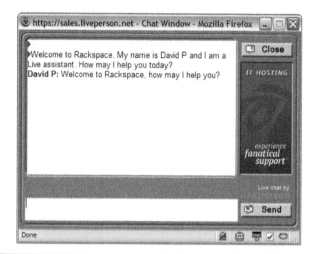

FIGURE 9-9 Visitors can chat with Rackspace representatives on the company's website.

"We want it to be green, but we have to balance it with business needs," said Enright. "We're also considering LEED certification. We're doing things on a lot of different fronts."

Supply Chain

Rackspace is looking beyond its walls to be environmentally responsible, and is trying to pull in their supply chain partners and whoever else they deal with.

"After Green Day, we started thinking about how we can reduce, reuse, and recycle," said Enright. "Then employees started thinking about relationships with vendors."

The company had already done away with paper manuals and then they started talking to server vendors about packaging. As a result, when possible, multiple servers are consolidated into a single package for shipment.

In 2007, Rackspace joined other environmentally conscious tech companies to be part of the Green Grid. The group is a consortium that advocates for ecologically responsible technology, and also serves as a knowledge clearinghouse for its members.

"The outcome is you have regular conversations about what they're all doing," said Enright. "It's better working together than working in isolation."

The rush to environmental responsibility is motivated by the desire to be responsible, but that desire is driven by business.

"It is market-driven," said Enright. "Datacenters are in short supply and you need to be able to fit more into the datacenter. For the suppliers, it's a competitive fear. If they don't do it, someone else will come in and do it."

Technology companies make a huge impact on the environment—both in what they make and how they make it. But the heads of many of these companies aren't evil villains, twirling their mustaches while they poison the planet. Although they still make an impact on the planet, they are trying to do what they can to minimize the effects. In the next chapter, we'll take a closer look at what some other, non-IT companies are doing to green their operations.

Other Organizations

G oing green" means different things to different organizations. Although the crux of this book is on Green IT, we don't want to forget other utilizations of technology to propel you toward your green goals. Green IT is, of course, very important, but it's helpful to see how other initiatives can help you.

In the preceding chapter, we looked at technology companies Dell and Hewlett-Packard. Let's now change gears a bit and look at organizations that aren't specifically technology based and see what sorts of unique things they are doing to reduce their carbon footprint.

We'll start off with an examination of the University of Wisconsin–River Falls. The university not only offers programs geared toward environmental responsibility, but is also practicing it, as well as reaching out to its community.

The second half of the chapter is an examination of the world's largest retailer—Wal-Mart. You might do a double-take to hear Wal-Mart being mentioned, but it's true: Wal-Mart is making great strides in going green. The company's ultimate goal is to have a zero impact on the Earth. Will Wal-Mart do this? Who knows, but you can't fault it for a lack of effort.

Although the measures taken by these organizations aren't directly related to IT, you should consider these case studies from the standpoint of what is possible for you to do. Although you may not pursue the sorts measures the University of Wisconsin–River Falls did, you can look at your own issues with innovation in mind. That's what both these organizations did.

University of Wisconsin–River Falls

The University of Wisconsin–River Falls (UWRF) is located in River Falls, Wisconsin on the trout fishing Kinnickinnic River. UWRF is a 226-acre campus that consists of 32 major buildings. The university also has two laboratory farms containing a total of 440 acres of land.

University staff and students have made a commitment to environmental efforts, not the least of which is the recent opening of a sustainable student center and its involvement with the community. The school's St. Croix Institute for Sustainable Community Development website contains information about the program and activities underscoring this commitment. It can be found at Link 10-1.

University Center

Throughout this book we've pressed the notion that it's really up to the CEO to drive ecologically responsible change. Although that's true the vast majority of the time, in some cases change can come from deep in the heart of an organization. Take UWRF, for instance.

In January 2008, the school opened its US$35 million University Center (UC). The center was the brainchild of two university students, and then backed by the student body. The center, shown in Figure 10-1, incorporates green and sustainable design principles.

The facility represents an enormous commitment by the students. All told, US$32.9 million of the project came from student fees—in essence, the students voted to tax themselves for the project.

"Thanks to the vision and determination of university leaders, and particularly our students, the UC will serve as a model for bringing people together to learn, collaborate, create, and enjoy," said UWRF Chancellor Don Betz. "It will also be a tangible example of UWRF's commitment to sustainability and to being good stewards of our resources. This is a defining moment in the 133-year history of this distinguished institution."

The 140,000-square-foot building signifies the nascent UW System sustainability initiative, announced in 2007 by Wisconsin governor Jim Doyle. The governor announced that four UW System campuses, including UWRF, UW–Stevens Point, UW–Green Bay, and UW–Oshkosh, will take the lead toward going "off the grid" in the next 5 years.

Practicing What They Preach

Kelly Cain, professor of environmental science and management, said that the facility also grew out of the need to put into practice what students were learning. Although the students were learning important lessons about environmental responsibility, the college wasn't doing what it was teaching.

"We are not walking the talk, in terms of what we were teaching in the classroom," said Cain.

A number of years ago, Earth Consciousness Organization (ECO) club members and 2001 graduates Rusty Callier and Phyllis Jaworski tracked energy use, water consumption, and waste generation in campus buildings for an academic project. Their project culminated

FIGURE 10-1
The University of Wisconsin–River Falls' University Center is a sustainable building, paid for by students.

in an outline of how sustainable and green design principles could be utilized in campus buildings starting with a student union.

"The students felt this offered a chance to move the university toward sustainability and set the example for the rest of the community and the UW System," said Cain, also an advisor to Callier and Jaworski's project. The pair presented their findings to the UW System Board of Regents, who embraced the guidelines. Another student, Ryan Perkl, was then instrumental in leading Student Advocacy to commit and contribute 1 million USD to the project. Using UWRF student funded fees helped make the new UC a reality.

Student Life

The University Center is the primary building for student life and serves as a student commitment that began with the initial idea and grew into a committee of students who helped oversee the planning and design process and continued as students helped complete and ready the building for use. Student positions include a building manager lead workers, receptionists, event coordinators, and food and retail services, according to Mike Stifter, director of student life programming.

"One of the underlying principles that predated my time in the student life programming area is that if we can put our jobs in the hands of students, that is a good thing," said Stifter. "We are in the process of hiring students in all areas."

In the last few months before the University Center opened, Stifter estimates that more than 2500 student hours were devoted to everything from planning grand-opening activities to final touches on the building, including computer wiring and installation by Frednet, the student-run computer center.

Green Building

A wall of glass spans the building façade on the south side, mirroring the gentle curve of the South Fork of the Kinnickinnic River, which it overlooks. The world-class trout stream offers a natural beauty that sets the campus apart from others in the region. In addition, the natural resource offers bountiful opportunities to learn about and protect the meandering waterway amid walking trails and native plants.

The commitment to reclaim and recycle materials started with the deconstruction of the Ames Education Building, the site on which the new UC is constructed. For example, several architectural elements from Ames were retained for their aesthetic qualities and used as seating as well as ornamentation and sculpture in the UC.

The design highlights local, natural materials, such as stone from Winona, Minnesota. The interior makes use of natural lighting and earth-inspired colors throughout. Green design principles include a 48,000 gallon storage capacity under the building for collecting rainwater from the roof that is filtered back into the building where it's used to flush toilets.

A white roof that reflects sunlight is intended to decrease summer cooling costs, and energy-efficient windows, LED and photoelectric lighting, and water-saving fixtures will maximize savings. All cleaning chemicals used in the building are nontoxic and environmentally friendly, and low volatile organic compound paints, sealers, and adhesives were used as much as possible.

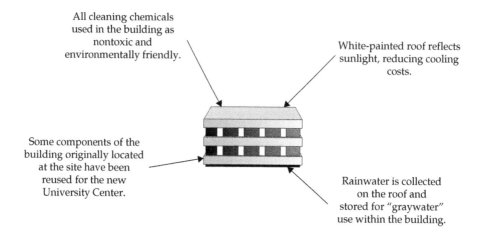

All cleaning chemicals used in the building as nontoxic and environmentally friendly.

White-painted roof reflects sunlight, reducing cooling costs.

Some components of the building originally located at the site have been reused for the new University Center.

Rainwater is collected on the roof and stored for "graywater" use within the building.

An environmental kiosk highlights campus sustainability initiatives and monitors the building's resource consumption, which is estimated to be 40 percent less than comparable buildings, according to energy auditors Arnold & O'Sheridan, Inc.

Features

The east area by the south entrance features an outdoor bonfire area with a natural landscaped amphitheater for up to 75 people. The North Mall commons is another area designed for outdoor events.

Meeting rooms are named after rivers in the Lower St. Croix and Upper Mississippi watersheds, including the Chippewa, St. Croix, Rush, Red Cedar, Kinnickinnic, Mississippi, Eau Galle, Apple, Willow, Trimbelle, and Wind.

Amenities in the new building include bi-level game room with Xbox 360, Nintendo Wii, and PlayStation 3 console cabinets, a state-of-the-art multimedia theater with seating capacity for 150, an entertainment complex with a second-level balcony, large-screen plasma televisions, and state-of-the-art staging, sound, and lighting equipment for concerts, productions, and special events.

The Cyber Café features 12 computer kiosks as well as coffee and snacks, and the building offers wireless access. Food service includes several retail outlets and Riverside Commons, a buffet-style dining area featuring various cooking stations.

A branch of the First National Bank of River Falls is also open in the University Center, along with an information desk, copy center, student involvement/services office complex, and convenience store, with Heritage Hall rounding out the new facility.

University Center Quick Facts

The University Center has a number of efficient systems in place. It's a testament to how ecologically friendly technologies are changing.

"The technologies we had to fight for 5 years ago are run of the mill now," observed Cain. Some of the building's features include:

- Materials from the deconstruction of the Ames Education Building, the previous building on the site, were reclaimed, reused, and recycled as much as possible by the demolition and salvage firm.

- Stone benches, metal tables and supports, and the Cup of Knowledge sculpture and support beam in the Heritage Hall of the University Center are elements reused from Ames.

- Waste from the construction of the University Center was reclaimed, reused, and recycled as much as possible by the general contractor.

- The roof rainwater collection system, mentioned earlier, will allow for filtered storage of up to 48,000 gallons of water under the building to use for gray water purposes, such as flushing toilets and exterior irrigation. This system will also drastically reduce stormwater surges that would normally end up in the Kinnickinnic River. Stormwater surges can deplete the amount of dissolved oxygen in the river, which can cause trout mortality. With a 1-inch rainfall, more than 34,000 gallons can be collected from the roof.

- The white roof is designed to reflect heat and decrease heat absorption into the building, thus decreasing cooling costs in the summer.

- Low-E thermoglass in a deep mullion cap on the south side bank of windows is an energy-saving measure.

- The efficient heat recovery system uses direct air exchangers.

- Photoelectric on/off lighting as well as motion lights and timers are connected with the facility scheduling system.

- Light-emitting diodes (LEDs) in the lighting system use much less energy than incandescent light bulbs or fluorescent lighting.

- An energy analysis determined that the building will be greater than 40 percent more efficient than buildings of a similar size and usage.

- Water-efficient landscaping plans utilize native plants and grasses, and require no freshwater for irrigation.

- The detention swale adjacent to the parking area retains and cools stormwater before it enters the surrounding river system.

- Nontoxic, environmentally friendly cleaning products are used throughout the building.

- A special pulp process for food service waste has been installed that uses less water than traditional "garbage disposal" methods and provides the ability to complement a food waste compost system planned for the future.

PART IV

- Furniture in the Involvement Center is constructed of wood from certified sustainable forests (CSFs).

- Use of bamboo flooring in the dining area utilizes a durable, readily renewable natural resource capable of rapid regrowth.

- Low volatile organic compound (VOC) substances such as glues, paints, and floor sealers were used in the construction of the building.

- An environmental education kiosk highlights UWRF sustainability initiatives as well as provides a continuous monitoring of resources used by the University Center, including current and average temperatures, gallons of stormwater used, gallons of freshwater used, and the amount of energy consumed.

- The design of the interior space and maximized use of natural light are intended to foster social unity in the building's common areas.

Power and Water

The university is making efforts to be environmentally responsible wherever possible. In addition to the UC, the university built a parking lot when neighbors objected to students parking on local streets. The result, however, was a lot with an impervious surface that caused a rainwater runoff problem. What's more, in the summers, the blacktop heated up from the sun beating down on it. When it rained, hot water then ran off into the Kinnickinnic River, thus raising the water temperature, which is dangerous for the trout that live in the river.

One of the solutions under consideration is to place a rack covered with solar cells over the Parking lot. The result would be a carbon neutral method of generating energy and would also serve to reduce the temperature of the runoff water destined for the Kinnickinnic River.

Community Development

Cain noted that nearly every college offers some program on sustainability. UWRF differs, however, in that it is actively engaging its community.

"We've gone after sustainable community development to solve issues at a community level," said Cain. "We framed the campus as a microcosm of the community."

The college has set a goal of being off the grid by 2012.

Good Neighbors

The college also has a strong relationship with the city of River Falls, the Municipal Utility, and Wisconsin Public Power (WPPI). WPPI even gave the university $75,000 for a campus wide energy audit.

Conventional thought might run contrary to the notion that electric companies are happy to buy back the electricity generated by an organization's solar panels and windmills. After all, how does the utility make any money if it's buying other people's power?

As it turns out—and is being played out at UWRF—the college's electrical provider, The Municipal Utility and WPPI is more than thrilled to buy back any excess electricity it produces in the future. That's because the price of coal is rising, so the company can resell the university's power without having to spend as much money on coal.

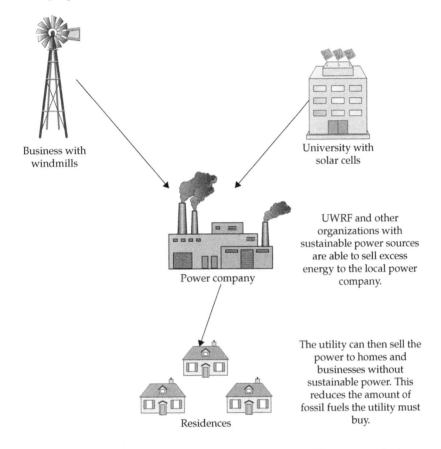

Business with
windmills

University with
solar cells

UWRF and other
organizations with
sustainable power sources
are able to sell excess
energy to the local power
company.

Power company

The utility can then sell the
power to homes and
businesses without
sustainable power. This
reduces the amount of
fossil fuels the utility must
buy.

Residences

Additionally, local companies who are adopting sustainable energy solutions are able to sell their excess electricity back to the co-op. The more local businesses sell to the co-op, the less coal the nonprofit needs to buy.

Monitoring
The university is working with the community's residents as well as its organizations. It has a number of remote sites that track performance—in real time—of various metrics.

For example, one farmer with a windmill is generating power for his home. The university is able to tap into the data coming from his windmill so it can study windmill performance.

Sustainability
The University Center is an important indication of the university's commitment to the environment. However, the impetus behind building the center was an issue of the school "walking the walk."

The UWRF has a rich history of supporting sustainability and sustainable community development both on campus and in its service area of the St. Croix Valley. The university defines sustainability principles in a broad context of economic, ecological, social justice, and human and physical resources that meet current needs without decreasing opportunities for future generations. Some of the formal and informal partnerships, events, and activities include:

- Faculty and staff are members of the UW-Extension Sustainability Team, which advocates for agent and community literacy in all aspects of sustainable community development. In addition, the campus members are involved with the Local Foods Network and Buy Local, Buy Wisconsin, which includes participation by UW-Extension, the Wisconsin Department of Agriculture, Trade and Consumer Protection, and local producers.

- UWRF has been a cosponsor and active participant in the ongoing "What We Need Is Here" community forums on sustainable community development.

- Faculty and staff are working with River Falls Municipal Utilities, the City of River Falls, Wisconsin Public Power Inc., Xcel Energy, and nongovernmental organizations to form partnerships to create opportunities for academic programming and installation and implementation of alternative energy generation. Other such partnerships include work with the City of River Falls, the Kinnickinnic River Land Trust, and the Kinnickinnic Priority Watershed Steering Committee for protection and enhancement of the river and Lake George.

- UWRF helped create and advises the board of the Western Wisconsin Intergovernmental Collaborative (WWIC), available to 99 local government units in Pierce, Polk, and St. Croix counties. The WWIC meets to share information and address the issue of sustainable communities, among other concerns.

- Sustainability principles are incorporated into many UWRF courses and programs. The university offers a major and minor in Environmental Science and incorporates the principles into majors and minors in Conservation, Geology, Land Use Planning, and Agriculture Engineering Technology, as well as a minor in Hydrogeology. Graduate offerings include a master's degree option in Sustainable Community Development.

- The College of Agriculture, Food, and Environmental Sciences has successfully instituted compost-bedded pack barns at its lab farm and offers the compost for sale to the public. The farm completely replaced its traditional liquid manure system and has implemented this environmentally sound method of reusing organic farm waste.

- UWRF students have actively encouraged energy conservation. During the 2007 spring semester the Student Senate, ECO Club, and several residence hall–based student groups encouraged students to be energy efficient, which resulted in a 7 percent reduction in water, heat, and electrical consumption in housing. The education program is being continued this academic year for the 2500 students who live on campus.

- UWRF has continued its energy efficiency monitoring for more than 30 years. Lighting and flooring replacement projects in residence halls are contributing to energy savings, as well as reducing maintenance and replacement costs. Toilet and light fixtures have been replaced with energy- and resource-efficient fixtures in academic buildings.

- The campus has an extensive recycling program that was implemented more than 25 years ago. In 2005, the campus recycled a combined 185 tons of plastic and Styrofoam containers, paper products, and food waste. Thousands more items also were recycled, including batteries, tires, oil, computer components, appliances, light tubes and incandescent bulbs, and pallets. Also, some 150 cubic yards of compost and chipping were produced.

Wal-Mart

A discussion of retailer Wal-Mart invariably brings up issues about its labor practices. However, Wal-Mart has to be given credit for its green initiatives. The company is making great efforts to reduce its impact on the environment. In 2007, Wal-Mart set out to achieve three laudable goals:

- To be supplied 100 percent by renewable energy
- To create zero waste
- To sell products that sustain resources and the environment

To achieve those goals, Wal-Mart unveiled a company-wide program called Sustainability 360. The program is targeted at its employees, customers, and suppliers.

NOTE *You can see more about the Sustainability 360 program at www.sustainability360.org, also found at Link 10-2.*

Even making small progress can mean big things. For example, Wal-Mart has set out to reduce 5 percent in all its products' packaging by 2013. Five percent? Big deal, right? Actually, this will result in 60,000 suppliers changing how they package their products and will result in a US$3.4 billion savings in Wal-Mart's supply chain. It has the potential to save US$11 billion in the global supply chain. That's nice for Wal-Mart's bottom line, but again, what does this mean for the environment? Turns out it's quite a lot, actually. Reducing packaging by 5 percent by 2013 would be the equivalent of

Reducing packaging by just 5% is equivalent to... Removing 213,000 trucks from the road. Saving 67 million gallons of diesel fuel.

- Removing 213,000 trucks from the road
- Saving 324,000 tons of coal each year
- Saving 67 million gallons of diesel fuel per year

Because Wal-Mart is the world's biggest retailer, look for other companies to follow suit. Again, if we look at just the supply chain, a reduction of packaging will likely mean that other companies will also get packaging that has been reduced for Wal-Mart. Also, other companies are likely to follow the example set by Wal-Mart.

As part of the Sustainability 360 program, Wal-Mart intends to introduce what it calls "Global Innovation Projects." One such project is a challenge for Wal-Mart associates and suppliers to start thinking about how to remove nonrenewable energy from the products the company sells.

"Perhaps the most far-reaching opportunity we have with our suppliers is a simple idea with potentially profound consequences," said Wal-Mart CEO Lee Scott. "Just think about this: What if we worked with our suppliers to take nonrenewable energy off our shelves and out of the lives of our customers? We could create metrics and share best practices so our suppliers could make products that rely less and less on carbon-based energy."

The steps Wal-Mart is taking aren't just in the United States. The company is making efforts worldwide. For example, Wal-Mart stores in the United Kingdom are looking at reduced packaging on food products by 25 percent and are selling more energy-efficient light bulbs.

And Wal-Mart isn't stopping at the intermediate goals it has set. The company strives to be supplied with 100 percent renewable energy and provide zero waste. It has also set goals of creating more recyclable materials and replacing PVC packaging in all Wal-Mart brand items with environmentally friendly materials.

Wal-Mart has already committed to selling 100 percent sustainable fish in its food markets, and is experimenting with green roofs, corn-based plastics, and green energy.

NOTE *In 2007 in Canada, Wal-Mart also signed a 3-year commitment to purchase 39,000 megawatt-hours (mWh) of renewable energy, the largest corporate purchase of renewable energy in Ontario's history.*

Partners

Remember, Wal-Mart's commitment to the environment involves its employees, customers, and supply chain. How are all these stakeholders being involved by the retailer? Wal-Mart is encouraging, recommending, and outright demanding change from the various people involved.

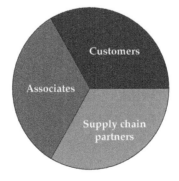

Consumers

Wal-Mart introduced its Live Better Index to help customers save money and "live better." The index is a barometer of consumer attitudes and shopping behaviors.

"Wal-Mart is uniquely positioned to be a barometer for America because of its scale, store locations, and affordable prices," said Stephen Quinn, Wal-Mart chief marketing officer. "The Live Better Index allows us to keep a pulse on what's important to our customers so we can continue to bring them unbeatable value on the products they want."

Wal-Mart has identified five everyday products to serve as nationwide trend indicators for the launch of the Live Better Index:

- Compact fluorescent light bulbs (CFLs)
- Organic milk
- Concentrated/reduced-packaging liquid laundry detergents
- Extended-life paper products
- Organic baby food

As a result of the study, Wal-Mart hopes to examine the products and attitudes surrounding environmental issues. The products the company is tracking were chosen because consumers make a conscious decision to purchase them for their environmental friendliness and potential for cost savings, versus conventional versions of the same products.

The items are also popular purchases in all store locations across the United States, so it allows Wal-Mart to have an apples-to-apples comparison of the entire country.

The Live Better Index is constantly changing and can be found at www.livebetterindex.com, also Link 10-3.

Figure 10-2 shows the Live Better Index.

Employees

Wal-Mart introduced Personal Sustainability Projects (PSPs) to its employees. PSPs are not necessarily work related, but rather efforts by Wal-Mart employees to be more environmentally responsible.

As of September 2007, associates have reported that they've voluntarily

- Recycled 675,538 pounds of aluminum
- Recycled 282,476 pounds of glass
- Recycled 5,953,357 pounds of paper and cardboard
- Recycled 3,177,851 pounds of plastic
- Walked, biked, and swam more than 1,109,421 total miles
- Lost a total combined weight of 184,315 pounds

What's more, 19,924 associates say they have quit or reduced smoking. Associates also state that they have shared the PSP program with 375,824 of their friends, family, and community members outside of Wal-Mart. The program extends beyond the associates' own efforts. They are encouraged to work in teams to undertake projects in their communities.

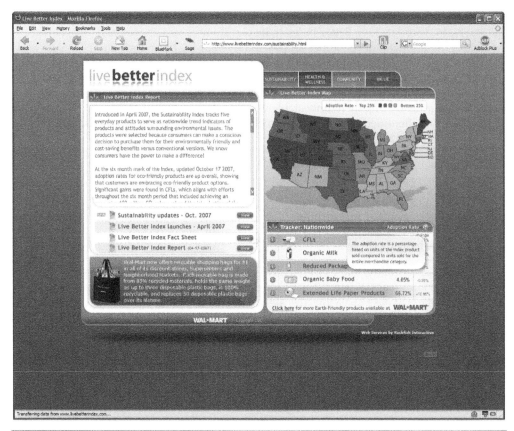

Figure 10-2 The Live Better Index is Wal-Mart's nationwide tracking tool to gauge how important environmental responsibility is to its consumers.

Wal-Mart says that because PSPs don't involve a large time commitment, monetary investment, or a major life overhaul, it is a great way for associates to improve their health and wellness, as well as the health of the planet.

Wal-Mart hopes to expand the program internationally.

Supply Chain

For its supply chain, Wal-Mart partnered with the Carbon Disclosure Project to find out ways for its suppliers to better manage their energy efficiency.

Note *The Carbon Disclosure Project is a not-for-profit organization that works with organizations to determine the greenhouse gas emissions of major corporations.*

The partnership will allow Wal-Mart to measure the amount of energy used throughout its supply chain. It will then use the information to look at a group of suppliers to examine ways to make procurement, manufacturing, and distribution more energy efficient.

Wal-Mart started its plan with a pilot group of seven of the most commonly purchased products:

- DVDs
- Toothpaste
- Soap
- Milk
- Beer
- Vacuum cleaners
- Soda

Suppliers are encouraged to monitor their greenhouse gas emissions, thus helping Wal-Mart reduce its total carbon footprint.

Experimental Stores

In 2005, Wal-Mart opened so-called "experimental" stores in McKinney, Texas and Aurora, Colorado. It did so in an effort to measure the benefits of implementing sustainable practices into Wal-Mart stores across the nation.

The experimental stores were built with recycled materials and employ energy-saving technologies. Over a 3-year period, independent labs will continue to monitor the progress of these experiments.

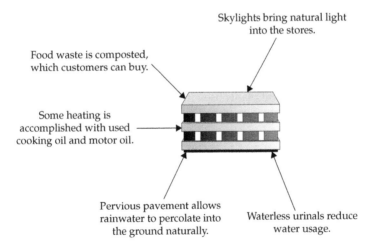

Initiatives taken at Wal-Mart's experimental stores

Energy Efficiency

In its experimental stores, Wal-Mart has taken a number of steps to improve its energy efficiency:

- LED lights are used in exterior signs as well as internal grocery, freezer, and jewelry cases. These have proven to use less electricity and last longer.

- Skylights and clerestories were built to direct natural light inside the stores. Dimming controls were installed to monitor the natural light and adjust the lights in the store accordingly.

- Evaporative cooling was installed in the Aurora store, which uses water sprayed into the air stream to cool the air as it evaporates.

- Air distribution system ducts are mounted 11 feet above the ground to distribute air closer to the floor. This system results in a reduced amount of energy needed to cool the store.

- A portion of the heating for the stores uses recovered cooking oil and motor oil, burned via a bioboiler, to heat water used in a radiant heating system. Heat recovered from the refrigeration racks is also used.

- New refrigeration display cases were installed in the Aurora store. These refrigeration cases have doors and use state of the art technology. The doors reduce air infiltration in the case, thus reducing electricity usage.

Although Wal-Mart has racked up some wins for its energy-efficiency measures, the stores have not been a complete success. There have been problems with the stores' solar panels and windmills, which requires them to still use fossil fuels. The company continues to work on these issues, however, which is the point of having such stores.

Water Conservation

Another effort that Wal-Mart set out to study with its experimental stores has been a reduction in water usage. Some of their achievements include:

- Since April 2006, the McKinney store has used approximately 85 percent less water for irrigation, compared to a conventional Wal-Mart. This decrease can be linked to the native, drought-tolerant plants used in landscaping as opposed to water-intensive lawns, and using drip irrigation instead of sprinklers.

- Native grasses and trees were planted to reduce water needed for irrigation.

- Waterless urinals were installed in the men's restrooms. The urinals were designed to save 1 to 3 gallons of water per use.

- Pervious pavement and/or concrete were used at both stores to assist with draining water from the parking lots. This pavement allows water to percolate through the pavement system and into the groundwater system.

Waste

Wal-Mart has also dealt with the sundry forms of waste generated at its stores through different measures, including the following:

- Food waste was reduced by composting spoiled items from the produce, deli, meat, and dairy departments. The compost is then available for Wal-Mart customers to buy.

- Waste created through the construction of the stores was recycled. At Aurora, approximately 50 percent of materials were diverted from the landfill. McKinney diverted 10 percent from the landfill.

Products

At its heart, Wal-Mart is, after all, a retailer. Although it's nice that the company has installed pervious parking lots and waterless urinals in some locations, it's only part of the story. To address what's going on inside the stores—specifically what's on its stores' shelves—Wal-Mart has set some goals there too.

Its plans range from altering the types of packaging used, to only stocking certain types of products. This includes the following:

- Stocking sustainable products, such as organic fruits and vegetables, fresh seafood, clothes made from organic cotton, and household products that are safe for families.

- Selling only concentrated liquid laundry detergent in all of its U.S. stores and Sam's Clubs by May 2008.

NOTE *The commitment is expected to save more than 400 million gallons of water, more than 95 million pounds of plastic resin, and more than 125 million pounds of cardboard. For water alone, this is the equivalent of 100 million individual showers.*

- Reaching its goal to sell 100 million compact fluorescent light bulbs (CFLs), a full 3 months ahead of schedule.

- Selling reusable bags in all its discount stores, Supercenters, and Neighborhood Markets for $1 each.

- Working with suppliers to develop "Extended Roll Life" products, which eliminate plastic wrapping from individual toilet paper or paper towel rolls by selling them as a multiple unit package.

NOTE *By selling twice as many "Extended Roll Life" Charmin 6 Mega Roll packs, the company can ship 42 percent more units on its trucks, eliminate 89.5 million cardboard roll cores, eliminate 360,087 pounds of plastic wrapping, and reduce its diesel consumption by 53,966 gallons.*

- Ensuring that its imported shrimp are farmed with environmental sustainability in mind. Wal-Mart partnered with the Global Aquaculture Alliance (GAA) and Aquaculture Certification Council, Inc. (ACC) to certify that all foreign shrimp suppliers adhere to Best Aquaculture Practices (BAP) standards.

Waste Reduction

Go behind any store, and you'll see at least one dumpster, filled to the brim with trash and refuse. Several years ago, progress was made in that a separate dumpster was set out for shipping containers, cardboard boxes, and other recyclables. As utilitarian as that is, it's not enough for Wal-Mart. The company doesn't want there to be any dumpsters at its stores, and no sign of Wal-Mart in any landfills.

PART IV

To help reduce the waste it produces, Wal-Mart has set a number of goals:

- Reducing solid waste from U.S. stores and Clubs by 25 percent
- Reducing overall packaging by 5 percent by 2013
- Becoming packaging neutral by 2025

NOTE *Wal-Mart is moving toward these goals by working with suppliers to ensure that their goods come in space-efficient packages and that the materials in that packaging are made from renewable or recyclable materials.*

Other initiatives include:

- In 2006, Wal-Mart's packaging team worked with a supplier to reduce excessive packaging on some of its private-label toys.

NOTE *By making the packaging just a little bit smaller, the company was able to use 497 fewer containers and generate freight savings of more than US$2.4 million per year. Wal-Mart will also save more than 3800 trees and more than 1000 barrels of oil.*

- Select produce packaged in corn-based NatureWorks PLA, made of their biodegradable polymers, can be found in all Wal-Mart stores.

NOTE *When Wal-Mart changed the packaging on just four produce items to PLA in 2005, the company estimated it saved approximately 800,000 gallons of gasoline and prevented more than 11 million pounds of greenhouse gas emissions.*

- Wal-Mart's sandwich baling program helps it recycle millions of pounds of plastic and cardboard in the back of its stores. This process allows all aluminum cans, plastic hangers, plastic bottles, office paper, and potentially other recyclable items to be "sandwiched" between layers of cardboard and bundled into bales, which are sent to certified recyclers. In 2007, Wal-Mart recycled more than 56 million pounds of plastic and 16 billion pounds of cardboard.

So, what should you take from the examples of the University of Wisconsin–River Falls and Wal-Mart? The main thing these two have in common is their desire to be responsible and innovative. Both organizations set a goal of environmental responsibility and are taking it on with creativity and originality in mind.

Although you might not want to funnel rainwater into a cistern for use when you flush toilets, there might be other opportunities to save water that you can embrace. There might also be opportunities to reduce power consumption in your datacenter; you just need to commit to the plan and follow through on it.

In the next chapter we'll talk about redesigning your datacenter and how you can save power and money.

V

The Greening Process

Datacenter Design and Redesign

Chances are you aren't sitting in an empty building, thinking about installing computers, and wondering, "If I do install computers, how can make the process as ecologically friendly as possible?" The reality is that there's probably already a computer on every desk, a datacenter humming away, and a throbbing electrical bill.

In this chapter we'll talk about issues that pertain to redesigning your datacenter. When it is time to replace equipment, how you can downsize your datacenter and replace equipment with energy efficiency in mind.

We'll talk about power consumption, how you can tweak your datacenter with that in mind, along with designing for optimal cooling. We'll also talk about the hardware in your datacenter and how that can be optimized.

Energy Consumption

Every 5 years computing capacity doubles. And when capacity doubles, so does everything that goes with it. For instance, between 2000 and 2005 the amount of energy consumed by datacenters and other infrastructure in the United States also doubled.

What accounts for this gorging? It's going on both in the datacenter and in the cubicle farm. Users are taking advantage of everything the World Wide Web has to offer: YouTube, music downloads, Internet telephony, and whatever else is popular this week. But in the server room, power consumption has spiked because of other trends, including the bloat of low-end servers that cost less than US$25,000.

Also, many IT managers are deciding to move to Linux and other free operating systems, rather than pay a charge for each server. As such, there's even more demand for a large number of low-end servers.

Growth

As Figure 11-1 shows, in U.S. datacenters in 2000 about 5.6 million servers were installed. Of those, 4.9 million were low-end, 663,000 were midrange, and 23,000 were high-end servers, according to a survey by Lawrence Berkeley National Labs in 2007.

By 2005, U.S. datacenters had 10.3 million servers. Of those, 9.9 million were low-end, 387,000 were midrange, and 22,200 were high-end servers.

The same study showed that it's not just the U.S. that spiked in its server growth. Around the world server demand expanded. In 2000, as Figure 11-2 shows, there were 14.1 million servers. Of those, 12.2 million were low-end servers, 1.8 million were midrange, and 66,000 were high-end servers.

By 2005, that number had swelled to 27.3 million servers. Of those, 26 million were low-end servers, 1.2 million were mid-range servers, and 66,000 were high-end servers. To feed that growth, in the United States, the amount of power necessary was equivalent to about five 1000-megawatt power plants. Worldwide, it was the same as 14 power plants.

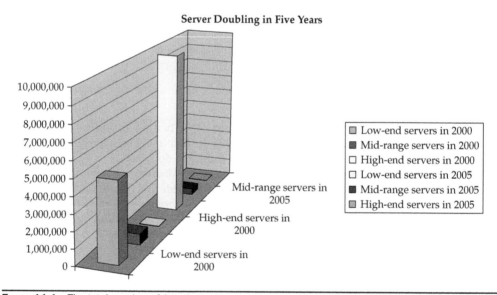

FIGURE 11-1 The total number of American servers nearly doubled between 2000 and 2005—and so did power consumption.

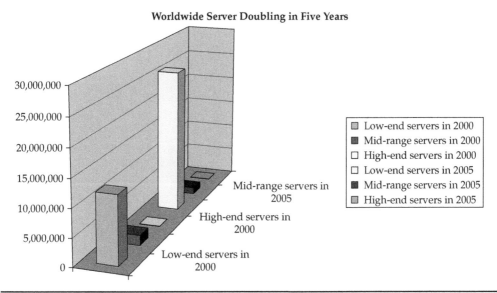

FIGURE 11-2   Around the world, server usage doubled.

Other Costs

Naturally, when we talk about energy consumption, we tend to immediately think of the power meter and just how fast it's spinning. But you might also want to think of your organization holistically. That is, how a change in one area can help another area.

For example, Isothermal Systems Research (ISR) in Liberty Lake, Washington offers a technology called SprayCool. SprayCool uses a fluid called Fluoinert, which is nonconductive. The coolant is sprayed directly on a chip or processor (the procedure is called "chip-based" cooling), and then cools the chip as the coolant is converted into a gas. This and other cooling technologies for the datacenter can be found at www.spraycool.com and at Link 11-1.

As Figure 11-3 shows, that gas is then taken down to a heat exchanger at the bottom of the unit, where the heat is transferred to another fluid, such as water. Because the water has been heated up, it can be used to regulate the building's temperature.

In a system with 10 racks of equipment, there is a 150-kW load just for cooling. Using the spray coolant removes a quarter of that cooling load.

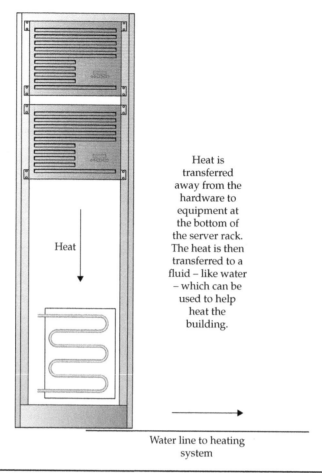

Heat is transferred away from the hardware to equipment at the bottom of the server rack. The heat is then transferred to a fluid – like water – which can be used to help heat the building.

Heat

Water line to heating system

Figure 11-3 The heat can be taken from servers and used to help heat the facility.

Design

When you design or redesign your datacenter with green in mind, approach it from the perspective of rightsizing the physical infrastructure. Use efficient devices, and design with energy efficiency in mind. The following sections will examine how you can make the most efficient decisions and plans for your datacenter.

Efficiency

You can ensure better efficiency in your datacenter by looking at some common sources of problems:

- Power distribution units operating well below their full load capacities
- Air conditioners forced to consume extra power to drive air at high pressures over long distances

- N+1 or 2N redundant designs, which result in underutilization of components
- Oversized UPSs to avoid operating near capacity limits
- Decreased efficiency of UPS equipment when run at low loads
- Under-floor blockages adding to inefficiency by forcing cooling devices to work harder

Floor Layout

As we discussed in Chapter 4, the way you lay out your datacenter has a huge impact on the efficiency of the air conditioning system. If airflow is blocked, it is not as efficient. If a hot-aisle/cool-aisle layout is not adhered to, you lose efficiency. When you design your floor layout, you want to do it with hot air and cold air segregation in mind.

Also, be mindful of where cooling systems overlap in your datacenter. This is the ideal location for equipment that runs especially hot or is especially important.

Server Configuration

It's not enough just to get the servers up and running; be sure that you enable any power-saving features on the servers. A lot of times IT managers don't set power-saving modes, rather opting for high availability. Setting power-saving modes will help save money by reducing power consumption and cooling costs.

Floor Vent Tiles

Vented floor tiles don't just look cool, they're designed to facilitate airflow. In many datacenters, however, vented tiles are either incorrectly placed or an insufficient or excessive number of vented tiles are installed.

If you use Computational Fluid Dynamics (CFD)—an analysis of airflow patterns—in your datacenter, you can optimize datacenter cool-airflow. This allows you to fine-tune the center's cooling by placing vented floor tiles in their optimal locations. Some vendors will even help you with CFD. By simply fine-tuning tile locations, some datacenters have achieved a 25 percent reduction in cooling costs.

Rightsizing

Datacenter design and redesign involves a lot of components. For instance, a seemingly small task such as the placement of vented floor tiles can lead to big savings. However, the biggest thing you can do to optimize your datacenter is to design with rightsizing in mind. That simply means building for what you need.

Rightsizing has the most impact on your datacenter's power consumption. Fixed losses in your power and cooling systems are present whether or not you have a datacenter in place. Organizations that have light IT loads might not even see an impact by its IT department. However, as the IT load gets larger, organizations will see power and cooling expenses climbing. Rightsizing can be accomplished through server consolidation and virtualization.

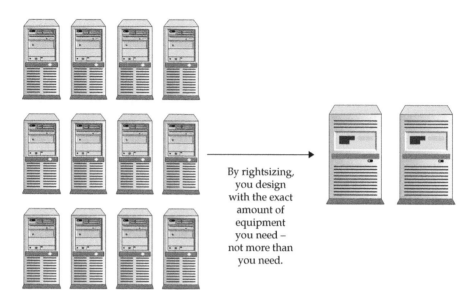

By rightsizing, you design with the exact amount of equipment you need – not more than you need.

NOTE *We talk about consolidation later in this chapter and show you how to do it in Chapter 12.*

When you redesign with rightsizing in mind, you must also be cognizant of the fact you will need additional capacity in the years to come. However, if you spend the time and money you need to predict the datacenter power and cooling load, it will pay for itself in both reduced capital and operational expense.

Upgrading to Energy-Efficient Servers

When you plan to green your datacenter, it would be nice if you could do it in one fell swoop. But, realistically, that's not going to happen. You can't really take down your entire system and replace it from scratch.

It won't work for a couple reasons. First, the cost would be too prohibitive. The budget just probably won't be there for so much expensive equipment. Second, there's the issue of workflow. Can anyone really envision being dark for the amount of time it would take to turn everything off and install new equipment? In most cases, when a new server is installed, it has to be hot-swapped in, so that there isn't even a fraction of a second of downtime.

So what you'll wind up doing is replacing your equipment with green alternatives as you would normally replace servers and storage units. When you do design your green datacenter, there are some issues to keep in mind and some practices you should follow.

Consolidation

The first place to start with any datacenter greening project is to consolidate servers. In some cases, you might find servers that you don't even need and you can just turn them off. Between 10 and 30 percent of servers aren't even being used and could be deactivated.

NOTE *If you take one physical server out of service, you'll save about US$560 in yearly electrical costs (that's assuming 8 cents per kWh).*

As soon as unused servers have been taken out, the next step is to consider consolidation. Many servers are underused, in terms of their processing power, as Figure 11-4 shows. Most physical servers run at a maximum of 15 percent.

Move as many server-based applications as you can to a virtual machine. A virtual machine is simply a software server installed on a physical server. You can put a number of virtual machines onto a physical server. This will result in a sharp drop in the number of physical servers in your datacenter. The servers that take on the additional roles will be more efficient in terms of their utilization levels.

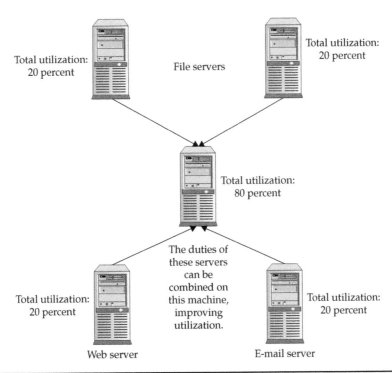

Total utilization:
20 percent

Total utilization:
20 percent

File servers

Total utilization:
80 percent

Total utilization:
20 percent

The duties of these servers can be combined on this machine, improving utilization.

Total utilization:
20 percent

Web server

E-mail server

FIGURE 11-4 By consolidating servers, you reduce the amount of servers you're paying to power, plus you are increasing the utilization of the tasked machines.

New Replacement Policies

The biggest place where you will see cost savings, power reduction, and cooling reduction is in server consolidation. It's a no-brainer—the less hardware you have, the less consumption will occur. When you replace servers, keep these guidelines in mind:

- Replace two or more old servers with a two-way server or dual-core, single-processor server.
- Replace old servers with a blade based on a low-voltage or mid-voltage processor.
- Replace dual-processor servers with a single, dual-core processor.
- Replace four-way servers with two-way, dual-core servers.

Use Power Management Features

It seems obvious, but some IT managers don't get it: Use your equipment's power management tools. Although electricity usage is reasonably constant, the IT load swings up and down according to the needs of the system. It can be as much as a factor of three.

By using your equipment's power management functions and turning off unused servers, you can cut datacenter energy usage by 20 percent. But it's not because IT managers are dimwits—rather, they're focusing on uptime and performance. In reality, however, turning on power management features can improve overall reliability and uptime because it reduces the stress on datacenter power and cooling systems.

NOTE *Experiment with your system, however, before turning on any power management features. In some systems running Linux, for example, waking up an idle server can cause unexpected behavior.*

Get Energy-Efficient Servers

As you upgrade to new equipment, look for energy-efficient servers. They're using less power than before, and they'll probably only get more efficient as new products are introduced.

The first generation of multicore chips resulted in huge reductions in power consumption. For instance, the Intel Xeon 5100 delivered twice as much performance with a 40 percent drop in power usage.

Use Energy-Efficient Power Supplies

Probably the biggest wastes of power in the datacenter are the power supplies. Inefficient units tend to ship with servers, and they aren't really selected based on how the server is configured.

Inefficient power supplies can waste almost half of the power before it gets to the server. Further, every wasted watt is turned into heat, which then requires at least another watt of power to cool.

Look for power supplies that achieve 80 percent or higher efficiency, even at 20 percent load. They cost more, as much of this type of equipment does, but they cost less to use. We'll talk about power supplies later in this chapter.

Talk to Your Facilities Manager

The IT department might keep scrupulous records and track the performance of its equipment, but most IT managers don't see the electrical bill. The facilities group does.

In order to truly understand how much power you're using (and costing the company), pick up the phone and punch in the facilities manager's extension. You might make his day. At the very least, open some communications with the facilities manager so that he knows that you are trying to address the power usage problem.

NOTE *This disconnect is also affecting how vendors develop equipment. Often, vendors just work on their one piece of equipment and don't worry about how their power needs will affect the rest of the datacenter.*

Refer to the Standards

If you're not sure which equipment to buy and you don't have the time, patience, or energy to sit down with product brochures and data sheets, you can still make wise procurement decisions.

A number of standards are out there that you can refer to. For instance, the 80 Plus certification program was initiated by electric utilities, and it names power supplies that achieve 80 percent efficiency at load levels of 20, 50, and 100 percent.

Energy Star is most commonly affiliated with desktop machines, but there is an effort underway to extend certifications to servers. Certainly, if you purchase a server in Europe, it will have to be RoHS and IEEE compliant. It's likely that vendors would tout that feature in other parts of the world, should their servers be so certified.

Ask for It

Remember 15 years ago when fat-free food was all the rage? To make it taste better it was jacked up with extra sugar. Remember 5 years ago when the Atkins diet made it forbidden to eat carbs, but you could eat steak wrapped in bacon and smothered with cheese? In each case, industry responded to demand. Fifteen years ago store shelves were stocked with fat-free foods. Five years ago store shelves were stocked with low-carb food.

Industry only responded because customers wanted it. It's the same way for Green IT equipment. If you don't ask your vendors for it, they won't see the need to make it.

Server Consolidation

Chances are you aren't going to shut down your datacenter for a weekend, wheel out the old servers, and install brand new, more powerful ones. It's more likely that you're going to bring in new equipment as your replacement plan dictates. However, when you do start replacing equipment, it's a smart idea to consolidate your servers.

By consolidating servers you can:

- Increase utilization of existing hardware from 10 to 15 percent, up to 80 percent
- Reduce servers at a 10-to-1 ratio
- Reduce hardware and operating costs by as much as 50 percent

Traditionally, servers were approached with a "one workload, one box" philosophy. That is, if you needed an e-mail server, you bought a new server. If you needed a file server, you bought a new server. However, each server is not used often enough to truly justify its location on a single machine. As mentioned earlier, most servers only operate at about 10 to 15 percent of their total load capacity.

The result of having a server for each network application is server sprawl. In this section, we'll talk about the merits of consolidating your servers into fewer machines.

Utilization

Server sprawl can be eliminated by consolidating and virtualizing your physical machines into virtual machines. Applications such as VMware run independently from the underlying hardware and are supported on a range of physical servers.

And if you have different operating systems for your different applications, that's not a problem. A virtual machine represents a complete system—processors, memory, networking, storage, and BIOS. This allows you to run Windows, Linux, Solaris, and NetWare operating systems and applications on the same server. This is illustrated in Figure 11-5.

Normally, a server running a lone application experiences total utilization of 15 percent, tops. That means all that processing power you paid for is being wasted—and all the power you're paying the electric company for to run that machine is also being wasted.

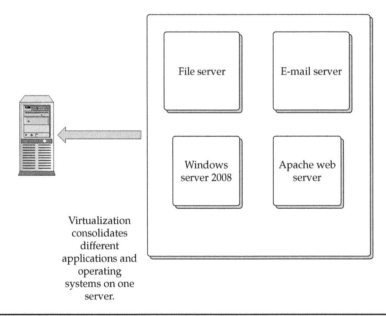

Virtualization consolidates different applications and operating systems on one server.

Figure 11-5 Consolidation and virtualization allows you to run multiple virtual servers on one machine, and each server can be a different operating system.

By running multiple virtual servers on one physical server, you're increasing your utilization of that machine from 15 percent up to 80 percent.

Hardware Reduction

Consolidation doesn't just mean that one server can do double-duty. It's more like a 10-to-1 ratio. For example, the VMware ESX Server can support more than 100 virtual machines.

You can also use the same strategy on storage and network consolidation, thus reducing more equipment from your server room.

Reducing Operating Costs

According to a study performed by Lawrence Berkeley National Laboratory, the servers in a datacenter account for about 55 percent of the electricity costs. The remaining power is spent to support that equipment—Lawrence Berkeley National Laboratory, 2007. So when you consolidate your equipment, you also need fewer pieces of equipment to play support roles, so there's more cost savings there.

Consolidating can save you about US$560 per year per server. So let's use the simple math example of consolidating 10 servers into 1. Consolidating 10 servers down to 1 results in a US$5040 savings per year. And that's at a smallish company. If you have thousands of servers, you'll recognize some big savings.

Consolidation also cuts down on the amount of heat generated in your datacenter. But, like power consumption, it isn't just the servers that generate the heat, it's also the equipment supporting the servers that add to the heat generation. Figure 11-6 shows this.

Repurposing Servers

As part of your green datacenter design process, you should also look at the equipment you have and evaluate its worth. You might have a systems life cycle that dictates that

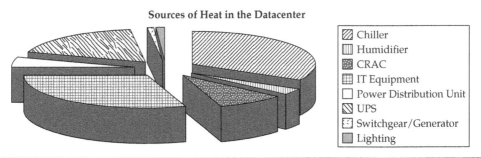

Sources of Heat in the Datacenter

- Chiller
- Humidifier
- CRAC
- IT Equipment
- Power Distribution Unit
- UPS
- Switchgear/Generator
- Lighting

Figure 11-6 Servers generate a lot of heat, but it's the equipment supporting them that adds up to create more heat.

the equipment needs to be phased out and replaced with new stuff. However, you might be able to save a few thousand dollars by simply repurposing the equipment.

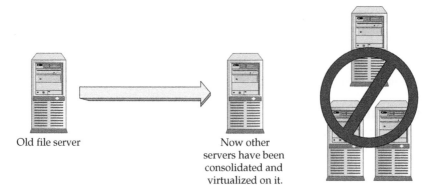

Old file server

Now other
servers have been
consolidated and
virtualized on it.

For instance, if you have a server that has sufficient processing power and memory, why not keep it, but consolidate and virtualize the duties of other servers? If it is equipment you already own, by repurposing the server you don't need to buy a new one (thus saving you the expense of buying a new one and recycling the old one), plus you maximize the server's utilization.

Cabling Considerations

Think of datacenter design as a Hollywood movie. The stars are the placement of servers and overall cooling. But the supporting actors in datacenter design are the small things you might not think about, such as cabling. True, cabling doesn't generate heat, and there are no toxic emissions that come out of your cabling. However, you need to make certain considerations when redesigning the cabling placement in your datacenter.

Largely, cooling is affected by your cabling choices. For the most efficient cooling, cabling has to be properly designed, remediated, and routed so that air flows optimally.

TIA-942

The Telecommunications Industry Association (TIA)—the same people who came up with CAT standards for unshielded twisted pair cabling—have published a definitive document encompassing best practices and design considerations for the modern datacenter.

The standard, titled "Telecommunications Infrastructure Standard for Data Centers, TIA-942," is 148 pages long and covers all sorts of issues, from site selection to rack-mounting methods.

TIA-942 is a best-practices document that aims to standardize a lot of requirements throughout a datacenter. One of the upshots is that by standardizing requirements for contractors, companies can save on one of IT's biggest budget items—IT management salaries.

You can order a copy of the standard from TIA at www.tiaonline.org (Link 11-2). They're not giving it away, though. The standard costs US$278, and you can buy either paper or PDF format.

Cable Routing

The key consideration in cabling your datacenter is keeping airflow in mind. TIA-942 and other datacenter standards advise horizontal and vertical cabling to be run accommodating growth so that you don't have to revisit cabling when your datacenter does grow (and it will). There are a number of reasons to do this:

- Eliminating the adverse affects of removing floor tiles and decreasing static pressure under raised floors during moves, adds, and changes (MAC) work

- Ensuring that pathways allow the flow of cold air in cold aisles to be unobstructed by cabling

- Installing cabling to provide a baffle of sorts, channeling cool air into cold aisles

Unless the issue of cabling is addressed every time a datacenter is changed, cabling can add to your cooling woes. A lot of older datacenters suffer because abandoned cabling channels are left behind, creating an air dam that can obstruct airflow.

In everyday use, cabling in and of itself isn't toxic, but given extraordinary circumstances it can be. Old cabling jackets might not meet current RoHS requirements. Older cabling also carries a significant fuel load, which can pose fire threats and can release toxins—such as halogens—if it catches fire.

Safety issues are important, but if you're removing old cabling, you also have to consider the disposal and recycling of cabling. Like with other IT equipment, you can't just chuck the cabling into the dumpster; it must be disposed of properly.

When you design your datacenter, you can save future problems and reduce the amount of abandoned channels through proper management. Infrastructure management systems (such as MapIT) can provide a detailed monitoring of any moves or changes in your datacenter. This gives you an up-to-date diagram of the physical layer connections so that channels can be managed and fully utilized before they become a problem. More information on MapIT and infrastructure management systems can be found at Link 11-3.

Bigger Bandwidth

When designing or redesigning a datacenter, there's a balance to be struck between what you need and what you can spend. If cost were no issue, you'd get the biggest, fastest equipment you could afford. However, there is a financial reality you need to keep in mind. That said, it is in your best interest to get the highest capacity equipment you can afford.

Currently, CAT 7/Class F cabling is the highest performing cabling on the market. CAT 7A/ Class FA is due soon, offering 1GHz per channel. This provides a high amount of bandwidth above the latest 10Gbps speeds for copper. The new cabling is backward compatible with older technology.

But what if you don't need CAT 7 cabling right now? Well, you will. And when you do, you'll have to take out the CAT 5 or CAT 6 cabling you've got and rewire with CAT 7. If you install the highest performing cable now, you will pay more upfront. However, it will cost significantly more if you have to keep upgrading every time your equipment gets a performance boost.

For instance, the installation of a CAT 5e system would need replacing in a few years as 10GBASE-T is implemented to the desktop. Once your organization outgrows CAT 6, you'll have to replace it with CAT 7, and so forth.

Installing high-performance cable not only saves you money, but copper, aluminum, and other natural resources are conserved. Further, the discarded cable doesn't have to be recycled or disposed of, thus saving some environmental impact.

Other Savings

Although optimization of airflow with proper cable planning and routing will save energy, there are other energy saving opportunities within the cable infrastructure.

For example, if you move to a higher performing class of cabling, you will reduce noise on the cabling channel, thus resulting in a significant power savings in the equipment by eliminating Digital Signal Processing (DSP) complexity used to reduce noise levels. In fact, using fully shielded cabling could save 20 percent in the overall power budget in 10BASE-T deployments.

Alien crosstalk (shown in Figure 11-7) happens in 10GBASE-T deployments when signals from neighboring cables bleed into other cables.

LEED Considerations

If you are concerned with LEED, good cabling practices can help propel you toward your certification goal. Buildings registered under the LEED system are awarded "credits" for reaching certain environmental goals, and are assigned a rating within the LEED system based on the following scale:

- **Platinum**   52–69 credits
- **Gold**   39–51 credits
- **Silver**   33–38 credits
- **Certified**   26–32 credits

Table 11-1 lists some design considerations, what they accomplish, and which LEED credits they can help you earn.

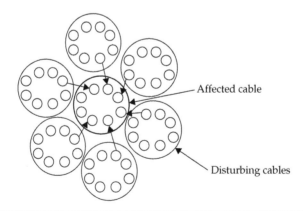

FIGURE 11-7   Alien crosstalk occurs when signals bleed from one cable to another.

Design Consideration	LEED Credit	Explanation
Using intelligent infrastructure management software	**MR 2.1** Construction Waste Management (50 percent)	Reduction of unnecessary channels due to undocumented or poorly managed movement, addition, or change work.
	MR 2.2 Construction Waste Management (75 percent)	
	MR 3.1 Resource Reuse (5 percent)	Identification and utilization of unused cabling channels to limit installation of new channels.
	MR 3.2 Resource Reuse (10 percent)	
	EA 1 Optimize Energy Performance	Maximization of active port usage to limit the installation of unnecessary active equipment.
		Identification and utilization or elimination of abandoned channels to maximize pathway space or increase airflow for energy-efficient cooling.
CAT 7 cabling and cable sharing	**MR 2.1** Construction Waste Management (50 percent)	Cable sharing as a means to reduce the number of installed cabling channels.
	MR 2.2 Construction Waste Management (75 percent)	Future-proof performance extends the life cycle of the cabling, decreasing the frequency of cable removal/disposal and installation of additional cabling.
	EA 1 Optimize Energy Performance	Shielded construction may limit noise sufficiently to reduce active equipment power consumption through elimination of DSP.
Using trunking cable	**MR 2.1** Construction Waste Management (50 percent)	Factory termination eliminates onsite waste created by field terminations.
	MR 2.2 Construction Waste Management (75 percent)	Efficient installation of trunk cables requires fewer contractor visits and smaller crews.
	MR 3.1 Resource Reuse (5 percent)	Modular design of trunks allows for onsite reuse.
	MR 3.2 Resource Reuse (10 percent)	
	EA 1 Optimize Energy Performance	Well-organized channels eliminate air dams in pathways caused by poorly managed individual channels to maximize airflow for energy-efficient cooling.

TABLE 11-1   Some Cabling Considerations Can Help Earn LEED Certification

Power Supplies

A couple of years ago, Google decided to build its new facility on the banks of the Columbia River in The Dalles, Oregon. The facility is two football fields in size with two cooling towers extending four stories into the sky.

But Google didn't move to this location on the Oregon/Washington border to get closer to Microsoft. In fact, Microsoft and Yahoo! are following suit and have plans to build their own massive datacenters upstream in Wenatchee and Quincy, Washington, 130 miles to the north.

Is there something gloriously beautiful about the area? Actually there is—the flowing rivers are harnessed to feed the power that these power-hungry datacenters need. It is the cheapest power in the country. This location underscores the needs of datacenters—they need lots of power.

Although you may not be able to uproot everything and move your organization next to a river, you still need to manage the power in your datacenter. That is a key consideration when designing or redesigning.

Too Much Power

When systems engineers design power supply requirements for enterprise servers, they approach it the same way a civil engineer designs a tunnel—they build it for the largest possible traffic that will ever go into it. Even though the vast majority of the traffic in that tunnel will be commuter vehicles, they still have to make sure it will be large enough to accommodate semis and tanker trucks.

It's the same way for servers. It's common to specify power supply requirements based on the maximum system configuration and load requirements. But systems engineers don't need to hit the gas so hard. They can specify different power requirements for different configurations. Naturally, this would cost manufacturers more money, so they tend to just put the biggest power supply needed in all of a line's models, regardless of how they will be used.

For instance, consider the servers in Figure 11-8. Both are from the same line—WasteTech's Escalenté line. The WasteTech Escalenté 5000SUX, shown on the left, is configured with enough hardware to only require 60 W of power. The 6000SUX, on the other hand, is fully maxed out and contains enough hardware to consume 540 W. Both servers use the same power supply. Although the power supply feeds the 6000SUX model with enough power, it provides more than enough power for the smaller server. So much so that it wastes energy.

But the issue isn't limited to servers in the same line. Many times manufacturers select a power supply that can fit all of their equipment. Again, cost is the issue. It's cheaper for the manufacturer to use the same supply in all their equipment—you're the one who ultimately pays for power inefficiency. Further, the planet pays a price, because of the carbon emissions spent to inefficiently power that device.

Thankfully, many companies such as Dell offer different power supply configurations so that the customer can choose the right size for the job a particular server is going to do. This can lower power consumption significantly, especially when factored over the life of the server.

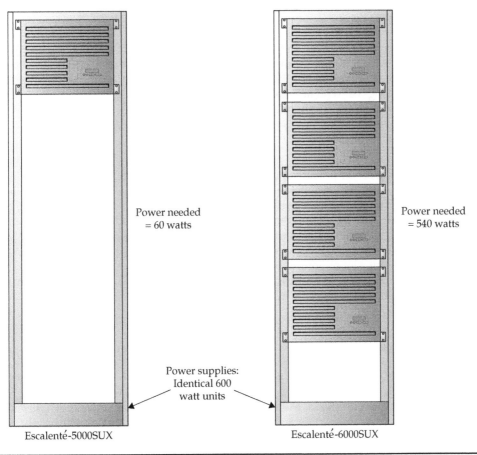

Power needed
= 60 watts

Power needed
= 540 watts

Power supplies:
Identical 600
watt units

Escalenté-5000SUX

Escalenté-6000SUX

Figure 11-8 Servers with different power needs are often fitted with the same power supply, leading to inefficiency.

Efficiency

A power supply's efficiency is calculated by taking the DC output of the power supply and dividing it by the AC input. If a power supply draws less AC to produce more DC, then the power supply is more efficient than one that uses more AC power than the DC power it generates. Here's the formula:

Efficiency = (DC output)/(AC input)

For example, if we have a power supply that's putting out 200 W and it's using 300 W from the wall, simply divide 200 by 300:

200 / 300 = 66 percent

The higher the efficiency, the better. In this case, 66 percent isn't so great. Typically, the efficiency of a quality power supply is between 75 and 85 percent. Using our calculation, the missing 34 percent doesn't just disappear. It turns into heat—that same heat you have to pay to cool off.

When power supply efficiency and system cooling are taken into account, the actual useful work done by the computer can be less than 50 percent of the total power draw of the system. That means over half of the power consumed is simply a drain on the ROI, an increased operating cost with no benefit to the client.

There are various power supply calculators available for different machine types and uses. At Link 11-4, we have provided you with a list of several that you may find useful.

Loads

In terms of efficiency, server power supplies are the least efficient when they are just idling. That doesn't mean they are using more power, they're just using power inefficiently. It's like an automobile. When you're parked with the engine running, you're still consuming gas, but not going anywhere. When you pull out of the driveway, you're finally going somewhere, but now wasted energy is a smaller percentage than it was when you were just idling. Now, consider a server that is configured minimally, but with a large power supply. The power supply is churning out a lot of unused power.

Manufacturers are trying to address this issue. However, as you've seen before, there will be more upfront costs, especially in the form of more expensive circuit materials.

Redundancy

Quite often, datacenters are configured with redundant power supplies. The reason is obvious—if one power supply fails, the other is there to keep the server online. In fact, in large datacenters, the power supplies are on separate power grids, so if the AC power goes out on one grid, the other supplies power and the servers keep working.

Redundancy is great for the sake of ensuring uptime, but it's tough on energy efficiency. For example, if a server needs 200 W to operate and it has a single 800 W power supply, then that server is using just 25 percent of the supply's total capacity. If a redundant power supply is added, power use is split between the two supplies and the draw on each is only 100 W. The efficiency then drops from 83 percent for a 25 percent load to 65 percent for a 12.5 percent load.

As with many issues in the datacenter, this comes down to a balancing act and some negotiations. How important is system availability versus reduced energy usage (and cost)?

The biggest thing you should take from this chapter is the importance of consolidating and virtualizing your servers. The technology now exists to run multiple servers virtually. In the next chapter we'll talk about server consolidation and show you how you can do it.

Virtualization

Virtualization is the technology that can set you free; it also provides most of the business drivers to make Green IT happen. No longer do you need to be shackled to dozens, hundreds, or even thousands of physical servers. No longer do you have to pay exorbitant electrical bills for power and servers. Virtualization allows you to condense equipment that normally filled racks upon racks in your server room into a much smaller amount. The benefits include less expense and a much smaller physical footprint.

As with so many other green issues, the benefit is twofold. You save money in electrical bills to power and cool the servers, and your reduced energy need means less CO_2 is generated to produce said electricity. In this chapter, we'll take a closer look at virtualization and how the process applies to both your servers and your storage area networks (SANs).

Server Virtualization

Walking into a server room can be a surreal experience. It's kind of like when Dave Bowman went inside the HAL 9000 Computer in *2001: A Space Odyssey*. Sure, it's not exactly the same—you're not wearing a spacesuit, floating inside a computer bent on your destruction—but the other stuff is the same. Blinking lights and expensive technology are everywhere.

In your server room is the hum from the equipment and the white noise of the constantly spinning fans. You can also feel the electricity as the servers do their work. It's sort of awe inspiring until you think about how much electricity you're using.

Until the day when servers run on perpetual motion, you'll always use some sort of electricity. We already talked about the merits of low-power servers, but "low-power" doesn't mean "no-power." Right now the only way to experience a no-power scenario is to just shut off and unplug your servers.

By consolidating multiple servers onto a single server, that's what you in essence do— shut off the power. Instead of your mail server consuming 560 watts of power, once its duties have been offloaded onto a virtualized server, the old server is consuming 0 watts of power.

Virtualization allows you to take all your existing physical servers and condense them into an amount about a tenth of the current size—although your mileage may vary, depending on what kinds of servers you're using and their importance to your organization.

Server Virtualization Explained

Put simply, server virtualization allows you to run multiple independent virtual operating systems on a single physical computer, which in turn allows you to squeeze the most utilization out of your servers.

For example, you know that 1U dual-socket, dual-core server in your datacenter that you think is near its end of life? By virtualizing it, you can turn it into ten (possibly even more) virtual servers running ten (possibly even more) virtual operating systems.

Although virtualization does not increase computing power (it actually decreases it because of the overhead involved in virtualization), it does increase server efficiency and utilization overall. Plus, because a reasonably powerful server these days is much less expensive than a top-of-the-line model was a few years ago, you can buy a new server and cost-effectively virtualize your existing machines onto it.

And, obviously, this results in less money being spent for hardware and less money being spent for power and cooling.

Advantages

The ecological advantages to consolidation are clear, and we've been eager to remind you about them in preceding chapters. However, not only will you save on electricity costs to operate and maintain the equipment, you will also save money outright with equipment costs.

Remote Users

By virtualizing terminal servers—that is, servers that present a remote desktop to your users—an organization can allow users to work remotely. Consider the organization depicted in Figure 12-1.

As Figure 12-1 shows, server virtualization allows workers to access the content of the server across a WAN link.

The application need not be installed on the employee's computer, and the application need not be installed on every desktop in your organization. Only those users who need to have access to their specific desktop environment can use it.

You can also provide a secure and standard corporate enterprise environment across your organization's desktops—whether they're in Beijing, Bali, or Branson, Missouri.

Fast Provisioning

Provisioning new infrastructure is less time consuming than it used to be. Virtual servers combine easy-to-use deployment software with preconfigured devices. This allows you to introduce new services and applications faster and easier than if they were rolled out conventionally.

Rehosting

There's likely some legacy software humming away on an old server (or two) somewhere in your datacenter. And more than likely, you haven't been eager to move that application to a new server in fear that it won't work. Further, chances are even better that this dinosaur of a physical server is inefficient, generates a lot of heat, and sucks up a lot of power.

Through virtualization, you can move those legacy applications to a new server, and you won't have to pay huge electrical bills. You'll still have that charming old application. And best of all, you can sleep at night, not worrying if the old server has finally died.

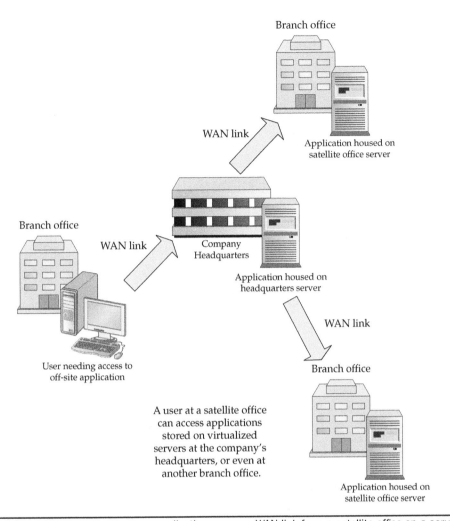

FIGURE 12-1 Workers can access an application across a WAN link from a satellite office on a server located at the company's headquarters, or even at another satellite office.

Best Practices

Of course, not everything can be virtualized, so there may still be some servers in your organization that are dedicated to sole tasks. However, those that can be consolidated should be.

Virtualization is ideal for applications that are used on a small or medium scale. It's your high-performance applications that need one or more clustered servers to get their jobs done.

Let's consider a 12GHz server (a four-core device with 3GHz per core). We can divide it into 16 virtual servers, each with 750MHz of processing power. This is illustrated in Figure 12-2.

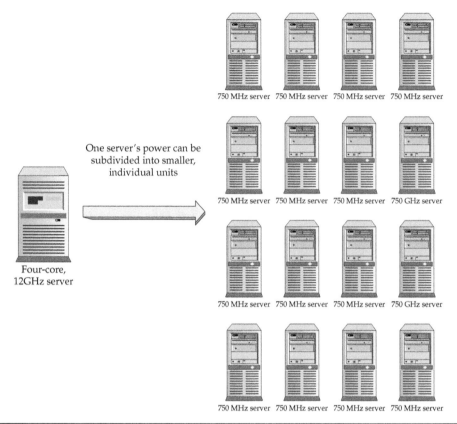

750 MHz server   750 MHz server   750 MHz server   750 MHz server

One server's power can be
subdivided into smaller,
individual units

750 MHz server   750 MHz server   750 MHz server   750 GHz server

Four-core,
12GHz server

750 MHz server   750 MHz server   750 MHz server   750 GHz server

750 MHz server   750 MHz server   750 MHz server   750 MHz server

FIGURE 12-2   For this example, a four-core server delivering 12GHz of power can be divided into sixteen 750MHz servers.

But it gets even better. If half of those servers are in off-peak or idle mode, the remaining servers have that much processing power available to them. So, in essence, if half of the servers are barely being used, the remaining eight servers have 1.5GHz available to them.

You can't expect the servers to run at optimal usage all the time. That's because the more the servers are called on to deliver this capacity, the less responsive the system will be. Rather, a good rule of thumb is never to let a server exceed approximately 50-percent sustained utilization, thereby reserving capacity for moments where usage needs may peak.

For instance, let's say that a group of servers are somewhere between 1 and 5 percent utilized and that they run different applications that are used at varying levels during different times of the day, week, year, or season. If you were to virtualize those servers onto a single machine so that you have about 50 percent utilization, you should be able to use peak capacity for the various applications during their individual peak times. All it takes is a little bit of planning to save a lot of energy and reduce waste.

Storage is another issue with virtual servers. Although we tend to look at CPU usage as our yardstick, input/output (I/O) considerations still need to be added to the equation. I/O overhead for storage and networking can gum up the works. If your server has high storage or hardware I/O requirements, it might be better to leave it on its own physical server.

NOTE *The second half of this chapter talks about virtualizing your data storage.*

Use Caution

Although the ideal for reducing power usage and hardware costs seems to be consolidating and virtualizing everything onto a lone server, that's really a bad idea. Yes, it's cheaper and there's less environmental impact, but you also run the risk of having an extended outage or losing everything should the server fail.

The easiest way to protect yourself is to ensure that your servers exist on more than one physical server, as shown next.

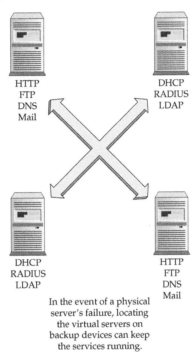

HTTP
FTP
DNS
Mail

DHCP
RADIUS
LDAP

DHCP
RADIUS
LDAP

HTTP
FTP
DNS
Mail

In the event of a physical
server's failure, locating
the virtual servers on
backup devices can keep
the services running.

If you replicate your HTTP server, for example, on two physical servers, you can roll it over easily enough if you have hardware problems.

This is easy to do with servers providing such services as the following:

- HTTP
- FTP
- DNS
- DHCP
- RADIUS
- LDAP
- Active Directory services

These types of servers are easy to switch over if there's a fault. If one server fails, the other can step in to pick up the slack.

PART V

But it's a different story for more complex services, including the following:

- Microsoft Exchange Server
- Microsoft SQL
- MySQL

These servers are more complex to cluster, and although it's a good idea to have redundancy in place, if one server goes down, it could take several minutes for the new server to be transitioned to. This isn't a virtualization issue; instead, it has to do with various implementations of clustering software, the complexity of the server, and even the application software.

These servers can be virtualized, however, if the service is transferred to a secondary physical server. But for it to work properly, the memory must be constantly synchronized so a switchover will be unnoticeable to users.

Server Virtualization Solutions

Server virtualization has picked up steam in the past few years, and plenty of companies are offering their own solutions. In this section, we'll take a look at two of the most prevalent companies—VMware and Microsoft—and talk about their solutions.

VMware Infrastructure 3

VMware is the big dog on the virtualization block. The company offers a number of applications for various virtualization needs and enhancements. Its flagship offering, however, is VMware Infrastructure 3. The suite comes in three editions: Starter, Standard, and Enterprise. Link 12-1 will get you over to VMware's server virtualization section of the VMWare website.

Let's take a look at the components and technologies in VMware Infrastructure 3.

VMware ESX Server

ESX Server is a virtualization layer that abstracts processor, memory, storage, and networking resources into multiple virtual machines. It virtualizes server storage and networking, allowing multiple applications to run in virtual machines on the same physical server.

ESX Server is also available as ESX Server 3i, which offers the same functionality as the original ESX Server, but with only a 32MB footprint.

VMware VMFS

The file system at the heart of VMware Infrastructure is the VMware Virtual Machine File System (VMFS). It is a high-performance cluster file system that allows multiple installations of ESX Server to access the same virtual image. This technology makes it possible for multiple users to access the same server image simultaneously.

VMware Virtual SMP

Processing performance is enhanced by VMware Virtual Symmetric Multi-Processing (SMP) technology. This allows a single machine to use multiple processors simultaneously.

VMware VirtualCenter

Management of the suite is done through VMware VirtualCenter. This provides centralized management, operational automation, and resource optimization to IT environments.

VMware VirtualCenter uses a number of web interfaces that allow integration with third-party system management products. It is also a control point for managing, monitoring, provisioning, and migrating virtual machines.

VMware DRS

VMware Distributed Resource Scheduler (DRS) can be used to automatically fine-tune processor, memory, and other resource allocations. You can do this manually, but DRS does a better job and with no need for intervention as server loads change.

VMware VMotion

The VMware VMotion technology allows live migration of virtual machines from one physical server to another for nondisruptive maintenance of IT events. This adds the ability to migrate live virtual machines from one server to another for both maintenance and load-balancing.

VMware Storage VMotion

Like VMware VMotion, the VMware Storage VMotion technology allows the live migration of virtual machine disks from one shared location to another. This is done with no downtime and no disruption to users.

VMware HA

VMware High Availability (HA) is another worthwhile option, adding automatic failover in the event of a hardware or software problem. This allows your servers to be automatically transferred to another machine in the event of trouble.

VMware Update Manager

VMware Update Manager busies itself with making sure all the ESX Servers are current with their patches and updates, and it also looks for updates to virtualized servers.

VMware Consolidated Backup

VMware Consolidated Backup enables virtual machines to be backed up via automated snapshots to a Windows server rather than running backup software on the hosts themselves.

Microsoft Virtual Server 2005

Microsoft has its own virtualization tools available. If you are considering virtualizing a number of Windows Server deployments, you can download Virtual Server 2005 from Microsoft—it's free. Link 12-2 will take you to the Microsoft TechNet Virtual Server website where you can download the latest version.

Virtual Server 2005 is used in conjunction with Windows Server 2003 and allows you to run most major x86 operating systems in a guest environment. Because it is a Microsoft product, it integrates with Windows Server 2003 fluidly.

Microsoft Virtual Server 2005 features these capabilities:

- It can be installed on servers with up to 32 physical processors.
- Host-to-host connectivity features allow you to cluster all virtual machines running on a host.
- It can run within a 64-bit Windows operating system. This provides increased performance and more memory availability.

Benefit	Description
Hardware-assisted virtualization	Supports both Intel Virtualization Technology (Intel VT) and AMD Virtualization (AMD-V) hardware-assisted virtualization.
VHD Mount command-line tool and APIs	Provides the ability to mount a virtual hard disk file as a virtual disk device on another operating system.
Support for Volume Shadow Copy Service	Allows backup of Virtual Server and its running virtual machines without the need to install backup agents inside the guest operating system of the virtual machines.
Larger default size for dynamically expanding virtual hard disks	The default size for dynamically expanding virtual hard disks has been changed from 16GB to 127GB, making the VHD file format even more useful for enterprise production, test, and disaster-recovery workloads.
Support for more than 64 virtual machines on x64-based hosts	Virtual Server can run more than 64 virtual machines on x64-based hosts. The 64 virtual machine limit remains when Virtual Server is running on 32-bit hosts.
Host clustering step-by-step guide	Host clustering allows you to extend the high-availability benefits of clustering to non-cluster-aware applications and workloads.
Virtual SCSI fix for Linux guests	This fix resolves an issue some customers encountered when trying to install certain Linux distributions inside a virtual machine on the emulated SCSI bus.
VMRC ActiveX control and Internet Explorer security zones	The Virtual Machine Remote Control (VMRC) ActiveX control now uses the security zone information in Internet Explorer to determine whether to prompt you for your credentials when you load the control.
Service publication using Active Directory Service Connection Points	Virtual Server service now publishes its binding information in Active Directory as a Service Connection Point (SCP) object.

TABLE 12-1   Some Microsoft Virtual Server 2005 Features

Table 12-1 lists other features available in Microsoft Virtual Server 2005.

Implementation

We've been banging the virtualization drum pretty loudly throughout this book, chiefly because it makes good sense. However, virtualization is not without its issues, many of which are related to the guest operating system you wish to "virtualize", and the applications you intend to run in them. Before you get started, be sure to check release notes and related documentation to see if there are any known issues or special requirements specific to your server and application environment. Remember, most issues are not insurmountable, but it is wise to go into this with your eyes open.

Migration

Most virtualization packages will include physical-to-virtual migration tools. That is, the tool will take an existing physical server and make a virtual hard drive image of the server (along with necessary adjustments to the drivers). Then the new server will boot up and run the virtual image.

You also get a nice measure of backup protection when virtualizing. This is because virtualized images can be used to recover any failed server.

Licensing Issues

Licensing can be an issue in your quest to virtualize. In our earlier example, we talked about having a machine that ran 16 servers. If you have expensive licensing costs, you probably don't want pay out all that money for licenses and then put them in one box. If you do have a server with a huge licensing cost, it's better to leave that one on its own machine—plus if it's that expensive, it's probably mission critical and you don't want to take any computing power away from it.

However, that doesn't mean licensing should stop you in your tracks. If you're using open-source software such as the Apache web server, it's free, so don't sweat it. But other servers—such as Windows, for instance—will require licensing fees. You may have to pay based on how many virtual servers are installed on a single physical server, or you may have to pay based on how many users are connected to the servers.

When you're computing your equipment costs as part of your virtualization strategy, make sure to figure in any licensing costs.

Storage Virtualization

In your datacenter, you likely have hundreds of disk drives spinning away like crazy, holding the treasure that is your organization's digital data. Although each of those drives contains your organization's cyber-gold, do you really need that many drives?

Like servers, each drive costs money to buy, to operate, and to cool. Storage virtualization—like server virtualization—allows you to reduce the sheer number of disk drive in your datacenter.

What You Can Do

Although the goal of our efforts here is to tout the green benefits of virtualizing, that's not the only benefit. Storage virtualization can help your organization in a number of ways, including providing a way to move data with as little fuss as possible. A number of benefits, beyond being green, stem from storage virtualization.

Data Migration

Another benefit of storage virtualization is the ability to migrate data from one location to another while maintaining access to your information.

The host only knows about the logical disc, so any changes to the metadata mapping goes on without the host knowing. This means that data can be moved or replicated to a different physical location without any effect to the client. If data has been moved or replicated, the metadata is updated to represent the data's new location, thereby freeing up space at its former location.

NOTE *Metadata is sort of a map of where your data is stored on the SAN.*

By migrating data, the IT manager can perform a number of day-to-day tasks much easier:

- Moving data off an over-utilized device
- Moving data to a faster storage device
- Migrating data off of older storage devices (for instance, those being replaced or returned when a lease period has ended)

Pooling

IT managers are able to better utilize their storage equipment through virtualization. This is accomplished through pooling.

For instance, when storage capacity is pooled, IT managers don't have to try and find open space on certain drives to allocate space for a host or server. When the system is pooled, a new logical disk can be allocated from the pool. It also allows an existing disk to be expanded.

This is an extremely efficient system. Through pooling, all the available capacity in your disks can be used. In a conventional environment, a whole drive would have to be mapped to the host. If the drive has more capacity than is needed, this space is wasted. If the drive is too small for this use, you run the risk of running out of space and having to add additional drives.

Storage can also be assigned when it is needed, so you don't have to guess how much space is needed. Also, if you need more capacity overall, simply adding extra drives can help your entire organization's storage needs. For instance, as Figure 12-3 shows, let's say your marketing, production, and administrative departments all need more capacity in their individual servers. If you are pooling your drives, you just need to add one drive. In a traditional environment, you'd have to buy (and install) three separate drives.

Ease of Management

Storage virtualization makes management of your data much easier. Even though data is scattered throughout many devices, it all appears to be in one place, on one storage device. This allows you to manage your data centrally.

Risks

Like a moon shot or dating an old girlfriend's best friend, there are risks involved in storage virtualization. Before moving all your data onto a new SAN, it's a good idea to understand what's involved with the transition.

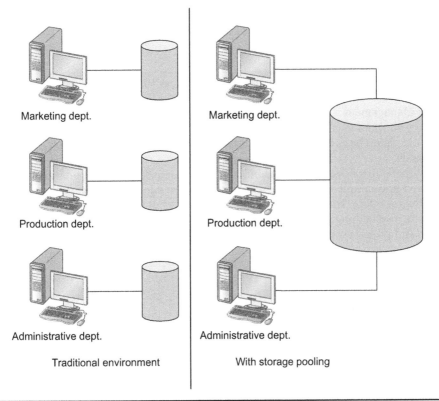

Figure 12-3 Pooling allows you to more easily expand the capacity of your storage system.

Problems Undoing What You Did

Once you virtualize your storage, only the virtualizer knows where data is actually stored on the drives. If you have to back out of a virtual storage environment, you need to reconstruct the logical disks onto physical disks that can be used in a conventional way.

Backing out of the system is normally possible, but it is time consuming.

Complexity

When you virtualize your storage, you can only imagine how complex the system must be, especially if you are pooling the entire data needs of your organization. And that complexity works on several levels.

Environment   It's fantastic to have all your data managed from one location and easily accessed by your users. However, when a problem arises (and it will), it's more difficult to handle. Isolating problems becomes very complex, because only the virtualizer knows where data is being stored.

Also, just because you have this beautiful symphony of virtualized data in place doesn't mean you don't have to maintain your hardware. Physical drives still need to be maintained and managed.

Software   Some software implementations are complicated to design and code. For example, network-based and in-band designs are especially complicated, so read and write requests can lead to latency problems.

NOTE *We talk more about network-based and in-band designs later in this chapter.*

Metadata Management

When you write data to your hard drive, you don't know exactly where, on your drive, it is stored. A piece goes here, a piece goes there. If you have to find the information, it is possible, albeit a hassle.

In a storage virtualized environment, not only is data scattered throughout a drive, it's scattered throughout several drives. The only way to know where everything is comes down to the metadata. The metadata is sort of the map your system uses to find data.

As such, if something happens to the metadata—while still located on your drives—for all intents and purposes, the data is gone.

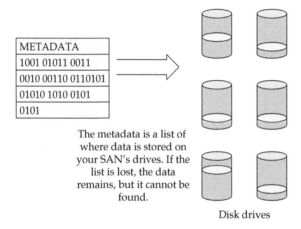

The metadata is a list of where data is stored on your SAN's drives. If the list is lost, the data remains, but it cannot be found.

Disk drives

Because metadata is so important, it is critical that the metadata is backed up and kept safe. But not only must metadata be recoverable, it must be updated quickly. If a file is saved on the system and others need to access it, that metadata must be updated so others can find the file.

Performance

You may also experience some performance problems if the system isn't properly tuned. Caching required data must be visible to input/output (I/O) requests. If the I/O request misses cached data, there is a performance hit as the request tries to relocate the data. If the software or the device is efficiently designed and tuned, this shouldn't be a problem, but it can be if the system is not properly optimized.

NOTE *It's not all bad news. You may also see a performance increase when the system is put together properly.*

However, just by the sheer nature of virtualization and the overhead of trying to locate data, there will always be some form of latency. How much will depend on the following factors:

- What data you're storing
- Where it has been virtualized to
- How efficient your system is
- The quality of your equipment

Throughput

The total amount of throughput available is also a concern. Bandwidth into and out of the metadata lookup application has an impact on your system's bandwidth. This isn't as much of an issue with asymmetric systems, because the metadata lookup occurs before any information is read or written.

In symmetric implementations, however, throughput is limited by processing power and connection bandwidths.

Best Practices

A SAN can just show up and do its job: It can store your data. But you not only want it to earn its living, you want it to excel. As such, there are a few things you should expect your virtualized storage solution to deliver in order to maximize the level to which you can consolidate.

Automated Tiered Storage

Many organizations maintain data in different classes, which adds to the complexity of maintaining a SAN. Organizations have faster (more expensive) and slower (more economical) storage classes in order to better balance cost and performance. Although this balance is important to strike, it is hard for IT staff to manage, because it is very labor intensive. Further, IT managers need to study data patterns to determine which data needs to be migrated to more economical storage so that it doesn't stay on faster, more expensive media.

Datacenters using this class system that want to employ a virtual storage system must have a mechanism to accomplish both. The system must be able to track data usage and automatically move data between storage classes based on predefined rules.

Data can't just be moved to the lower, slower, more economical class. It also has to be able to be promoted to the faster, more expensive drives in case a piece of data becomes particularly popular with your users.

Green Advantages   Automated tiered storage provides a number of significant ecological advantages. First, by automatically moving infrequently accessed data to energy-efficient, higher capacity SATA drives, your organization will reduce the number of power-hungry drives and reduce the cost of powering your system. And, as we've said before, less heat is generated, thus reducing the amount of cooling that is necessary. As a result, fewer CO_2 emissions are produced.

For example, over 5 years, an enterprise-class 15,000 rpm 146GB drive with a RAID 10 configuration might produce 32 tons of CO_2 emissions. This includes the power to cool the datacenter as well as humidification, UPS support, power distribution, and so on. Over that same time span, a 7200 rpm 1TB drive with a RAID 5 configuration would produce a bit more than 2 tons of CO_2.

Again, this is just the case for one drive. If your organization replaces hundreds or thousands of similar drives, you can see the level of impact realized.

NOTE *Typically, 80 percent of user data is inactive and best suited for storage on a SATA drive.*

Real Estate   Using fewer disks also helps reduce real estate costs. By using 21 spindles instead of 274, a company can reduce its total storage footprint by 92 percent. Not only do you have the potential to lease less space, you also have the opportunity for future growth.

Space-Efficient Snapshots

Data protection brings its own set of headaches to the SAN. Datacenters that use RAID storage experience higher costs as capacity is added because RAID overhead increases. Storage preallocated for specific applications is inefficient, because a lot of expense comes from unused space. To protect data, data snapshots guard again loss or corruption, but full-volume snapshots add even more expense.

Space-efficient snapshots do not require full-volume clones for creation or recovery. This allows for more snapshots to be maintained on your system. This allows you to restore a virtual server in a few seconds.

NOTE *These snapshots allow you to test new applications and service packs before deploying them to the organization.*

Virtualization Types

Storage virtualization can be implemented the following three ways:

- Host based
- Storage device based
- Network based

This section examines all three.

Host Based

Host-based virtualization occurs on a user's PC. It uses physical disks on the host system and is managed by software just above the physical device that performs metadata lookup.

Most operating systems have their own form of host-based storage virtualization. In Windows it's called Logical Disk Manager and was introduced with Windows 2000.

Pros

- No additional hardware (aside from extra disk volumes) is required.
- It's simple to implement.

Cons

- It is performed on a host-by-host basis, so it doesn't have organization-wide impacts.
- Replication and data migration are only possible locally to that host.
- No easy way of keeping host instances in sync with other instances.

Storage Device Based

In the past, devices such as RAID controllers provided logical and physical abstraction, but didn't provide the ability to migrate data. Just recently, new RAID controllers have made it possible to allow downstream attachment of additional storage devices.

It works through a primary storage controller that manages virtualization services and allows additional storage controllers to be added. The primary controller manages metadata services and provides pooling. It can also manage replication and migration services to other devices.

Pros

- No additional hardware (aside from extra disk volumes) is required.
- Gives most benefits of server virtualization.

Cons

- Storage is optimized only across connected controllers.
- Replication and migration are only possible across connected controllers and may only be possible in homogeneous environments.
- Higher latency. The primary storage controller must issue a secondary downstream I/O request for content not in the cache.
- Higher bandwidth consumption. The primary storage controller needs the same amount of bandwidth as the secondary storage controllers to maintain the same level of throughput.

Network Based

The preceding types of storage virtualization really aren't ideal for a large organization. They can be used, of course, but the one you are most likely to use is the network-based implementation. This is a SAN connected to a network-based device. This device sits in the SAN and provides the management duties of processing I/O requests and managing the metadata.

Pros

- Heterogeneous storage virtualization.
- Data caching can be performed in-band.
- Single management interface.
- Replication between heterogeneous devices.

Cons

- Metadata is hard to update in switch-based devices.
- Out-of-band requires specific host-based software.
- In-band may add latency to I/O.

Implementation

Implementing network virtualization involves either a standalone appliance (appliance based) or a switch (switch based). Both architectures give the same services—pooling, data migration, and so forth.

Appliance-Based Devices   Appliance-based devices—such as the one shown in Figure 12-4—are devices that provide SAN connectivity. They sit between the hosts and the SAN.

I/O requests are sent to the device, which handles the metadata mapping before the request is redirected to the storage devices.

Switch-Based Devices   These devices reside in the switch hardware used in the SAN. These also sit between the hosts and the SAN, but might use different mechanisms to provide the metadata mapping.

In-Band   In-band (or *symmetric)* virtualization devices sit in the data path between the host and the storage. Hosts send I/O requests directly to the device, and they don't directly communicate with the storage themselves. Data caching, statistics, replication, and data migration are all possible in an in-band device.

Out-of-Band   Out-of-band (or *asymmetric)* virtualization devices just perform metadata mapping services. When an I/O request is made from the host, it is first processed at the host using special software. Then a metadata lookup is requested from the out-of-band device, and the location of the data is sent back to the host.

NOTE *This method prevents caching of data because the data never passes through the device.*

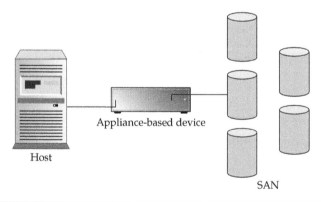

Host

Appliance-based device

SAN

FIGURE 12-4   Appliance-based devices sit between the SAN and hosts.

Storage Virtualization Solutions

Vendors understand the need for streamlined SAN solutions, and they're introducing new and ever-efficient technologies all the time. In this section, we'll take a closer look at some of the better SAN solutions out there and talk about how they can help you virtualize your storage.

Compellent Storage Center

Storage vendors are seeing the benefits of going green and reacting to market pressures to churn out smart products that balance performance, power, and consumption. One such company is Compellent. Compellent offers a number of SAN enhancements with its Compellent Storage Center 4.0. In fact, Compellent is not only concerned with providing an effective, efficient SAN, but is also taking strides to address ecological considerations through its products.

The company uses such technologies as the following:

- Automated tiered storage
- Thin provisioning
- Advanced virtualization

Compellent notes that a fully featured Storage Center SAN can save companies up to 93 percent of the power consumption and power costs of storage when compared to conventional solutions.

For instance, the company observes that a typical 20TB storage system configured with RAID 10 and utilized at 50 percent might require 274 enterprise-class disk drives. Using 10,000 rpm 146GB drives could consume 6020 watts per year (52,740 kWh). If the company pays $0.10 per kWh to power those drives, it would cost US$26,370 over the drives' 5-year lifespan.

However, a Compellent SAN with its proprietary technologies—thin provisioning, advanced virtualization, and automated tiered storage—might require just 14 of the same enterprise-class disk drives configured at RAID 10, and seven 7200 rpm 750GB SATA storage disks, configured at RAID 5.

This configuration would consume just 429 watts—or 3758 kWh—for a total cost of just US$1879 over the drives' 5-year lifespan.

Let's take a closer look at the technologies Compellent uses to reduce the size of a SAN.

Thin Provisioning

Compellent's thin-provisioning software is called Dynamic Capacity, and it helps increase storage utilization, thus lowering the overall number of drives required for a SAN.

Dynamic Capacity allocates storage only when the data is written to the disk, instead of preallocating storage capacity to volumes before they are used. The result is that administrators don't have to overprovision capacity to plan for future growth.

By purchasing and operating fewer disk drives, companies significantly reduce power, cooling, and real estate costs. If you were to just use Dynamic Capacity, you could reduce the number of drives you need by 75 percent.

Automated Tiered Storage

We talked about the advantages of tiered storage earlier in this section. Although the concept of moving less-often used data to slower, less expensive drives is a great idea, it's time consuming for IT managers to physically perform.

However, for organizations that haven't embraced the concept, the result is more expense and more energy usage. For instance, many businesses deploy the fastest—and most power-hungry—Fibre Channel disk drives in a single tier. All the organization's data is in that pool, which is great for the current data, but the Third Quarter Operations Department Report from 1997 doesn't need to be on such a system.

Compellent takes the person out of the process with its automated tiered storage solution, which adds more economical drives to the SAN. The architecture now has two or three layers of drives, as shown in Figure 12-5.

At the top in tier one are the fast, 15,000 rpm Fibre Channel drives. This is where the mission-critical data is stored. Beneath it in the second tier are the 10,000 rpm drives. But most of the data in your system—about 80 percent—is rarely accessed. This data is relegated to the 7200 rpm SATA drives at tier three.

Boot from SAN

Datacenter power requirements can be further shrunk through the use of Compellent's Boot from SAN solution. By maintaining an operating system boot volume on the SAN, rather than the server, you have no need for server-attached disks. By eliminating the need for

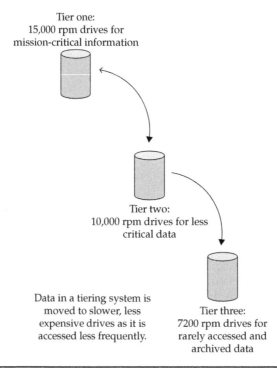

Tier one:
15,000 rpm drives for
mission-critical information

Tier two:
10,000 rpm drives for less
critical data

Data in a tiering system is
moved to slower, less
expensive drives as it is
accessed less frequently.

Tier three:
7200 rpm drives for
rarely accessed and
archived data

Figure 12-5　Compellent's automated tiered storage reduces the cost of drive acquisition and operation.

server-attached disks, you can use diskless blade servers, thus reducing hardware acquisition costs, power, cooling, real estate, and cabling costs.

Using Compellent Server Instant Replay can reduce the space needed to store multiple copies of the same OS boot volume on the SAN. If an OS boot volume for each server is stored on the SAN, it will consume storage space. However, Server Instant Replay can use the same image, with some adjustments to the name and IP address, so that the same image can be used over and over.

You can learn more about Compellent, its products, and technologies at www.compellent .com, or by following Link 12-3.

Incipient

Another SAN management platform is offered by Incipient. Incipient's solution is two enterprise-class software products managed by a common administrative console called Incipient Storage Administrator (iSA). The two products are Incipient Automated Data Migration (iADM) software and Incipient Network Storage Platform (iNSP) software.

Incipient Automated Data Migration (iADM) Software

iADM is targeted at customers who need to move their data with very little planning. Data migration includes:

- Datacenter moves
- Storage array refreshes
- Application tiering
- Storage resource balancing

iADM boasts an intelligent automation of end-to-end migration processes, and it supports heterogeneous SAN environments as well as various storage vendors (including 3PAR, EMC, IBM, and Sun).

Further, the software can run on off-the-shelf servers and is designed to automate end-to-end workflow and provisioning tasks that occur with migration projects. iADM also allows you to perform datacenter moves with reduced downtime, as well as to perform all tasks from a single console.

Incipient Network Storage Platform (iNSP) Software

The iNSP platform is targeted at customers who have ongoing data mobility needs, but can't have any downtime. iNSP combines storage virtualization tools with powerful management tools, which allows customers to move data across the SAN with no downtime.

iNSP is located on a director-class SAN switch and provides a suite of network-based storage services that can be deployed SAN-wide or across heterogeneous storage arrays. These services provide:

- Nondisruptive data migration
- Network volume management
- Storage provisioning
- Point-in-time copy

PART V

iNSP allows you to migrate data with no disruption to applications and hosts. You are also able to increase storage utilization, as well as enable tiering and cross-tier copy services.

iNSP abstracts the SAN data path. This eliminates application downtime that normally occurs with data migrations and device reconfigurations. iNSP software supports Cisco MDS 9000 SAN switches, along with storage vendors such as 3PAR, HDS, IBM, and Sun.

You can learn more about Incipient, its technologies, and products at www.incipient.com, or by following Link 12-4.

Both server and storage virtualization can accomplish some important things for your organization. First, there's the obvious honey we're trying to sell here: You become a more green organization. By consuming less power, you're generating less CO_2. By having less equipment, less needs to be discarded at end-of-life.

However, there are also overall organizational benefits, such as the ability to access applications from any branch office (or anywhere in the world, for that matter). Also, adding more storage to your SAN can be as easy as slapping on a new hard drive and letting your virtualization system use it as necessary.

Savings

So how much can you save by virtualizing your servers and storage? Let's consider the fictional software giant CompuGlobalMegaWare, which has decided to make the switch and is going to virtualize and consolidate its servers and storage. It will be reducing the amount of physical servers it has from 1000 down to 72—a 14:1 reduction.

The company is also going to reduce its 1000TB of storage spread across 13,700 hard drives down to 1050 drives, or a 13:1 reduction. Let's take a closer look.

Server Savings

In terms of storage, an average, run-of-the-mill server will cost US$9052 per year in costs. Those costs include:

- US$4000 for purchase, support, and maintenance costs. This amount is amortized over 3 years.
- US$1100 for storage and networking costs.
- US$333 for server provisioning and life cycle replacement costs, which consume 20 hours per server. That also assumes a 10 percent server growth. If your environment is growing especially fast, expect this amount to be higher.
- US$2720 in ongoing administration.
- US$589 in power and cooling costs.
- US$310 for datacenter space costs.

In the CompuGlobalMegaWare example, reducing its physical servers from 1000 to 72 has the same carbon impact as removing 1124 cars from the roads.

Here's the cost savings:

- The company can expect a saving of US$5.9 million per year.
- A US$14 million net present value (NPV). This is the amount of value added to the company.
- A 670 percent (or more) return on investment (ROI).

Storage Savings

CompuGlobalMegaWare isn't just interested in reducing the amount of spindles turning in its SANs. The company is also interested in deploying some intelligence to the system. This will include thin provisioning and automated tiered storage.

The company has 1000TB of data on 13,700 146GB drives, each spinning at 10,000 rpm. The drives cost—over 5 years—US$1.3 million just to power.

As part of its storage consolidation plan, CompuGlobalMegaWare will employ an automatic tiered system. As such, 13,700 drives will be reduced to 1,050. Of the new drives, 700 will be the same size as before, whereas 350 will be 750GB SATA drives.

This new deployment will cost US$93,950 to power, over 5 years, resulting in more than US$1.2 million in savings.

Bonus Savings

As we've mentioned before, savings manifest themselves in many different ways, some of which are difficult to quantify, because they will differ based on the company.

You can first realize savings based on what we've already stated. Although the price of a server and the act of consolidation can bring different results—based on what you buy, who you buy it from, and so forth—the savings are clear. But if you want some icing on your cake, you can measure some extras that you might not have thought about.

Start by taking some measurements at your organization. Before you virtualize, jot down what you're spending on:

- Security technology
- Staffing
- Training
- Application development
- Testing
- Support contracts
- Anything else you can think of that relates to your servers and storage

After you have been virtualized for a quarter or so, go back and revisit those numbers. You're likely going to be saving quite a bit of money you hadn't planned on.

Over the past few chapters, we've thrown a lot of concepts and technologies at you. In the next chapter, we'll take these pieces and show you how they all fit together as we show you how you can green your IT department, step by step.

Greening Your Information Systems

In the preceding dozen chapters, we've looked at various issues germane to your organization and its environmental impact—specifically we've focused on your IT department and its actions. In this chapter, we'll take all the various information we've covered and show you how you can lessen your IT department's impact on the environment.

Initial Improvement Calculations

Let's say you're overweight and one day you decide, "That's it. I've had enough. I'm losing weight tomorrow!" For the next 6 months you eat right, you exercise, you get plenty of rest, drink lots of water, and the weight is just pouring off. It's coming off so nicely that a friend comes up to you and says, "My gosh, you look great. How much weight have you lost?"

It feels good to have lost weight, but because you didn't step on the scale for a starting weight, you have no idea how much weight you've lost.

It's the same way with greening your organization and IT department. If you don't know how much power you're consuming, you won't be able to compare it to results as you proceed. But unlike someone who has lost weight, it'll be harder to see the benefits of your efforts. True, you can compare electrical bills from when you started to when you finished, and you'll see results there, but you can also take advantage of other opportunities to track your progress.

Selecting Metrics

There's a lot you can measure—and a lot of it isn't even that difficult—to see you how you're doing in your efforts to go green. Let's take a closer look at the metrics you can use.

Power Usage Effectiveness and Datacenter Efficiency

Two metrics have recently been introduced that help measure data center efficiency: Power Usage Effectiveness (PUE) and Datacenter Efficiency (DCE). PUE is defined as

PUE = Total facility power/IT equipment power

whereas DCE is defined as

DCE = IT equipment power/total facility power

Total facility power is the power as it is measured at the meter for the datacenter. IT equipment power is defined as the power needed to manage, process, store, or route data within the datacenter.

NOTE *Total facility power means just the power to the datacenter, not your whole building. Using the power to the whole building will give you false numbers.*

IT equipment power includes the load associated with all the IT equipment, including the following:

- Computers
- Storage
- Network equipment
- KVM switches
- Monitors

Total facility power means everything that is used to support that equipment, including the following:

- Uninterrupted power supplies
- PDUs
- Batteries
- Cooling system

These metrics can tell you various information:

- When you can improve your datacenter's operational efficiency
- How the datacenter compares with competitors
- If datacenter processes are improving with your changes
- Opportunities to repurpose energy for extra IT equipment

These metrics can be used to illustrate how energy is being used in the datacenter. For example, if the PUE is 4.0, you know that the datacenter demand is three times greater than the energy needed to power the IT equipment.

You can also use these numbers to calculate how much power a new piece of equipment will need from the power grid. For instance, if you add a new server that demands 250 watts of power to run, and that multiplier is 4.0, you know that the utility grid will need to deliver 2000 watts.

DCE is probably even more useful. Using the same example of a 4.0 PUE, the DCE equivalent is .25. Therefore, we know that IT equipment consumes 25 percent of the power in the datacenter.

The PUE can range from 1.0 to infinity. In the best case, a PUE reaching 1.0 would show 100 percent efficiency. Currently, most datacenters are in the 3.0 and higher range, but properly designed, a PUE of 1.6 is attainable.

Datacenter Density

Datacenter density is a measurement of your CPU cycles over square footage. The higher the CPU cycles, the better. Datacenters with more rack density and higher space utilization score higher. And as you virtualize and remove old equipment, you'll see this number get larger.

Storage Utilization

This metric compares how much storage you are using, compared with how much you have available to use. This can be a hard one to measure, because storage is such a moving target.

For instance, do you count virtual memory for live applications? How about backup data? Duplicate data? It's really up to you to decide what you will include in your calculations, but it's important to be consistent. That is, if you opt to use duplicate data in your initial computations, it's important to always include that data for an apples-to-apples comparison.

Storage Density

This is similar to datacenter density, but rather than measure CPU cycles per square foot, you're comparing the amount of storage to your datacenter's area. This helps you determine whether you are making the best use of your facilities.

CPU Utilization

This measurement examines the percentage of utilization of your servers' CPUs. This can be measured with a number of commercially available performance measurement tools. For instance, you can track CPU utilization through System Monitor on Windows Server, as shown in Figure 13-1.

If your server is running just one task, as the one in Figure 13-1 is, utilization is very low, and not very efficient. As you add virtualized tasks to your server, utilization will increase.

Optimally, you want server utilization to be somewhere over 50 percent, perhaps as high as 80 percent, with the actual target depending on the applications, how predictable demand is, and other factors. This space capacity gives you some headroom in case services experience a spike in demand.

SWaP

When considering purchasing new servers, there's more to consider than just overall performance. Sun Microsystems has developed a metric that calculates such issues as floor space and power used, along with performance. The metric, known as Space, Watts, and Performance (SWaP), is expressed as:

$$\text{SWaP} = \text{PERFORMANCE}/\text{SPACE} \times \text{POWER CONSUMPTION}$$

On its own, the metric doesn't mean a lot. For instance, let's consider a server with the following characteristics:

- 400 operations
- 4 rack units
- 300 watts

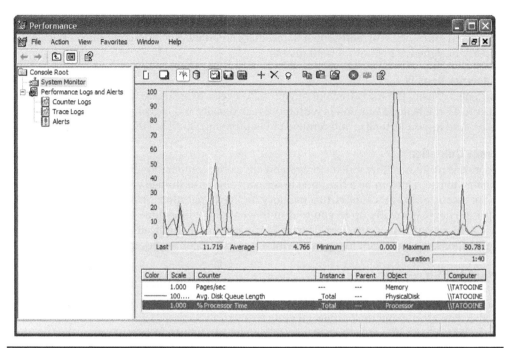

FIGURE 13-1   System Monitor is one of many tools that will help you monitor your CPU utilization.

The SWaP rating is .33 (400/4 x 300). So what does .33 mean? Nothing on its own. It's best used when comparing two servers. While the servers might be equivalent in performance, they could differ in the other areas, so the metric helps making a comparison.

Access the Sun SWaP calculator via Link 13-1.

Tracking Progress

Once you make your initial readings, it's important to make note of those measurements. You can do this simply using a tool such as Microsoft Excel and just add data as your project progresses. However, other tools are available that you can use.

BI Tools

In order to measure and track your data, you can use business intelligence (BI) tools, such as the following:

- **Digital dashboards**   These are also known as business intelligence dashboards, enterprise dashboards, or executive dashboards. They give you a visual summary of the data you want to track as well as an at-a-glance understanding of business conditions.

- **Online Analytical Processing (OLAP)**   This feature allows some information systems to analyze data from different perspectives and give you the results.

- **Reporting software**   These applications generate aggregated views of data you are tracking. They can compare different times so you can get a good understanding of your overall conditions.
- **Data mining**   This allows you to go back through your data and search for a specific piece of information. For instance, if you've decided to track a metric you hadn't previously thought to track, with data mining you can go back through existing data and make your new measurements.

Microsoft SQL Server

To keep track of your data, you can use a product such as Microsoft SQL Server, which is a relational database management system. It can be used in conjunction with a product such as PerformancePoint Server. Alternatively, if you are so inclined, you can build your own database.

Microsoft SQL Server is very powerful and includes such services as the following:

- Service broker
- Replication
- Analysis
- Reporting
- Notification
- Integration
- Full-test search

For instance, SQL Server's Analysis service adds OLAP and data-mining capabilities. The service includes various algorithms such as decision trees, clustering algorithm, naïve Bayes, time series, sequence clustering, linear and logistic regression, and neural networks.

Microsoft PerformancePoint

PerformancePoint Server 2007 busies itself with three missions:

- Planning
- Monitoring
- Analytics

Monitoring and analytics are delivered through a Monitoring Server, which includes two interfaces:

- Dashboard Designer
- SharePoint Web Parts

The Dashboard Designer allows you to perform the following tasks:

- Define the data you wish to monitor.
- Create views that allow you to monitor that data.

- Assemble the views in a dashboard.
- Deploy the dashboard to Microsoft Office SharePoint Server 2007 or Windows SharePoint Services.

The content that Dashboard Designer collects is saved to a SQL Server 2005 database that is managed through Monitoring Server. Data connections, like OLAP or relational tables, are managed through Monitoring Server.

Once a dashboard has been published to the Monitoring System database, it can be sent to Microsoft Office SharePoint Server 2007 or Windows SharePoint Services. The information can also be viewed in a web browser.

The server also comes with an API that allows developers to add extensions to the Dashboard Designer to develop custom reports, wizards, and so forth.

Change Business Processes

The way you run your business also has a huge impact on the environment in how much power you consume and waste you generate. In this section, we'll take a closer look at how you can streamline your organization to reduce the amount of waste you generate in the following areas:

- Worker time
- Power
- Inefficiency
- Paper
- Materials

Customer Interaction

Your company can save a lot of time and money by making some changes to the way it interacts with its customers. This has to do with its relationship with the customers, tracking their interaction with your company, and making the lives of the customers—as well as your own—as easy as possible.

Customer Relationship Management

When a customer looks at your company, they only see one thing: The Company. The customer doesn't see all the cogs and wheels spinning behind the front door. But customers aren't stupid. They know that if they buy something, someone has to process the payment. Someone has to package the product for shipping. And someone else has to perform the actual shipping.

Customer Relationship Management (CRM) is a philosophy of coordinating among all the players in an organization so that the customer is served well and has the best experience possible being your customer. To that end, several application packages help streamline the process.

Rather than Gladys typing out an order form and putting it in her "Out" basket, Corky from the mailroom picking it up and delivering it to the warehouse, and then Bud taking the ordered item from the shelves and sending it out, CRM applications allow Gladys to enter the order into her computer, which is then instantaneously sent to Bud. What's more, while he's packaging the item, a shipping label is printed so that the order is ready to go.

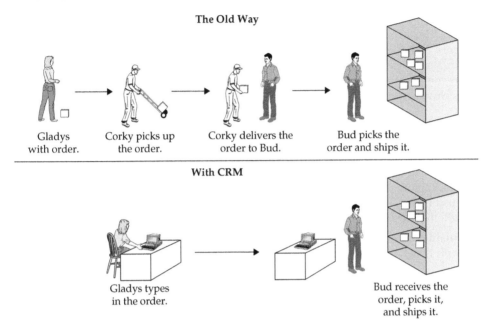

Who's Who   The preceding is a wholly simplistic example. CRM is intricate and places the various people within your organization in the following groups:

- **Customer Facing Operations**   These are the people and technologies a customer experiences when he or she interacts with the company. This can include face-to-face interactions, telephone calls, instant messaging, web chats, e-mail, and so forth. This can also include kiosks and web self-service.

- **Internal Collaborative Functional Operations**   These are the people and technologies that support the company policies and back office operations that have a direct impact on the activities of the Customer Facing Operations group. This includes IT, billing, maintenance, planning, marketing, finance, and manufacturing.

- **External Collaboration Functions**   These people and technologies support the organization in its cultivation of relationships with outside groups. These groups include suppliers, vendors, distributors, lobbying groups, and trade associations.

- **Customer Advocates and Experience Designers**   These are the people and technologies that help deliver value to the customer and profit to the organization.

- **Performance Managers and Marketing Analysts**　These are the people and technologies that design key performance indicators and collect metrics and data that help keep CRM on track. This is the group that establishes milestones and data to determine if the CRM process is being effective.

- **Customer and Employee Surveyors and Analysts**　These are the people and technologies that determine whether customer and employee relationships are getting better—or getting worse.

Technology　The technology you need to drive your CRM solution has many specific components. Although there are unique pieces to your CRM puzzle, they all fit together to present an overall view of who your customer is and what value they get from interacting with your company.

The technological components of your CRM system include the following:

- **Database**　A database for customer information and their interactions with the company, which includes order information, support information, requests, complaints, and survey responses.

- **Customer Intelligence**　You need a system for translating customer needs and profitability projections into plans that can be segmented for different types of customers. Then, you need to be able to track whether those plans are followed and whether desired outcomes have been achieved.

- **Business Modeling**　This piece analyzes your customer relationship strategy along with the goals. In the end, this will tell you whether you are meeting your goals.

- **Learning and Competency Management Systems**　This component helps you get closer to the results you desire and the goals you've set. Complex systems need time to be implemented and tweaked, and this component can help you analyze your processes.

- **Analytics**　This piece is used to analyze customer relationship policies and activities, using such technologies as voice recognition and statistical analysis.

- **Collaboration**　This component allows your customers to interact with your business and their fellow customers.

Each of these components can be implemented one by one over time, but the end goal is for them to be configured to benefit one another. SAP (Link 13-2) and Oracle (Link 13-3)—among others—offer CRM solutions.

Billing and Online Forms

We talked briefly about paperless billing in Chapter 6, but it is an issue your company should embrace. This process is not only ecologically responsible, but also convenient for you and your customers. It provides also a huge cost savings for your organization. Consider Figure 13-2.

As the figure shows, it costs money for someone to physically create the bill and mail the bill. Then, after the bill comes back, it costs money for someone to open the envelope, enter data from the enclosed form, and handle the customer's payment.

NOTE　*In this case, the customer could be either an individual consumer or a business-to-business buyer.*

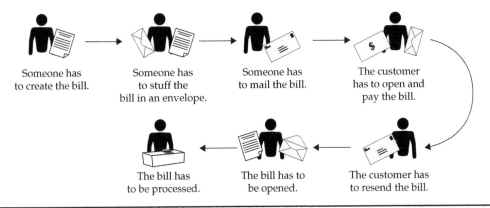

FIGURE 13-2   Conventional billing adds time and expense to your organization.

It costs between US$0.75 and US$2 for each document to be generated and mailed. If a paper check is eliminated, another $1.25 is saved. You also see a benefit from the elimination of inbound and outbound float. Electronic funds transfers offer next-day availability of funds.

Autoscribe (Link 13-4), ACHWorks (Link 13-5), and InterceptEFT (Link 13-6) are companies that offer online payment services. Figure 13-3 shows an example of the ACHWorks web interface.

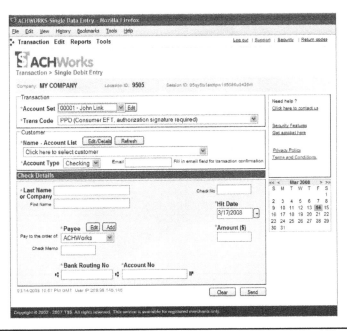

FIGURE 13-3   ACHWorks is one of many companies that allow you to set up online billing and payment processing.

The Council for Electronic Billing and Payment maintains a list of companies that can help provide online billing and payment systems. The list can be located by following Link 13-7.

Is paperless billing right for you? If you send out bills to consumers or other companies, then the answer is "Yes." What's more, the trend is moving that way.

Microsoft Surface

If you really want to be ahead of the curve and your organization is one that will accommodate it, you might consider using the Microsoft Surface. This touch-sensitive computer is a standalone device about the size of an old arcade Pong machine. A picture of it is shown in Figure 13-4.

Surface is, basically, a Windows Vista PC inside a table and topped with a 30-inch touch-sensitive screen. A projector beneath the screen projects an image onto its underside, while five cameras in the machine record reflections of infrared light from the user's fingertips.

The cameras can also recognize objects placed on the surface. If those objects have tags applied to them, Surface can access a database to gather information about the objects. Surface can recognize finger movements, and if a customer sets down a wine glass, the Surface can recognize the glass and offer dinner suggestions. Initial plans for the Surface call for it to be used in hotels, restaurants, and retail stores. The Surface costs around US$10,000.

FIGURE 13-4 The Microsoft Surface is a touch-screen computer that allows customers and guests to interact with the company in various ways.

Paper Reduction

A big way you can save money and help the planet out a little is by reducing the amount of paper you use. The paperless office isn't an absolute. There are some who will be able to embrace the philosophy and completely show paper the door, whereas others may only be able to handle one change, such as turning their fax services into a paperless endeavor. Regardless of what you are able to do, here are some of the tools that can help you reduce the paper you use.

SharePoint Server

Once you go paperless, you need a mechanism in place to ensure that you can find what you want when you want it. It's best to have a system that will help you logically organize your information.

Microsoft SharePoint Server, which we talked about in Chapter 6, is one such option. SharePoint is a web-based collaboration and document management platform. It can also be used to host websites that can then be shared across workspaces and documents. SharePoint sites are ASP.NET applications that are served using IIS and a SQL Server database for data storage.

Workflow Management

If you are totally embracing a paperless environment, but have filing cabinets full of old documents, you should let your departments know that the documentation needs to be scanned and saved on your SAN.

Supply your departments with scanners and give them a deadline. You must be realistic about becoming totally paper-free. This will depend on how much hardcopy you have on hand and how much of your staff's time you wish to dedicate to the project. A good idea is to have weekly goals in place. This allows the project to get done, but you're not totally overwhelming your company and you're not grinding the gears of your business to a halt.

Also, be aware of what type of paper you're scanning. If you have blueprints or oddly sized paperwork, you may need to buy scanners that can physically accommodate that paperwork.

An easy place to start the changeover is to simply stop producing paper. When you generate a document, just save it to the network as a Word or PDF file. If someone else in your organization needs a copy of the document, just e-mail it to them.

Green Supply Chain

The greening of your organization doesn't just stop at your front door. Think about the loading dock as well. The companies you are in business with and the companies you buy parts and services from should also toe the line when it comes to being ecologically responsible. True, you might not want to be too draconian about it, but think about companies such as Dell. As we mentioned in Chapter 9, Dell has a whole rating system in place for its vendors. If a vendor doesn't meet Dell's minimum standards, the company finds someone else.

We don't mean to tell you with whom you should do business, but you should evaluate to what degree greening is important and then decide whether your vendors are acting in a manner with which you are comfortable.

Green Procurement

When you need to acquire products, you can ensure you're doing so ecologically by engaging in *green procurement*. This requires an organization to perform an assessment of the environmental consequences of a product at the various stages of its life cycle. This means considering how the product was made, how it will be transported and used, and how it will be ultimately discarded.

A good green procurement program will include these steps:

- **Get organizational support**   Policies and procedures need to be changed to accommodate such a change, and the organization needs to be completely on-board. Those responsible for making purchasing decisions must be involved in the implementation process, because their suggestions and support are crucial.

- **Conduct a self-evaluation**   Take a look at your current purchasing practices. This gives you a starting benchmark and will help you clarify what you purchase, how much you purchase, where it comes from, and how much it costs. This gives you a baseline so you can measure the success of your green procurement efforts.

- **Set goals**   Set big goals that have specific measurements.

- **Develop a strategy**   Once you set the goals, figure out how you will reach those goals. Identify how you will implement changes necessary to reach those goals. You need to determine both short- and long-term solutions. Identify the products and vendors you want to work with.

- **Run a pilot project**   Don't jump into it all at once. Start small and run a pilot project. By starting small, you can see where the bumps are in the road and you can then figure out how to implement the program better, in a larger fashion.

- **Implement the plan**   When you put your green procurement plan in place, you will have to assign accountability and develop a communications plan that addresses employees, customers, suppliers, partners, and the public.

- **Review the program**   You want to periodically review your green procurement program to make sure you're still getting what you want. At regular times, look at whether the plan is meeting its stated goals and objectives. This review should also look at your organization's changing environmental goals.

Just-in-Time Buying

Not to keep banging the same drum, but Dell features another attribute that can help your organization. Just-in-time buying reduces the sheer amount of product in your warehouses. Rather than have a million connifilin pins on the shelves waiting to be installed in your gonkulators, set it up so that the connifilin pins are delivered right before you need to install them.

Dell does this with its computers. Rather than have warehouses bursting at the seams with product, the company has a system in place where, when a certain component is running low in stock, new ones are shipped. Dell builds computers to order so that there aren't built-out machines waiting to be purchased, or facing obsolescence.

Of course, for just-in-time buying to work right, you need reliable vendors and a good system in place to let the vendor know you need more product. But the benefits can be huge. You save money because you're not warehousing so much product. You don't need as much real estate to store product, and you're not buying more than you potentially need.

Improve Technology Infrastructure

The whole crux of this book is revealing the energy hogs in your organization and showing how you can make changes so that those systems and processes are less piggish. This section takes the IT issues we've already talked about and shows you how you can put them into practice in your organization.

Reduce PCs and Servers

A big undertaking—in the scope of the project, as well as your ultimate payoff—is reducing the sheer amount of computers and servers you have in your organization. The biggest change comes by virtualizing your servers, but there are other opportunities to reduce the amount of infrastructure you have in place. Let's look at how you can cut back on the humming boxes in your organization.

Virtualization

We can't give a definitive answer for how many servers you can eliminate by virtualizing. It's a moving target. The ratio of server virtualization will vary based on how powerful the original server is, how powerful the destination server is, the roles of your servers, how you need your servers physically distributed, and so forth. Your best bet is to pilot your consolidation, virtualizing servers onto a machine and checking the processor utilization to make sure it doesn't exceed the 50 to 80 percent mark.

NOTE *We talked about virtualization and its merits in the preceding chapter.*

As previously noted, several tools are available for virtualization. For the sake of understanding how virtualization can be implemented, let's take a look at the most popular tool—VMware—and discuss how to install it on a server (or workstation). It doesn't take very long, and heck, you might be the very first CIO in your organization to have actually installed one of the technologies you talk about in the boardroom. So go get a spare machine from your desktop or server group (ask for one with plenty of memory), and give it a shot—you may be surprised at what you learn.

Prerequisites

VMware Server runs only on Intel machines—Windows or Linux. Once you install VMware, however, the operating system can be just about anything you want. VMware will use a lot of RAM. You can control the amount of RAM that each virtual server uses, but a minimum of 256MB per virtual server is required.

Be sure you allocate enough memory for each server. Don't try to cram as many 256MB servers as you can on your physical server, because you'll experience sluggishness and other problems. At the minimum, you want 1GB or 2GB per virtualized server.

Remember that disk space and CPU utilization are also affected by how many virtual servers you have installed. Make sure you have enough CPU power and disk space to accommodate your virtual servers.

Obtaining VMware

You can download VMware from the company's website for a free 2-month evaluation. After that you will have to pay for it, based on how many images you have deployed.

For this example we're installing VMware Server. That and other flavors of VMware can be located via Link 13-8.

Installation

Installation is as straightforward as installing most any Windows application:

1. Go to the VMware download site and click the link that allows you to register. Once you provide some information, your serial number will be e-mailed to you.

2. Double-click the VMware Server icon to install.

3. In the VMware installation wizard, click Next to start.

4. Accept the license agreement and click Next.

5. Click Next again to start a default complete installation.

NOTE *If you are installing VMware on a Windows XP client for any reason, you'll get a warning message advising against the practice, but you can click away the warning and proceed. If you are performing a Windows XP install, be aware that VMware won't support it. Naturally, you won't install VMware on production equipment as a rule, but you may try it if you're repurposing an old machine.*

6. You're given the option to enter the default folder destination. Click Next.

7. If Autorun is enabled on your machine, you'll get a warning message that recommends disabling it. Take the default action of disabling Autorun and then click Next.

8. Click Install to begin the installation process.

9. Once the installation is complete, you are asked to provide customer information, including your username and a serial number. The serial number was provided earlier in the process, so enter it here and click Enter.

10. Restart the server.

When the server has been restarted, open the newly installed server to see two icons added to your Start menu: VMware Server Console and Manage Virtual Networks.

Clicking the first icon brings up the VMware Server Console – Connect to Host dialog, which is shown in Figure 13-5.

NOTE *The VMware Server Console also allows you to connect to remote virtual servers as well as local ones.*

Create a Virtual Server

To create a new virtual server, follow these steps:

1. Click OK to connect to your local host VMware system. Then click the New Virtual Machine link, as shown in Figure 13-6.

2. This starts the New Virtual Machine Wizard.

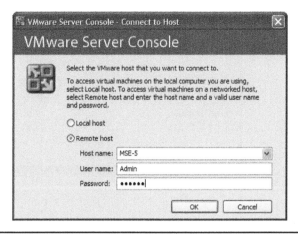

FIGURE 13-5   The VMware Server Console allows you to connect to your virtual servers.

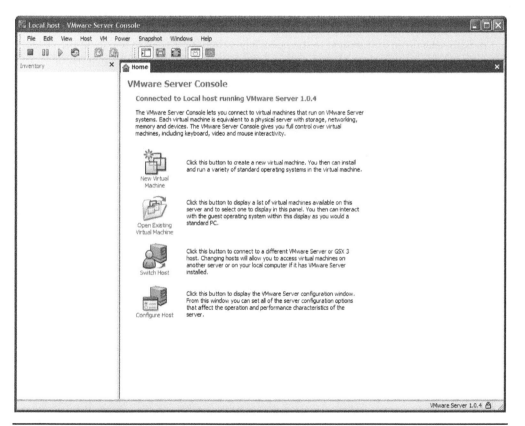

FIGURE 13-6   You create new virtual servers by clicking the New Virtual Machine link after you've connected to a VMware system.

FIGURE 13-7
FIGURE 13-7
Select the type of
operating system
that will be used
on your virtual
server.

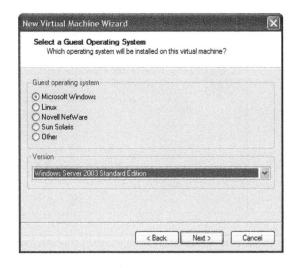

3. Click the Typical radio button and then click Next.

4. Select the radio button next to the operating system you wish to reside on the virtual machine. If you select Microsoft Windows, you also get to pick from a list of Windows flavors in the dropdown box. This screen is shown in Figure 13-7.

5. The next window gives you the opportunity to name the server and select its location. When you are finished, click Next.

6. The next screen gives you the chance to select what type of network you'll be adding. You can choose from bridged networking, network address translation, host-only networking, and no network at all. This is shown in Figure 13-8.

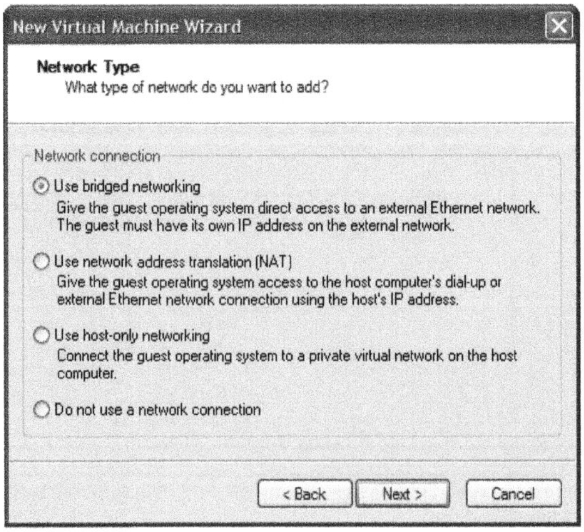

FIGURE 13-8
VMware allows you
to define what type
of network your
virtual server will
be a part of.

FIGURE **13-9**

FIGURE 13-9
You can set the size of your server's virtual hard drive. It can never be larger than the amount you specify.

7. As Figure 13-9 shows, VMware allows you to set the maximum size of the disk drive. It can never be larger than the amount you specify.

8. Click Finish, and your new virtual server will be created.

You can access your new server through the tool shown in Figure 13-10.

Thin Clients

As part of your virtualization efforts, don't forget to virtualize your everyday server. That is, if you use Microsoft Windows Server 2003, be sure to virtualize it. That way, as part of your client replacement strategy, you can replace costly, hardware-intensive clients with thin clients.

You can buy new thin clients, but don't overlook the opportunity to save money and not have to recycle an old computer. Because the processing and data storage is done at the server, you can absolutely use existing clients and simply deploy your day-to-day functions and applications onto your server. Even if your old clients aren't up to specs to act as thin clients, it may be possible to simply add a couple sticks of memory to get them up to snuff.

Rationalization

Take a look at your datacenter. Are there any servers that you, honestly, don't use anymore? Some servers may be running legacy applications that you really don't need to keep around. If that is the case, simply switch them off and get them ready to be recycled.

Check your business operations, anything that is running on a server, to verify which services are needed and which are not. If you find a service that's barely being used, ensure it's still a necessary function of your organization. It may be possible to just change the way you do business, stop using the service altogether, and turn off that server.

If you do have a server that is running a legacy application that you just can't do without, maybe you'll find that it uses such a low amount of CPU power that it can easily be moved onto a server with several other virtualized servers.

PART V

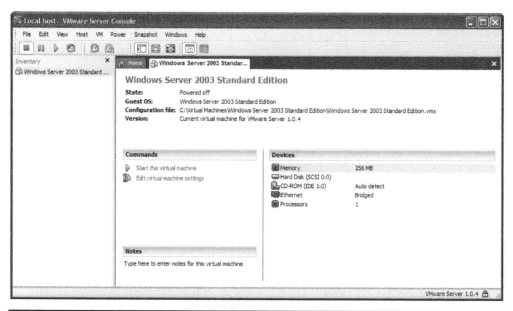

Figure 13-10   Your virtual servers are managed and viewed with VMware.

Terminal Services

The driving technology behind Microsoft's virtualization efforts is Terminal Services. This is a component of both Windows servers and clients that allows a user to access applications and data on a remote computer across any type of network.

Terminal Services is Microsoft's implementation of a thin-client terminal server computer. With it, Windows applications or the entire desktop of the computer running Terminal Services is accessible from a remote machine.

The computer accessing the server doesn't even have to be a flavor of Windows; it just has to be running the Terminal Services protocol. Alternatively, it could be a stripped-down PC or thin client that is running the protocol. With Terminal Services, only the user interface of the application is presented to the client. All input is sent back to the server where processing takes place.

Terminal Server is the server component of Terminal Services. This is the piece of software handling the connection on the server's end of the connection. It authenticates clients and makes the applications remotely available. It is also responsible for restricting clients based on the access level they have.

Terminal Services Web Access makes a session possible through a web browser. A session can also be initiated by tunneling through a gateway via the TS Gateway service.

This allows the server to be available over the Internet or by tunneling the Remote Desktop Protocol data over a secure HTTP session.

Software as a Service (SaaS)

For some applications, you may not even need to have the software installed on your servers at all. This is another way that equipment can be eliminated from your company—just don't install the software to begin with.

Characteristics   Software as a Service (SaaS) is a model where a software vendor offers its software for use over the Internet. You don't house any of the equipment needed to run the software; you simply log on with the provider and run the software virtually. Also, you don't pay to own the software. Instead, you simply pay whatever fees are charged to you.

Another upside to SaaS is that you don't have to worry about buying upgrades to the application, performing upgrades, and troubleshooting any problems. Any upgrades are performed by the SaaS provider.

According to IDC, key characteristics of SaaS software include the following:

- Network-based access to, and management of, commercially available software.

- Activities that are managed from central locations rather than at each customer's site, enabling customers to access applications remotely via the Web.

- Application delivery that typically is closer to a one-to-many model (single instance, multitenant architecture) than to a one-to-one model, including architecture, pricing, partnering, and management characteristics.

- Centralized feature updating, which obviates the need for downloadable patches and upgrades.

SaaS applications are priced on a per-user basis. Additional fees can be added for extra bandwidth and storage. Revenue for SaaS vendors is generally smaller up front (as compared to buying licenses and selling software packages), but much larger on the back end as companies subscribe to the service.

ASP Differences   This concept may not sound new, especially if you have been using application service providers (ASPs). But SaaS is different from an ASP. It's easier to think of SaaS as ASP version 2.0.

ASPs host applications on behalf of their clients. But ASPs generally don't create their own applications. SaaS vendors, however, create their own applications and run them on their own.

PART V

SaaS vendors also use a multitenant architecture. This means that multiple customers are running the same software, but the data is kept separate. ASPs, on the other hand, typically deploy one instance of each type of software for each customer, as illustrated next.

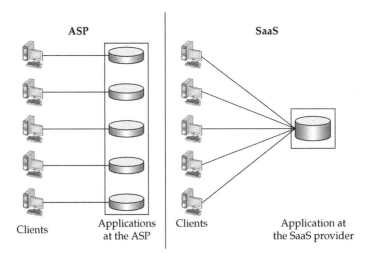

Telecommuting   You can save a lot of money and reduce your carbon footprint by allowing employees to telecommute. As we explained in Chapter 5, your company can reap significant cost benefits by implementing a telecommuting program, including the following:

- Less cost for hardware purchases and maintenance
- Less carbon emissions by commuting employees
- Lower real estate costs
- Lower electrical costs
- Less need to cool the facility

For more information on telecommuting and how to implement it in your own organization, flip back to Chapter 5.

Shared Services

An organization's common IT functions can be consolidated via a shared services system, rather than spread across the enterprise, implemented separately by each department. For example, when a new employee is hired, he or she is automatically added to all databases in the organization with no extra work performed by the HR department.

Another way to look at it is that IT acts as an internal service provider—one that essentially competes with the quality of service, cost, and value that an external service provider might provide.

Using shared services, common distributed IT functions are consolidated and delivered over a shared infrastructure to the enterprise. This results in lower costs, higher service levels, and greater responsiveness.

A Shared Service Center can be established as a distinct organization to provide shared services to business groups using a customer/supplier model. Services provided are defined by the needs of internal customers and delivered by the Shared Service Center.

Hardware Costs

When it comes time to buy new computers and servers, you're looking at a lot of specifics—the speed of the machines, how much RAM they have, the size of hard drives, and so forth—not the least of which is cost. When you look at new hardware with ecological responsibility in mind, you should also be looking at how much power is consumed and what components you absolutely need.

If you are performing a virtualization project that needs thin clients, you can save money there. However, if you are still putting a tower in every cubicle, that's fine, but maybe you don't need computers with DVD drives. If you send software updates over the LAN, you needn't spend the extra money per machine for DVD drives.

Also, consider your server needs. As we talked about in Chapter 11, get your servers tailored with the correct size of power supply. It may cost more up front, but you'll save money in the long run because less power is wasted, less heat is generated, and less cooling is required.

Wherever possible, be sure to look for low-power models of monitors, servers, towers, and thin clients. Also, look for Energy Star, RoHS, and EPEAT certifications. This ensures that the hardware meets some sort of environmental standard.

Cooling

You can look at the issue of cooling—and reducing your cooling bills—from two perspectives: You can cool more efficiently, or you can reduce the overall need to cool. Actually, both approaches should be pursued.

If you cool more efficiently, you do things like we discussed in Chapter 4. You can organize the physical layout of your datacenter to accommodate cooling. This means making sure cabling is routed so that airflow isn't restricted. This means laying out your servers to follow the hot-aisle/cold-aisle philosophy. This means adding supplemental coolers that use cool outside air as much as possible.

But in addition to striving for more efficiency, you should reduce the need to cool as much as possible. This means using power supplies that are appropriate for the load being supplied. Too much extra power turns into heat. Remember that 1 watt of unused power turns into heat that requires 1 watt of power to cool.

Will you ever find a Zen-like balance between your power supplies and the exact amount of power you need? Likely not. But get as close as you can.

Now that you've greened the various aspects of your IT department, you want to make sure you keep making progress—at the very least, you want to make sure you don't take any steps backward. In the final chapter, we'll talk about how you can keep checking up on your IT department's green initiatives and what you can do if you start to slip.

14

CHAPTER

Staying Green

Most of a rocket's fuel is spent getting into space. Once the rocket is out of the atmosphere, it's easier—takes less energy—to keep it moving toward its destination than it did to get it 100 feet off of the ground. It's the same way with greening your IT department. The hardest part is figuring out how to do it and actually getting started. Once you figure out what to do, how to do it, and actually get going, it'll be easier to maintain your momentum.

But once you get going, you still need to make some in-flight corrections in order to get to your destination. This chapter looks at some of the things you should do to keep on target and to help your organization get the greenest IT department it can get.

Organizational Checkups

There are some overall adjustments you might consider for your organization—not just in the details of your green plan, but in how you approach the plan's implementation. This will involve putting people in new roles and keeping important people—such as the CEO—sold on the merits of a green plan.

Chief Green Officer

It's no secret that going green is a one-two punch of benefits—the environment benefits, and your organization benefits. However, it's not an easy process. Many organizations, as part of their green initiatives, are adding to their C-suite by introducing a Chief Green Officer (CGO). This person has the overall responsibility to make sure the company is meeting its green goals and looking for ways to do an even better job.

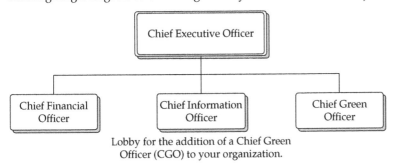

Lobby for the addition of a Chief Green Officer (CGO) to your organization.

The CGO, ultimately, is going to be responsible for three things:

- Reducing the organization's environmental footprint
- Engaging diverse stakeholders
- Discovering new revenue opportunities

Transitioning

Although it would be wonderful to say that companies are choosing to go green because it's the right thing to do, that usually isn't the case. True, many companies have a long commitment to the environment, and they should be commended for that activity. But the fact of the matter is that many companies started their eco-friendly behavior because, at first, it was the law—they were simply trying to achieve a certain level of environmental responsibility because of compliance issues.

But a good thing has happened. Even though the companies started out with their arms twisted behind their backs, the momentum remained and they've started going beyond what was required. What tends to happen in cases like this is a four-step process:

- **Compliance**   Put simply, in order to obey the law, organizations started taking steps to meet the minimum requirements. Compliance costs money, and businesses do not like to cut into their bottom lines, but the end result is that they got the ball rolling.

- **Personal commitment**   A company can only be as dedicated to environmental friendliness as its leaders are. Although being green can be important to the CEO (and therefore the organization), if that CEO leaves, there's potential for green initiatives to go out the window. It's important for the entire organization to sign on to the notion of being green.

- **Public trust**   The public can be skeptical of your purported greening. Although the public wants you to be responsible, it's easy enough for a company to tell everyone that it is being responsible, but still consuming way more power than it needs, throwing computers in dumpsters, and using tons of paper every year. Although advertising your green efforts is good for your company, you have to actually back it up with action.

- **Sustainable growth**   Once the organization has met its green goals, it's all done, right? No. Now is the time to set new goals and look for ways to develop greener products, increase energy efficiency, and reduce waste further.

This sort of evolution is great, but it needs some sort of guidance. It is really easy to simply meet compliance goals and then stop forward momentum. To help guide your organization to the next steps, you need to ensure that someone is continually driving your green initiatives. This is where the CGO comes in.

The ultimate goal of organizations trying to stay green is to have zero impact on the environment. But in addition to this goal, it is important for organizations to have a good level of trust with the public. As we mentioned before, you can't just talk the talk without walking the walk. You can improve your company's image by forging closer bonds with organizations such as the National Resources Defense Council (NRDC).

In order to keep steaming forward, it is important that you make not only internal efforts, but also external ones.

Structure

The CGO, most times, reports directly to the CEO. This makes sense (the CEO is the boss after all), but it is also good for the CGO to have the CEO's ear, because the CEO has influence in the entire organization. It's important to stress that going green is an organizational change—not a departmental or single business unit change. That is, if the shipping department, for example, can save money by restructuring its shipments, the CGO can recommend changes to the CEO, who can then trickle them down to the shipping department, as shown next.

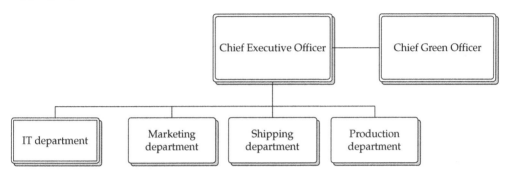

The CGO isn't just reading from the company's greening plan. They also need to have their nose stuck into the daily activities of the organization's various departments. The CGO will also be responsible for environmental stewardship, corporate communications, strategic partnerships, and product development.

With all this responsibility, the door seems wide open for a huge and bloated green staff. However, that doesn't have to be the case. Rather, the CGO needs to have strong relationships with the department heads, and a program management office should be established. The management team can then guide programs that are developed.

Once the strategy is set and metrics are established, it's up to the CGO to make sure they're being met. The CGO and their staff can find which goals aren't being met and what can be done to help reach them.

Evolution

Perhaps you've already achieved your organization's green goals. That's fantastic, but you're not done yet. At least you shouldn't be. Greening your datacenter and IT department shouldn't be a destination, it's a journey.

Be sure to continually evaluate your organization, equipment, and processes to make sure you're being as green as you can be. The rewards remain the same—you lessen your environmental impact and you save money.

PART V

From an environmental standpoint, the equipment today is better than it was 5 years ago, but the stuff available 5 years from now will be better than what we have today, as shown next.

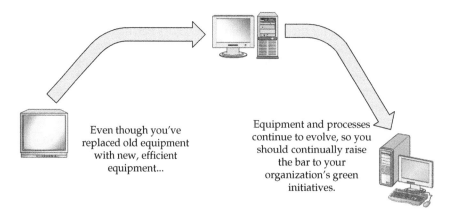

Even though you've replaced old equipment with new, efficient equipment...

Equipment and processes continue to evolve, so you should continually raise the bar to your organization's green initiatives.

Plus, a lot of wheels are in motion from different companies and organizations to improve your processes, from a more ecologically responsible perspective. For example, although you might adopt a plan today that lessens the environmental impact of your organization's SAN, in the future there will be a smarter, safer way to deploy your SAN. As such, if you keep up on what's evolving, the next time you replace your SAN, you can keep moving forward toward zero impact on the environment.

Also keep in mind the need for expansion. Even if you initially condense the size of your datacenter through virtualization, make sure you have the room to expand. That is, don't give up all your datacenter space for some other use, because if you do have to expand and don't have the room available to you, you run the risk of making bad decisions because you're backed into a corner (no pun intended).

Sell the CEO

The benefits of going green seem obvious to us. But they aren't obvious to everyone. Unless your management—especially your CEO—buys into the notion that going green is a good idea, nothing will change.

Although people are inherently good at heart, and they know they should reduce greenhouse emissions, CEOs also know that their company needs to make money. So the best way to explain the benefits of going green is by explaining the monetary benefits.

For instance, don't just say, "Converting our datacenter from old rack servers into new consolidated blade servers, with the responsibility of old servers virtualized onto the new blades, will be more efficient."

You will have lost your CEO at "datacenter."

Rather, if you can explain that changing from old rack servers to blades will save US$560 in electrical costs per server per year (and by the way, we have 5000 servers), you will have the CEO's ear.

Here are some other strategies that can help win over upper management:

- **Keep contacts updated**   It's important to have a personal relationship with management to be able to communicate how these programs are contributing to corporate value. If upper management is engaged, it's easier to sell your projects.

- **Talk to the investor relations staff**   Meet regularly with your investor relations staff and explain the value of energy management, not only to the company's bottom line, but also to socially responsible investors and the company's overall reputation. For that matter, make sure your internal HR and communications departments are aware of what your company is accomplishing. Although we all know how much consumers are interested in buying from a company that is doing right by the environment, employees will enjoy working for a company they know is environmentally responsible.

- **Gain recognition for your "wins"**   If you are participating in a program such as LEED, for example, when you achieve goals in the program, you can communicate these "wins" to senior management, employees, customers, and investors.

SMART Goals

Most executives have heard about SMART goals. This concept is something that should be applied to your green goals. It is a mechanism that helps you set and achieve certain goals. SMART is an acronym for

SMART Goals

Specific
Measurable
Attainable
Realistic
Timely

- **Specific**   A goal should be precise and put in terms people can relate to. Rather than "We're going to reduce our greenhouse gas emissions," a specific goal states the following: "We are going to reduce our greenhouse gas emissions by 30 percent by the end of next year, and this is like taking x number of cars off the road."

- **Measurable**   Develop concrete criteria for measuring progress toward a goal. By measuring progress, you stay on track, achieve milestones, and maintain motivation to keep moving forward.

- **Attainable**   When you identify your goals, you think of ways to achieve them. You identify previously overlooked opportunities and identify new ones.

- **Realistic**   Although it's laudable to have a goal such as "We're going to have zero impact on the environment by the end of the quarter," it's just not realistic, and you're setting yourself up for failure. Set high goals, to be sure, but do a reality check and make sure they're something you can actually achieve.

- **Timely**   You need to have a timeline in mind. There should be a definite date by which you intend to meet your goals. If you leave things open-ended, or if the end date is too far out in the future, there's no sense of urgency to meet the goals, so you run the real risk of languishing and not getting anything done.

PART V

SMART goal setting is just one way to meet your green goals. We mention it here as a mechanism to help keep you moving forward. However, if there is another way you've had success with, by all means keep doing what you're doing.

Equipment Checkups

In the previous chapter, we talked about some metrics you should use—first to find out where you are, and then to keep track of your progress. In this section, we'll talk in more depth about that data, how you can measure it, and how it can be used to keep you moving forward.

Gather Data

Figuring out how well you're doing in your efforts to save energy starts with having good information on how much energy you're using. You should start by gathering baseline information that you can use to measure future readings against.

When you're collecting data, keep these issues in mind:

- **Determine the level of detail**   The scope of data collection is going to vary from organization to organization. Some will just look to their monthly utility bill, whereas others will check power consumption at submeters.

- **Detail all energy sources**   Take readings of all the energy you use that is purchased from offsite vendors. This includes electricity, gas, and so forth. Record those amounts consumed (kWh, MMBtu, and so on) and the amount of money you spend on each.

- **Document energy use**   For the energy you pay for, gather energy bills, meter readings, and any other documentation that might contain a history of your power use. You may be able to find this in your own records, or you can contact your utility companies and request that data. It's best to have about 2 years' worth of data (or more) on hand.

- **Gather facility data**   To normalize your data, you may have to collect non-energy-related data for your facilities, such as the building size and hours of operation.

Tracking Your Data

When you've established which data you'll be monitoring, you need to have a tracking system in place to help compare your results. It can be as simple as an Excel spreadsheet, or you can get something as in-depth as SQL Server. To decide which tool is best for you, consider these issues:

- **Scope**   The type of system you use will be dictated, largely, by how much data and what types of data are being measured and how often those measurements are taken.

- **Ease of use**   Although SQL Server databases are very powerful, they aren't for the squeamish. And although an Excel spreadsheet is easy enough to use, it might not be powerful enough to track and cross-match the sorts of data you want to measure. Your tracking system needs to be something that's powerful enough for your needs, yet easy enough to use.

- **Reporting**   Not only is your tracking system good for monitoring your data, it can also be used to communicate your energy performance around your organization. This is an effective method because it can help encourage change.

When collecting data, keep these issues in mind:

- Collect data from submeters when possible.
- Use actual, not estimated, data.
- Use data that is current.
- Develop reports that analyze power usage every quarter.

Baseline Data

The next step is to establish a baseline for your data. This allows you to know where you're starting and also to establish realistic goals. In order to establish a baseline, you need to keep these issues in mind:

- **Establish a base year**   Establish a base year or an average of several historical years. Use as complete data as you can.
- **Choose your metrics**   Select what you are going to measure based on your organization's performance desires. For instance, if your overall goal is to reduce power consumption, you should be measuring and monitoring kilowatt hours (kWh).
- **Share your results**   Make sure you share the baseline results with managers, departments, and other stakeholders.

Benchmarking

You can compare your own organization's results against others through benchmarking. The procedure doesn't necessarily propel you toward your power reduction goals; however, it can be useful to monitor your progress and to compare your organization to others.
   Benchmarking can be performed in a number of ways:

- **Past performance**   Compare your current status to historical performance.
- **Industry average**   Compare your organization's results to an average of other organizations in your industry.
- **Best in class**   Compare your organization to the best in the industry, not just the average.
- **Best practices**   Compare your organization's results to established practices that have been deemed to be the best in the industry.

Analyze Data

Once you get all your data, what then? Sure, a table of numbers looks impressive, but what can you glean from it? There's a lot of information you can divine from your collected data. As shown next, you can look at it from two standpoints: quantitative and qualitative.

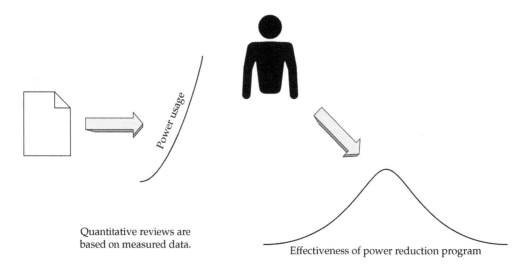

Power usage

Quantitative reviews are
based on measured data.

Effectiveness of power reduction program

Qualitative reviews are
based on interviews or
other subjective sources of
information.

Quantitative Reviews

Quantitative reviews are the meat and potatoes of data review. This involves looking at the numbers and figuring out what they mean based on the data available. You can look at such details as the following:

- **Usage profiles**   Look for consumption peaks and valleys, and figure out how they relate to your overall operations.

- **Performance comparisons**   Use the data to compare two similar facilities in your organization. For instance, if you have branches in Spokane, Washington and Albany, New York, how do the same facilities in these branches stack up against each other?

- **High costs**   Look at the data to see where you are spending a lot of money on energy use.

- **What's missing**   Look for any areas where you feel like you need more information, and then start collecting it.

Qualitative Reviews

Qualitative reviews are fuzzier than quantitative reviews. Whereas quantitative reviews focus on cold, hard numbers, qualitative reviews try to put numbers in a context to explain them. Such data can include the following:

- **Interviews**   Talk to colleagues and employees to seek informed opinions, anecdotal information, lessons learned, and in-house audits.

- **Review policies**   Look at your organizational policies and procedures to figure out what impact they are having on your energy use.

Conduct Audits

Baselining and assessing your performance are great to do, but these tasks are only part of the story. You should also periodically assess and audit the performance of equipment, processes, and systems to help identify opportunities for improvement.

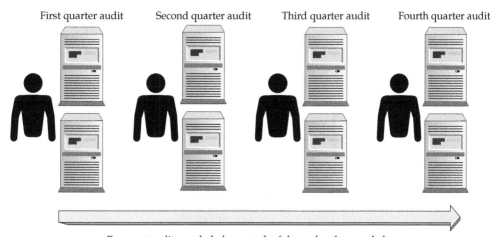

First quarter audit   Second quarter audit   Third quarter audit   Fourth quarter audit

Frequent audits can help keep track of data, plus they can help you find problems as they arise.

An energy audit is not something you can likely assign someone to conduct. It's usually done by energy professionals. In order to conduct an energy audit, you need to follow these steps:

- **Assemble your team**   You need to bring together a team with experience and knowledge of all energy-using systems, processes, and equipment. You can use your system specialists and facilities engineers, but you may discover that you need to hire an outside expert for objectivity and expertise.

- **Plan and develop a strategy**   Figure out which systems you are going to evaluate and then assign team members to perform those tasks. Use benchmarking information to identify facilities and systems that aren't performing properly.

- **Generate a report**   Based on your audit results, write a detailed summary of steps that can be taken to reduce energy use. The report should also recommend actions that should be implemented.

PART V

Get Back on Track

Once you have reviewed and analyzed your performance data, the next step is to understand what is influencing your results. Your review should be especially critical of your action plan, and it should detail which activities were successful and which were not. Based on that you can reevaluate your plan and decide how to proceed next.

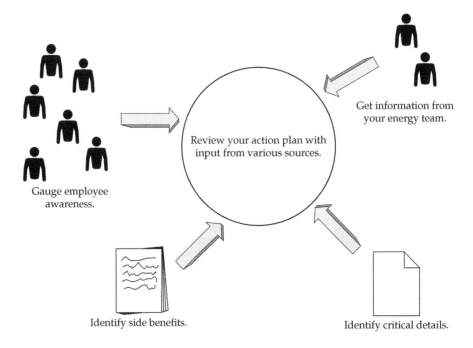

Reviewing your action plan involves these key strategies:

- **Get feedback**   Talk to people in your organization and get feedback information from the energy team and others in your organization.
- **Gauge awareness**   Find out whether employees are aware of energy issues.
- **Identify critical details**   Figure out which details contributed to your plan failing or succeeding.
- **Know your side benefits**   List—and if possible, quantify—any side benefits that arose from your action plan. This could be employee comfort, any impact on sales or operations, and so on. It could be a boost in community relations.

Reviewing your action plan can be a heady undertaking, but it's worth it. Doing so allows you to do the following:

- Identify new sources of action.
- Avoid repeated failures by identifying the actions that were not successful.
- Evaluate the usefulness of the tracking system, and make appropriate changes.

- Communicate your successes to your staff.
- Communicate successes to stakeholders inside and outside the organization.

Certifications

If you want to go green, there are plenty of certifications out there that can help guide you. For example, Energy Star, EPEAT, and RoHS can help you find equipment that does a good job of lessening your power consumption and the toxins introduced into the environment. If you want to build or remodel your facilities with environmental responsibility in mind, LEED can certify your efforts.

However, at this point in time there is no certification, specifically, for a green datacenter. Do you need any sort of certification to go green? Technically, no. However, having a formal certification in place could be a good idea.

Benefits

First, a certification would mean that industry has come together and agreed on what parameters must exist for a datacenter to be so certified. Industry would have to decide on such factors as the following:

- Maximum power consumption
- The types of equipment allowed
- Cooling guidelines
- The materials allowed in equipment
- End-of-life procedures

This wouldn't be a draconian edict handed down by industry. However, it would dictate what needs to exist for your organization to achieve this future green certification.

A green datacenter certification would be a great thing. Not only would it give organizations the opportunity to say, "We just got our green certification," but it also would provide a roadmap to achieve that certification. Just looking back through this book, you can tell that greening your organization is a lot like eating an elephant. Where do you start? The answer to both eating an elephant and greening your organization is simple: You start anywhere.

A green datacenter certification would give you the exact things you need to do, so you don't need to get bogged down in so much detail. Instead, you can focus on the exact things you need to achieve to gain certification.

Realities

Is a green datacenter certification a pipe dream? We don't think so. Although there's nothing front and center right now, the fact that greening your organization in general and your datacenter in particular are big issues right now—and with the state of our environment being what it is (not to mention the price of a gallon of gas)—you can expect that greening the datacenter is going to become more prevalent and that a certification will be developed sooner rather than later.

PART V

Certification can be a double-edged sword, however. Although many organizations will pursue greening just for the sake of earning that certification—and that's way better than not pursuing it at all—many organizations will also just do the minimum and stop. It's important to not only achieve the certification, but keep going.

Ideally, to maintain the certification, a metric will be in place that requires certified datacenters to continually improve.

Helpful Organizations

Going green can be daunting, but you're not in it alone. You can find help from peers as well as organizations, worldwide. Table 14-1 lists just some of the organizations out there that can help you achieve your green goals.

Organization	Website	Description
Business for Social Responsibility	Link 14-1	Helps companies that are endeavoring to engage in ethical business practices while being responsible to people, communities, and the environment.
Center for Clean Products and Clean Technologies	Link 14-2	The Center is located at the University of Tennessee, Knoxville, and develops, evaluates, and promotes clean technologies.
Climate Savers	Link 14-3	The World Wildlife Foundation's initiative for power consumption and waste in industry.
Consortium on Green Design and Manufacturing	Link 14-4	Formed in 1993 at the University of California, Berkeley, the Consortium works to encourage multidisciplinary research and education on environmental management, design for environment, and pollution prevention in critical industries.
Design for the Environment's Computer Display Project	Link 14-5	Part of the U.S. Environmental Protection Agency's Design for the Environment program, the Computer Display Project evaluates the life cycle, environmental impacts, performance, and cost of liquid crystal displays and cathode ray tubes.
Design for the Environment's Printed Wiring Board Partnership	Link 14-6	Part of the U.S. Environmental Protection Agency's Design for the Environment program, the Printed Wiring Board Partnership examines alternatives to traditional printed wiring boards—the foundation for virtually all electronic components.
Electronic Power Research Institute	Link 14-7	EPRI was established in 1973 as an independent, nonprofit center for public interest energy and environmental research. EPRI brings together members, participants, the Institute's scientists and engineers, and other leading experts to work collaboratively on solutions to the challenges of electric power.

TABLE 14-1   Organizations That Can Help Your Green Efforts (www.greenitinfo.com/links)

Organization	Website	Description
Electronic Products Stewardship Canada	Link 14-8	Electronics Product Stewardship Canada (EPS Canada) is developing a national electronics end-of-life program in Canada. EPS Canada works with an array of partners and stakeholders to design, promote, and implement sustainable solutions for Canada's electronic waste problem. EPS Canada was created to work with both industry and government to develop a flexible, workable Canadian solution.
Energy Efficiency Industry Partnership	Link 14-9	ASE's Energy Efficiency Industry Partnership (EEIP) works with organizations around the world to promote energy efficiency in industry. EEIP provides energy efficiency companies with a platform to promote their products and services.
Greenhouse Gas Protocol	Link 14-10	The Greenhouse Gas Protocol (GHG Protocol) is the most widely used international accounting tool for government and business leaders to understand, quantify, and manage greenhouse gas emissions. The GHG Protocol works with businesses, governments, and environmental groups around the world to build a new generation of credible and effective programs for tackling climate change.
Global Reporting Initiative	Link 14-11	Developed guidelines to help businesses prepare sustainability reports. GRI works with the private sector, nonprofits, universities, and other groups to develop guidelines.
Green Grid	Link 14-12	The Green Grid is a global consortium dedicated to advancing energy efficiency in datacenters and business computing ecosystems. The Green Grid Board of Directors is composed of the following member companies: AMD, APC, Dell, HP, IBM, Intel, Microsoft, Rackable Systems, SprayCool, Sun Microsystems, and VMware.
INFORM Inc.	Link 14-13	INFORM, in conjunction with businesses, communities, and governments, helps businesses ensure environmentally sustainable growth. It helps organizations avoid unsafe use of toxic chemicals, protect land and water resources, and conserve energy.
International Association of Electronics Recyclers	Link 14-14	The IAER represents and serves the interests of the electronics recycling industry for managing the life cycle of electronics products.
International Facility Management Association	Link 14-15	A professional organization for facilities managers.

TABLE 14-1 Organizations That Can Help Your Green Efforts (www.greenitinfo.com/links) (*Continued*)

Organization	Website	Description
Journal of Industrial Ecology	Link 14-16	A quarterly journal published by MIT that covers such issues as energy flow studies; dematerialization and decarbonization; life cycle planning, design, and assessment; design for the environment; and extended producer responsibility.
National Electrical Manufacturers Association	Link 14-17	The association develops technical standards for the electrical manufacturing industry. It also provides industry-specific information.
Scientific Certification Systems	Link 14-18	An independent provider of certification, auditing, and testing services and standards.
Silicon Valley Toxics Coalition	Link 14-19	The organization labors to reduce negative impacts of the high-tech industry by promoting environmental sustainability and clean production.
Sustainable Enterprise Program	Link 14-20	The Sustainable Enterprise Program is an effort by the World Resources Institute to partner with corporations, investors, and business schools to "create profitable solutions to environment and development challenges."
WasteCap Wisconsin	Link 14-21	The organization helps Wisconsin companies find cost-effective ways to reduce waste, including electronic waste, building waste, and manufacturing waste.
World Computer Exchange	Link 14-22	The organization already has offices across the United States, but has plans to expand around the globe. WCE tries to make the process of donating old computers as easy as possible for companies and individuals.

TABLE 14-1   Organizations That Can Help Your Green Efforts (www.greenitinfo.com/links) *(Continued)*

Well, that's our pitch for greening your IT department. Although we've said it often throughout this book, the fact of the matter is that by making ecologically responsible changes to your organization and your IT department, you can lessen your organization's impact on the environment and the impact on your bottom line. There's an initial cost up front, but in the end you'll save money.

Don't think you need to do everything at once and expend a huge amount of money up front. Changes can be made gradually and over time. For instance, when it's time to replace your client workstations, consider going with thin-client or low-power options rather than buying overpowered computers.

The important thing is to make any change. Whether you decide to jump into greening efforts with both feet and revamp your whole system, or you just decide to virtualize a few servers, you're still making progress. Hopefully, if you do opt to make one small change, it will inspire you to make many more.

Index

Lightning Source UK Ltd.
Milton Keynes UK
UKOW05f0838240416

272806UK00001B/3/P